On the evening of June 9, 1912, the Moore family—Josiah (43), Sarah (39), Herman (11), Katherine (10), Boyd (8), Paul (5)—and overnight guests Lena Stillinger (11) and her sister Ina (8) attended a highly anticipated children's program at the local Presbyterian church. The program ended late, after 9:30 P.M. The town of Villisca was dark. There was no moonlight, and a dispute between the municipal power company and city officials had resulted in the streetlights being turned off.

The Stillinger girls, afraid to walk alone through the darkened streets, telephoned home seeking permission to stay with the Moores. The family and their young guests made their way home and settled into bed sometime around 10 P.M. When the sun came up Monday morning, a neighbor doing her wash noticed how unusually still the Moore house was. By the time the clock struck 7 A.M., curiosity turned to concern and she telephoned Ross Moore, Josiah's brother.

Ross telephoned the house. Getting no answer, he called his brother's store to find he had not yet arrived at work. Growing more concerned by the minute, Ross made haste to the Moore house. Along with the neighbor, Ross circled the house, calling out to his brother's family, looking for any signs of life.

At 8:30 Ross pulled out his keys and opened the locked door. Once inside he made his way through the kitchen and parlor toward the downstairs bedroom. Almost immediately, he was confronted by the horrific sight of two bloody and lifeless figures lying in the small single bed in the downstairs sewing room.

Ross stopped and immediately called Villisca marshal Hank Horton, who arrived promptly to investigate. Once inside, Horton methodically went through the tiny house of horrors.

"There's someone murdered in every bed!" he exclaimed in disbelief.

AMERICA'S MOST HAUNTED

The Secrets of Famous
Paranormal Places

Theresa Argie
and Eric Olsen

BERKLEY BOOKS, NEW YORK

THE BERKLEY PUBLISHING GROUP
Published by the Penguin Group
Penguin Group (USA) LLC
375 Hudson Street, New York, New York 10014

USA • Canada • UK • Ireland • Australia • New Zealand • India • South Africa • China

penguin.com

A Penguin Random House Company

This book is an original publication of The Berkley Publishing Group.

Library of Congress Cataloging-in-Publication Data

Argie, Theresa, author.
America's most haunted: the secrets of famous paranormal places / Theresa Argie and Eric Olsen.
pages cm
ISBN 978-0-425-27014-1 (paperback)
1. Haunted places—United States.   I. Olsen, Eric, 1948– author.   II. Title.
BF1472.U6A74   2014   2014009101
133.10973—dc23

PUBLISHING HISTORY
Berkley trade paperback edition / October 2014

PRINTED IN THE UNITED STATES OF AMERICA

10 9 8 7 6 5 4 3 2 1

Cover photo: Shutterstock.
Cover design by Chelsea McGulkin.

ACKNOWLEDGMENTS

Theresa Argie: I want to thank the many people, living and dead, who made this book possible by sharing a story, photograph, experience, or haunted venue with me. Special thanks to my co-author Eric Olsen for bringing out the writer in me; Cathi Weber for sharing in my haunted adventures; Michelle Belanger for inspiring me to find my voice; my mother, Rose, for being my best friend; my beautiful children—Elijah, Karen-Mackay, and Jack—for dealing with my unpredictable moods and odd wardrobe choices; my wonderful and incredibly handsome husband, J, for allowing me to embrace my strange fascinations even though he'd prefer "less haunted and more housewife"; and finally, my grandfather, who quietly sparked the fire that led to my passion for the paranormal.

Eric Olsen: I thank my amazing co-author Theresa Argie, whose knowledge, experience, and insight made the project possible and fun. Thanks to Steve Troha for making it happen, and Danielle Stockley for her deft and delicate editing touch. Special thanks to my patient and supportive wife, Dawn; my children, Kristen, Christopher, Lily, and Alex; and my parents, Ray and Barbara, who really shouldn't have to worry so much about me at this stage of the game.

Willoughby Coal and Garden Center

Willoughby, Ohio

INTRODUCTION

Willoughby Coal is not your typical haunt—it's a fully operational coal company and hardware store. In an era of "super haunts," it's refreshing to know that some of the most interesting places, the most haunted places, are little-known local treasures just waiting to be explored. Willoughby Coal represents that one place in every community that only the locals know about, a place so amazing they almost don't want to share it with anyone. But they should.

Before the simple, beautiful Willoughby Coal building of today, a series of other structures and businesses called the property home, including a train depot, a flour mill, a cheese factory, and numerous inns and lodges such as the Zebra Stagecoach House. The Zebra, named for its unusual striped paint job, was destroyed by a fire in 1879.

In 1893, the current building was built for use as a flour mill, well placed between two railroad lines that made it convenient to move product to market. The mill was successful until automation killed it, and a coal company took over in 1912. The Golf-Kirby Coal Company provided essential fuel to the city, CP&E—the local interurban railroad—and the burgeoning Andrew School for Girls.

In the 1930s, Henry Windus and William "Don" Norris, ambitious employees of Golf-Kirby, joined forces and bought the business. They renamed it Willoughby Coal and Supply, a title it retained until a relatively recent change to Willoughby Coal and Garden Center.

After many successful years of operation, the owners decided to remodel the third floor of Willoughby Coal in 1947. Don Norris kept a watchful eye on progress, taking notes and making recommendations to the construction crew. On the morning of April 2, Norris, who lived nearby, kissed his wife, Maude, goodbye and headed off for work early at 7:10 A.M.

When the shop foreman arrived at Willoughby Coal at 7:40 A.M., he was greeted by a gruesome sight: A man's mangled body lay facedown at the front entrance in a pool of blood. The entire left side of his head was bashed in, his face an unrecognizable mess. His outstretched arms were broken at the wrists. If not for the car still parked in its usual spot and the wallet in his pocket, the identity of the dead man would have been a mystery.

At first authorities thought Norris might have been robbed, but over $400 in company money was still on his person; his wallet was full of his personal cash; the keys to his brand-new car were still in the ignition; and his gold wristwatch, stopped at 7:26, was still on his broken wrist.

The investigators' next thought was that for some strange reason Norris had climbed the coal uploader on the side of the building to go up to the third floor, fallen, and somehow crawled to the front of the building. This idea was quickly dismissed when investigators realized that the extent of Norris's injuries would have made it impossible for him to crawl anywhere, let alone from the side of the building to the front.

Norris's bloody, battered body was sent to the local funeral home, where the director, oddly, found over a cup of coal dust in the dead man's clothing. The clothes Norris had worn that morning had been freshly laundered. How could he have collected that much coal residue in such a short period of time? The director also found a small hole in Norris's left boot.

The grieving family and stunned community wanted answers, and the police cobbled together a theory. Don Norris had arrived at work early, as was his habit, to check on the previous day's renovations. He had climbed up to the third-floor rafters to examine progress there. A circular window space approximately three feet in diameter, just under the crest of the roof, was open in the front wall. Norris's foot had gotten caught on a nail sticking up from the wood. He had lost his balance and pitched forward through the open window space, tragically plummeting three stories to his death.

This tenuous sequence of events was accepted as the cause of death for decades. To those unfamiliar with the building, or basic physics, this closed the case. But the dots never really connected: Norris would have had to *dive* toward the circular opening like Superman in order to get there from the rafters; simply tripping would not have propelled him that distance. Also, the mystery of the coal dust was never officially addressed.

There was nothing in the contract that provided for the widow or the family of the deceased partner. Maybe Norris never gave much thought to dying so young. Maybe he wasn't aware of the death clause in the contract, or maybe he never suspected his partner would leave his poor widow and children high and dry.

Maude Norris took in boarders and laundry to make ends meet. All she was left with was a bucket of tears and baskets of dirty laundry.

Many decades later, in the fall of 2011, Cathi Weber led a small group on her usual Willoughby Ghost Walk rounds. When they arrived at Willoughby Coal, Cathi told the ghostly tales and haunted happenings surrounding the building, including the story of Don Norris, which she had researched extensively for her book, *Haunted Willoughby, Ohio*. When she got to the details of his death, a hand went up in the crowd.

"Excuse me, I have something to add to that story," said a young man.

Cathi was surprised but intrigued. "Of course, if you have any information I'd love to hear it."

The young man introduced himself as the grandson of William "Don" Norris. He said the official cause of death was incorrect, it hadn't been an accident. His grandfather had been murdered! Now that his grandmother had joined her husband in death, the family felt compelled to speak out about what had really happened that fateful morning.

Cathi was speechless. The young man did indeed know many details that only someone who had extensively researched the case—or who was a family member—would know. According to the Norris family, Henry Windus had wanted the business, the whole business. He had tried to buy his partner's half, but Don Norris had not been interested in selling. A clause in the partnership agreement between Windus and Norris stated that upon the death of one owner, the other would retain full control of Willoughby Coal and Supply. After several attempts to get control legally, Windus had allegedly hatched a dastardly scheme.

Windus knew of his partner's early-morning habits, this version goes, and on April 2 he was waiting for him. With the help of someone or several "someones," Windus jumped Norris when he arrived at the store, dragged him up to the third floor onto the scaffolding at the front face of the building, and viciously tossed him out the window opening, whence he plunged fifty feet to his death.

This version of the incident would account for the injuries to his face and hands and the mysterious coal dust found on the dead man's clothes. Intriguing and logical, yes, but there is no way to prove any of it and the case has long been closed.

Don Norris's spirit haunts Willoughby Coal because not only was it the place of his untimely death, it was the place of his life. He poured his blood, sweat, and tears into his work, and now his essence remains, crying out for justice, for someone to hear the truth, whatever that may be.

The untimely and mysterious death of Don Norris isn't the only recorded death on the grounds of Willoughby Coal. Another man, an employee, died inside the building in the 1970s.

Zip was an older gentleman who was fond of the drink. His problem with alcohol led to the breakup of his marriage and loss of his home. He had no family to speak of, so the owners of Willoughby Coal took pity on this troubled man and let him stay in the building at night, watching over the place as a quasi security guard.

People knew him as an eccentric character who kept to himself for the most part. He had some unusual habits and odd mannerisms, often mumbling to himself. He was also very protective of the few belongings he actually owned.

Zip lived inside the building for many months, making his home in the back of the first floor until he died of a massive heart attack prepping a load of coal for delivery. The rumor that he had hidden something in the walls began to surface immediately after his death. Some thought it was money; others thought it was a collection of antique guns. Myriad tall tales turned a nondescript Willoughby Coal employee into a legend.

No one knows what Zip hid, if anything, inside Willoughby Coal, but apparently he is still guarding it. His apparition has been seen on the first, second, and third floors quite frequently over the last four decades. He's careful not to show himself completely, letting you catch only quick glimpses of his disheveled form. His footsteps echo off the brick walls, fading into silence once you've tracked their source.

Invasion of the Body Snatchers

The settlement that became Willoughby was prime real estate along the Chagrin River about twenty miles east of Cleveland. In the early 1830s, a group of enterprising young physicians began a quest to start a medical college in the hamlet, called Chagrin at the time. The townsfolk of Chagrin weren't sold on the idea of a medical college—medical colleges were notorious for obtaining cadavers for anatomy training through sometimes unscrupulous methods.

The schemers, led by Dr. John Anderson, petitioned esteemed doctor Westel Willoughby Jr. to come and preside over their fair institution of higher medical learning. The good doctor was flattered but reluctant to leave New York. Anderson and company tried another tactic—they renamed the town after Willoughby. The great man, while thanking them for such an honor, never set foot in the town that still bears his name.

In the sultry summer of 1843, the restive spirit of one Eli Tarbel, a mature gentleman dead three days from typhoid fever, revolted against his defilers, protesting to his widow in a vivid and disturbing dream that his "body was being taken apart piece by piece at the Willoughby Medical College." When Mrs. Tarbel awoke, she gathered her daughter and they went immediately to the cemetery. After discovering his grave empty, the alarmed woman alerted neighbors and the Lake County Guard, who stormed the school with pitchforks and torches looking for Eli's missing parts.

The enraged mob invaded the college grounds, demanding answers and demanding justice. Mr. Tarbel was found and a sophisticated grave-robbing and body-snatching ring was uncovered and thwarted by an outraged spirit and his widow.

The college was unable to recover from this stain; enrollment dropped, staff left the school, and the curtain closed on the medical college for good in 1847. But various uprooted doctors and trustees went on to establish the Starling Medical College (now the Ohio State University College of Medicine), the Medical Department of Western Reserve (now Case Western Reserve University School of Medicine), and an all-female seminary that went on to become the Lake Erie College for Women.

Not a bad legacy for a bunch of grave robbers.

Take the Haunted Tour—The Parking Lot

This haunted tour is unusual because it begins outside the building. This location is so active that the hauntings spill out onto the property. Willoughby Coal is more than just the brick-and-mortar building that we see today, it is a place full of memories, ripe with history. Who's to say that the ghosts that haunt Willoughby Coal weren't here long before the current stone structure was built? Or that the land itself isn't thick with the spirits of Native Americans, foreign explorers, and early settlers?

Personal Experience—
Theresa Argie: The Haunted Housewives Meet

I'll never forget the first time I laid eyes on Willoughby Coal in September 2009, a pivotal moment in my paranormal career—the night I met my Haunted Housewives partner Cathi Weber.

Cathi ran a popular historic ghost walk in downtown Willoughby. Her reputation as a storyteller and historian preceded her. I was teaching ghost-hunting workshops and seminars at the time but wanted to get more involved with community events. I hoped to learn from her experience and wisdom.

Cathi invited me to join her on the ghost walk so we could meet and discuss the possibility of working together. We shared a love of the paranormal and history, and I was excited to see her in action.

Cathi was a natural. Her recitation at each stop was colorful and detailed, complete with profound personal observations and the perfect mix of horror and humor. The history of Willoughby was fascinating, and every stop intrigued me more than the one before.

After a short walk out of Willoughby's bustling downtown, we made our way across the railroad tracks to a large gravel parking lot. Set about a hundred yards back, behind a smaller building that resembled a barn, was a three-story brick structure: our destination, Willoughby Coal.

As we moved closer to the building, I noticed other structures around it: a small red one-story "barn" with plants and outdoor décor used as a garden center; the Willoughby Area Welcome Center, set in an old silver train car painted with stripes of red, white, and blue; and a large white storage shed adjacent to the train tracks that run alongside the parking lot.

I moved slowly across the parking lot, the loose gravel crunching under my feet. I was mesmerized by the simple façade of the building, its candlelit windows peering at me like eyes. There was a round, bricked-up hole at the top center of the third floor, and I couldn't take my eyes off it.

But as I approached, my body reacted in a surprising and painful manner: With each step my stomach churned more uncomfortably. One moment I was completely fine and the next I was overcome with nausea. I stopped, startled by the sudden sickness.

"Whew . . . wow," I said out loud as I buckled over in pain.

Cathi noticed and immediately stopped. "What's wrong?" she asked.

"I don't know, I just suddenly feel awful." I'd barely gotten the words out when I began to dry-heave.

"I'll be fine, I'll catch up in a minute." I was totally embarrassed.

Reluctantly, Cathi continued with the rest of the group toward the front of the building. She stood atop the platform outside the main door with her candlelit lantern as the small crowd oohed and aahed at her story. I couldn't hear her over my own noisy stomach. I took a sip from my water bottle, composed myself, and started walking again. The sick feeling returned, with a vengeance.

I stopped again and waited for the feeling to pass before I dared take another step.

After another brief pause, I started toward the group, but the discomfort continued to build. I felt the blood drain from my face and a cold sweat cover my body. I was shaking, trembling, weak in the knees. I thought I might fall to the ground. I couldn't stop the feeling of dread from overtaking me. Now I really did have to throw up. I staggered over toward the garden center and vomited into a garbage can.

That was it for me. I wasn't going any farther.

Cathi finished telling her tale and returned to check on me. She tried to sit me on the platform by the front door, but every time I moved in that direction I just got more nauseated. I was mortified by the scene I was making—nice first impression, Theresa! Cathi took my arm and walked me away from the garden barn back toward the parking lot entrance.

The farther I got from Willoughby Coal, the better I felt. Like breaking away from the pull of some invisible force field, the bonds magically loosened as I headed back toward the street.

The color returned to my alabaster face and the dizziness passed as my equilibrium stabilized. By the time we crossed the railroad tracks I was fine, except for the total humiliation.

I believe I was overwhelmed with the paranormal energy emanating from the three-story brick structure. It was oozing out like invisible waves, all focused directly at me. There is so much activity there, so many stories, so many spirits all fighting for attention, needing to be noticed, to be remembered.

Take the Haunted Tour—The First Floor

The moment you set foot inside Willoughby Coal, you know it's no ordinary place. Part coal company, part hardware store, part curio museum, Willoughby Coal is definitely unique. Once, the need for coal was essential to the townsfolk in the area. It was a source of power and warmth in the days before electric or gas furnaces. Today only a few patrons actually come to Willoughby Coal for coal, but the resourceful owners have found other ways to stay in business.

Crossing the threshold of the front door, you enter a world filled with the past. An assortment of unusual antiques are displayed on walls, hanging from the ceiling, tucked in every corner. A seven-foot-tall railroad crossing light looms as you enter the store. An old barber's chair sits in a corner next to a vintage phone booth and wooden wheelchair. A series of barbaric-looking handsaws hang from the rafters, dangling like deadly stalactites. A large rusty scythe is secured to the brick support column across from the counter.

There are classic children's toys, outdated musical instruments, old faded advertising materials, even rusted push-pedal scooters scattered about in deliberate disarray all over the store. It is like a bizarro-world TGI Friday's.

To the right of the front door, there is a large work counter where the proprietors do their business with the public. Several signs, both old and new, hang above the cash register and on the walls. Behind the counter is a door that leads to the offices and employee restroom. Directly across from the counter are the wooden stairs that lead to the second floor.

One thing that people notice, besides the antiques everywhere, is how dark it is inside the building. There are two front windows and two on the side, but even in the light of day and under fluorescent artificial light, it remains dark on the merchandise floor, which adds to the eeriness of the store, setting the scene for some good ghost stories!

Personal Experience—
Theresa Argie: Shadows Everywhere, Ho Hum

The first time I actually made it *into* Willoughby Coal was a few weeks after my queasy introduction on the ghost walk with Cathi. She invited me back to check out the inside and get a better feel for the place. I was a bit apprehensive, having become so violently ill in the parking lot, but I told myself this time would be different: no bad vibes, no stomach issues, no headache, no dizziness.

I thought it an odd building to be haunted, but Cathi assured me it was. As I walked through the door, I saw peculiar objects everywhere. It was as if I'd stepped into an exploded antique shop or wind-torn garage sale. But then I saw the store counter, the register, the security camera, things that indicated it was indeed a place of business.

My mind was bombarded with visual input from all around; I didn't know where to start. Cathi suggested we tour the entire place first so I could get oriented. As we walked methodically through each area, my eyes darted back and forth rapidly, scanning each dimly lit corner. We were alone at Willoughby Coal, or so I thought. My heightened peripheral vision noticed a dark shadow peeking around the door to the back storage room. When I turned to face it, it disappeared only to reappear seconds later behind some shelving on the back wall.

"So, do you ever see shadow play in this area?" I asked as my eyes continued to search the dark.

"Oh yes, lots of shadows. I catch glimpses of them out of the corner of my eyes. Why? Did you see something?" Cathi was not the least bit surprised.

"Well, I'm seeing something, some sort of movement in the back there." I pointed to the rear of the store.

"They're everywhere in this building. I think they're checking us out." Cathi was unfazed by this familiar visual phenomenon.

"Let's check out the stockroom. It's a great place for EVPs, and it's where I had my first paranormal experience inside this place," Cathi said as we headed back into the storage rooms and loading dock area.

Personal Experience—
Karen-Mackay Argie (Daughter of Theresa Argie)

Having a mom who's a ghost hunter can be, well, awkward. But growing up with the paranormal has become normal for me and my family. My little brother, Jack, and I have been around the ghosty stuff all our lives. We even get to participate in some of Mom's projects. I help Cathi and her with the ghost walks in the fall, pushing tours and answering questions. It's kind of fun, and I really like the history part!

Sometimes I help out with ghost classes: my mom's Ghost Hunting 101 and Cathi's Junior Ghost Hunting classes held at Willoughby Coal. The junior class is fun; it has lots of other kids, even some around my age. I feel more comfortable around the kids and they usually like hearing my stories. I've learned a lot about ghosts over the years!

Paranormal Activities

Shadow Play: the visual phenomenon of unusual, distinct, and/or intelligent movement of shadows, typically with no apparent natural source.

Electronic Voice Phenomenon (EVP): ghostly voices or sounds not audible to the unaided ear that are captured on electronic recording devices, which detect a broader range of frequencies than the human ear.

In the summer of 2012, Jack and I were at the Junior Ghost Hunting class at Willoughby Coal. There were about a dozen kids there, ranging in age from about six (Jack) to eleven (me). A few of the parents stayed as well, just in case someone got scared. Mom and Cathi gave a presentation about ghosts and what to do if you want to find them. After a quick lesson on how to use the equipment, we started investigating.

We were all on the first floor, near the stockroom. There were all kinds of tools, industrial buckets, and boxes of tile stacked on the floor. There were huge shelves with lots of plumbing and building material on them as well. All the kids were huddled together between the shelves and the back stock area.

Mom led an EVP session. "Are there any spirits here that would like to come out and say hello? We've brought visitors today."

Cathi joined in: "The children have come to meet you. No one will hurt you; we just want to prove to them that you're here."

Mom continued, "If you're here, can you make a noise or move something for us?"

Right after my mom finished asking that question, we all heard this really really loud crashing sound. BOOM!!! It was such a big sound, I could feel the concrete floor vibrate.

"AAAAAAAAHH!" All the kids screamed at the same time. I'm pretty sure some adults did too.

Mom and Cathi ran over to where the crash had come from. We could see dust particles rising from the floor right next to one of the large shelves. Something big must have fallen off the top shelf. We all crowded in around Mom and Cathi. The parents waiting in the other room came in to investigate as well.

There was nothing on the ground—I couldn't believe it! We had all heard it and seen the dust. I was sure it would be a huge box or large piece of *something*. Cathi looked all around with her flashlight, making sure something hadn't dropped and maybe rolled away, but she found nothing.

A few of us had voice recorders running and you could hear the crash on playback.

To this day, I have no clue what made that noise or why nothing was there when we went to look. Mom and Cathi had everyone's full attention for the rest of the class!

THE STOCKROOM

To the right of the main entrance is a doorway that separates the showroom from the stockroom. Once you go through that door, another side of Willoughby Coal is revealed. The stockroom is a place where merchandise is delivered, received, and stored. Past the stockroom is the loading dock, a raised platform that drops five feet into a ground-level pit filled with metal machines and stacks of unprocessed merchandise. The store's first floor is elevated, hence the stairs at the front door.

Without the aid of artificial light, the stockroom is dark, very dark. But many reliable sources have reported seeing eye shine peering out at them from the gloom. Several years ago, during a routine "rattling door" check, a rookie Willoughby patrol officer stopped by Willoughby Coal on a winter evening to make sure everything was locked up tight and nothing was out of place.

Paranormal Activities

Eye Shine: the glowing reflection created when light from an external source strikes eyes, alive or otherwise.

These door checks help businesses ward off crime and foster good community relations.

Upon finding the front door ajar, the officer entered the store, looking for a presumed intruder. On the first floor he thought he heard someone right behind him, but when he turned, nothing and no one was there. This disturbing sensation was repeated on each subsequent floor of the store. After determining there was no *human* intruder inside Willoughby Coal, the cop made a mad dash for the front door.

During another routine check of the building, a different officer noticed some strange shadows in one of the downstairs windows. He climbed the front stairs and shined his flashlight inside but could find nothing out of place. He repeated this procedure at all the first-floor windows but couldn't see anyone inside.

He ventured to the back side of the building near the loading docks. There was no window for him to investigate, so he shined his light through the slats on the large bay door. He cautiously placed his face up to the tiny opening and peered inside.

His heart nearly stopped when his light beam hit what appeared to be two glowing eyes glaring back at him! These faceless eyes appeared right at head level, so they couldn't have been an animal, but they certainly weren't human. The stunned officer beat a hasty retreat back to the safety of his patrol car and drove off.

Trying to rationalize the experience, he immediately telephoned the owner and asked who was living inside the storeroom. The owners assured him the place was empty; no one was inside Willoughby Coal, except for the ghosts.

Personal Experience—
Cathi Weber (Haunted Housewives Co-Founder, Paranormal Investigator, Author)

Willoughby is a magical place and I'm proud to call it my hometown. I started the Willoughby Ghost Walk because I was fascinated by all the history around me. Where there's history, there's haunting. I grew up surrounded by the iconic buildings and storefronts of this town and I was dying to know their stories, their *real* stories, the ones left out of the history books. My research had uncovered many ghostly happenings at Willoughby Coal and I needed to have an experience of my own!

It didn't take much effort to persuade the then-owners of Willoughby Coal, Jay Byram and Dan Garry (Dan sold his interest in 2011), to let me do a paranormal investigation. They were curious to see what I would come up with spending the night inside the store.

I invited a small group to join me; some were experienced paranormal investigators, some just curious ghost enthusiasts. Since there were more than a dozen of us, I thought it best we break into small groups and take turns inside; this way we could avoid audio contamination.

The first group went in while the rest of us waited patiently outside. Not long after they entered the building, one young lady came bounding out the front door. She was terrified, shaking uncontrollably and nearly in tears. As she had entered the stockroom area, something very large had come rushing at her. She described it as big, dark brown, and hairy like an animal.

"Oh my God, that was so scary! I thought I was about to be attacked!"

I asked her to keep this incident to herself until the end of the night. I didn't want to scare anyone or put ideas regarding what to expect in their heads.

The next group took its turn inside. When they came out, I asked if anything had happened. "No, it was really quiet. We didn't hear anything at all. We didn't see any shadows either," a member of the group replied, a tinge of disappointment in her voice.

"Wow, really? Nothing, huh?" I was kind of surprised myself.

"Well, the only weird thing was the smell. It was awful," she said.

I was confused. "What smell?"

"Oh God, the horrible smell back in the stockroom. It was overpowering. Gross."

I'd been in the building dozens of times and never noticed any unusual smell, certainly nothing "gross."

But the group insisted. "It smelled like old wet dirty dog or something. Yuck!"

Group three entered the building. When they came back out, I noticed confused looks on their faces. I asked if anything had happened. The group leader said they hadn't seen anything, but their audio recorder had picked up an unusual sound.

When we played it back, there was a low growling noise. The animalistic sound was unmistakable and terrifying.

Now I was really puzzled. What was going on inside Willoughby Coal? I'd soon find out for myself, as it was my group's turn to go inside. We headed immediately toward the stockroom, where everyone else had had their experiences. We gathered by the loading dock, careful not to fall off the ledge. Tiny slivers of streetlight peeked through the slats in the loading dock door from the security light outside. Other than that, it was pitch black.

We stayed perfectly quiet for a few minutes, hoping to hear the growl or see some sort of strange movement. I strained my eyes in the darkness trying to make out any shadow forms in the area. My nose prepped for a foul odor, but there was nothing unusual in the air. It was time for some EVP work.

"Is there anyone here with us? Are you trying to get our attention?" I asked.

At that moment, I felt the sensation of a large furry animal scurrying over my sandal-clad skin.

"OH MY GOD! There's something by my feet!" I screamed.

I didn't have a flashlight to see the fifty-pound tarantula that *must* have been attacking me in the dark. My companions rushed to my aid, but we could find nothing. No giant spider, no rabid squirrel, no rat. But this was no small rodent or bug, this was something large, with weight and mass to it, not a tiny mouse tickling my toes.

Well, that was enough for us, and out we went to share our story with everyone outside. We packed it up for the night and headed home. I pondered the strange happenings at Willoughby Coal. It certainly wasn't what I had expected.

The next morning, I went back to the store to return the keys to owners Jay and Dan. They were curious and anxious to hear what had happened during our investigation. I recounted our experiences, thinking they were odd and unrelated. I saw a knowing grin spread across Dan's face.

I asked, "What? What is it?"

"Well, Cathi, there are a few things I didn't tell you about this place. Maybe this will make sense to you now."

Yukon was a large chocolate lab Dan had had since he was a puppy. Yukon often came to the store with his master and was very comfortable around customers. He had the run of the place and went in and out as he pleased. In his later years, Yukon had still come to work with Dan, but the years had taken their toll. He was losing his hearing and partially blind. Instead of happily greeting customers with a wagging tail, he would often rush up to them growling, then sniff and circle around their feet before retreating to his spot by the door. He also hated taking a bath. The poor thing smelled awful, like an old dirty dog would.

One cold winter day Dan was ready to close up shop. He noticed Yukon was not in his usual spot, curled up in front of the warm potbellied heater by the door. The employees frantically called for the dog and looked around the store, but he was no-where to be found. Finally they looked outside, where they found paw prints in the snow leading to the railroad tracks. They rushed over to the tracks and found poor Yukon, lying motionless on the side of the rails. He had been hit by a train. They carried his battered body back to Willoughby Coal and laid him down by the front door, where he passed away in the loving arms of his master.

After we heard the story of Yukon, things clicked. Everything that had happened the night before made sense: the growling, the lunging shadow, the rancid smell, and the furry encounter at my feet! Yukon was still watching over Willoughby Coal, greet-ing guests who entered his territory and letting them know he was there.

Yukon is one of the many resident spirits at Willoughby Coal. He's used to me now and no longer scares me when I come to visit.

A psychic friend of mine who had never heard the story of Yukon asked me on her first visit, "Who owns the big choco-late lab?"

I was stunned. "A lab? Where?"

"Right there," she said, pointing to the door. "He's lying right there in front of the door. He's kind of dirty, actually, but he's not going anywhere. He thinks he owns the place."

Personal Experience—
Daniel Hooven (Paranormal Investigator) with
Rebecca Kirschbaum (Psychic)

Last year Theresa and Cathi introduced me to Rebecca Kirschbaum at the Para-Ex 2012 fund-raiser for the Lake County Historical Society, an event Cathi puts on every November. The event always features celebrity speakers and guest investigators such as Michelle Belanger (A&E's *Paranormal State*) and Jackie Williams.

Rebecca was introduced as Michelle's good friend and newest protégé. I was impressed by her undeniable gift and easygoing personality. We hit it off immediately. We'd both been featured on a Syfy show called *School Spirits*, so we had quite a bit in common. I enjoyed watching her gentle and personal approach to the paranormal. Rebecca and I have been working together ever since.

Rebecca lives in Ohio, not far from Willoughby, the hometown of my favorite Haunted Housewives, so I visit as often as I can. In June 2013, Rebecca and I joined Cathi one evening after one of her ghost walks. Rebecca had never been to Willoughby before, so I asked Cathi if she could show us around.

We were intrigued by Willoughby Coal—the building has an energy about it that draws you in. Rebecca felt it right away; something was calling to her. We went inside and Cathi gave us a quick tour but didn't give away any of the history. She didn't want to influence Rebecca's impressions.

As soon as we walked in the front door, Rebecca asked, "Whose dog is that? I see a big dog, a black lab maybe?"

Cathi grinned. "You're not the first psychic to pick up on the dog. That's Yukon."

We continued inside, heading toward the loading docks and stockroom. I couldn't shake the sensation of eyes watching us from the dark. Rebecca walked slowly toward the back corner of the stockroom and spotted something only she could see.

Calmly and quietly, she said with a comforting smile on her face, "Hey there, don't be afraid. You don't have to hide from us."

She said an older man and a young boy were cowering in the corner. They were very thin, wearing tattered clothes and no shoes. They were African American.

Turning back to Cathi, she asked, "Was this place part of the Underground Railroad?"

"Not that I know of, but that doesn't mean it wasn't. They didn't always keep records of that kind of thing back then. But this location, right by the railroad and near the water . . . this could have been a safe house." Cathi pondered the idea.

Rebecca tried to talk to the two spirits, but they were frightened of us. "They saw our lanterns and think we're slave catchers. They're afraid of the dog too!"

Cathi was surprised. "Yukon? Wow, they can see Yukon? He's from a totally different era."

I was amazed by the possibility. Could ghosts from the antebellum era be aware of a ghost from the 1990s? Since Rebecca was the only person who could see the two slave spirits, I thought I'd try another avenue of communication. I pulled out my recorder and started an EVP session.

"Can you see us? We won't hurt you. We want to help you. We are not slave catchers." The light on my voice-activated recorder was solid red, indicating an EVP had been captured. I anxiously played back the file.

"*We're still scared*," came the heartbreaking response. We all heard the fear in the whispered voice on the recorder.

Rebecca tried to psychically communicate with these two poor souls and assure them that we would not hurt them, and they had no reason to be afraid of us. But I knew that even after we left for the night, they would still be stuck in the building with the spirit of the dog. I hoped Rebecca had convinced them the dog was harmless, the war was over, and they were now free.

What a horrible way to live your afterlife: hiding and afraid, huddled in the corner of an old dusty building far away from home, yearning only to be free. It makes me wonder how much choice we have in what happens to us after we die. I couldn't imagine anyone would choose to stay in this frightened, confused state, and my heart broke a little.

Take the Haunted Tour—The Second Floor

A set of wooden steps leads from the main floor of Willoughby Coal up to the second. An old Inuit dogsled hangs overhead—it's an unusual sight to see, even in a place full of unusual things.

The second floor is beset with more bizarre items: A battered table and child's school desk are positioned next to an old steamer trunk; the skin of a white wolf hangs on display by the dressing rooms; a black baby carriage, a rusty tricycle, and a vintage Singer sewing machine are scattered about. Interspersed between these treasures are rows and rows of brand-new jackets, overalls, and work wear, neatly arranged for easy shopping, if you don't mind walking around the fully intact, highly polished speedboat that takes up about a third of the showroom area. If the owner knows how it got up there, he isn't saying.

Personal Experience—
Theresa

On a spring 2013 investigation at Willoughby Coal, I endured the frustrating experience of "chasing shadows." Sometimes the ghosts in the building like to toy with us, make us question our sanity. As I stood on the first floor, the footsteps I heard above me were so loud, so clear, I thought there *had* to be someone up there!

Cathi was accustomed to this phenomenon and it barely fazed her, but I implored her to investigate with me.

"Come on, Cathi, let's check upstairs. Something is up there. Don't you hear it?"

Cathi shrugged. "Yeah, I hear it, but we won't find anything."

Still, I needed to find out for myself. The sound of quickly moving footsteps resounded above me, as if someone were rushing into position, angling into a hiding spot.

We grabbed our recorders and cameras and headed up to the second floor. The first thing that greeted my eyes was a tall shadow darting across the room at the top of the landing.

And so it began.

"Did you see that?" I asked Cathi.

"Oh yeah, I saw it. Let's see if we can get it on video."

We took our places, sitting side by side in the middle of the

Paranormal Activities

Cold Spot: a distinct and presumably unnatural area of cold air that can manifest and dissipate suddenly and/or move with intelligent intent. Cold spots are thought to form when a spirit absorbs energy (heat) from the air.

room. I faced the north wall; Cathi faced the south. With our cameras and recorder ready, we tried an EVP session.

"Okay, we know you're here. We heard you walking around. I also saw someone when we came up the stairs." I tried a straightforward, logical approach.

Cathi chimed in, "You must *want* to be seen; you play this game with us every time we're here! Don't be shy now. Tell us what your message is."

Suddenly, it was very cold—I could almost see my breath.

"Damn, do you feel that? It's cold."

Cathi felt it as well. "Are you making it cold in here?"

I continued questioning. "Please just tell us who you are. What do you want to say to us?"

When we played back the audio file, "*Get out!*" was the response on our recorder.

This answer just pissed us off. My dander was up and I wasn't going anywhere. "Now why would you so obviously want us to know you're here and then tell us to get out? Who are you?"

Our session was interrupted by the sound of more footsteps, precise and rhythmic, coming from the *third* floor this time! Whatever was walking had moved up to the top floor of the building.

"You're kidding me—do you hear that? Now it's upstairs!" Cathi was amused. I was not.

"Why do they do this to us all the time? What do they want?" We headed up to the third floor to investigate the footsteps, even though we knew we wouldn't find anything. When we got upstairs, the footsteps stopped . . . momentarily.

Less than a minute later they started up again, but this time they were coming from downstairs. We heard the strike of each heel and the distinctive squeak of the floor.

Back down we went, frustrated. This was the behavior of an intelligent and very annoying spirit. Or maybe there was more than one.

Cathi tried reasoning with our invisible guest. "We don't mean you any harm, but we would like to know why you're doing this. Why do you stay here?"

When we played back the recorder, an angry voice on the tape screamed at us, "*AHH! GO!*"

At that point we stopped our investigation. We packed up our stuff and headed down to the main floor, but not before witnessing another strange sight. This wasn't a shadow but more of a mist, light in color, semitransparent with an undefined shape and erratic movement that appeared right in front of the stair landing on the first floor, blocking our descent. It hung in midair, pulsating for a few seconds before fading into nothingness.

"Um, okay. That was weird," I noted. Was this something good? Something evil? Was it a spirit or something completely different? It moved with intent, one last show of power from an entity inside Willoughby Coal.

Cathi said, "Yeah, I think something is mad. We'd better not push our luck tonight. We'll be back."

The shadows, the footsteps, the cold spots, and the EVPs all added up to a successful night of ghost hunting. The spirit we encountered wasn't shy; it wasn't afraid to let us know it was there. It was angry or at least seemed that way.

I theorized that sometimes the ghosts try extremely hard to get their voices heard. Sometimes it works, sometimes it doesn't. Maybe they get upset when they're unsuccessful. Or we were dealing with multiple spirits, with different agendas and personalities.

Take the Haunted Tour—The Third Floor

When empty, the third floor of Willoughby Coal is like an enormous attic. The wood floor creaks as you tread upon it, and the arched ceiling is crisscrossed with thick beams. The dark redbrick walls are broken only by the six windows paired on three of the four walls. Remnants of old scaffolding remain sticking out from the rafters. The point of the roof ends above the round bricked-in circle that was once open to the outside directly above the front door, the spot of the mysterious Norris death in the 1940s.

The proprietor of Willoughby Coal uses the third floor for a number of different purposes: storage, meetings, it's even a great spot for photography. But even when empty, it isn't vacant. Many of the resident spirits of Willoughby Coal like to hang out on the third floor, occasionally making their presence known.

Personal Experience—
Theresa

Whenever Cathi and I get the ghost-hunting bug, we head on over to Willoughby Coal. It's where we teach our classes and do all our training, and whenever we get a new piece of equipment, we try it out there first. It offers as close to a controlled environment as we can hope for, and being accustomed to a place helps us separate normal from paranormal experiences.

In August 2012, we bought an expensive new audio recorder, one we'd been dying to get our hands on for years. We were headed down to Waverly Hills Sanatorium in a week's time, so we wanted to get familiar with the device before the trip. Late one Monday night, after the kids were safe and snug in their beds and the town was shut down for the night, we met at Willoughby Coal for the christening of "the Oracle," the name we chose for our new, completely overpriced recorder.

Conditions were superb for spirit communication. Although the Oracle is highly sensitive and picks up sounds barely audible to us, noise contamination from outside was minimal. The occasional train rumbling down the track next to us made a distinct sound we could easily identify later.

I felt called to the third floor—someone or something was waiting for us. I love the third floor. It's different every time I visit, so I never know what to expect. Voices echo and sound carries up there, making it perfect for EVP work, since spirit voices don't usually echo and are therefore easily discerned from those of the living.

It was hot and muggy, the air thick and stifling around us. "How about right here?" Cathi asked, pointing to the desk. I pulled up a chair and we proudly set out our new recorder next to an older model.

We began with short-burst sessions, anxious to hear the results immediately. "Hello. It's me, Cathi. Theresa is here with me tonight and we're hoping we can talk again."

I joined in, "You remember me, don't you? Tonight there's only the two of us. There's no need to be afraid. We're trying to understand your story."

After a few minutes, with the formalities out of the way, it was time to get specific. We referred back to the history of Willoughby Coal, and specifically the strange death of Don Norris in 1947.

"Mr. Norris, are you here?" Cathi asked.

"If you're *not* Don Norris, what is your name?" I asked.

The Oracle responded with, "*Mike,*" an all-too-familiar name to us. "Mike" shows up at many of our investigations, even coming through at Cathi's house once.

"Mike? Are you the same Mike from the Ohio State Reformatory?" I almost didn't want to know. The idea that a ghost can follow you from one place to the next is creepy and disturbing.

"*Yes . . . NO!*" the Oracle screamed at us. Now we were confused. Was Mike here or was he not? Was someone else here too? I asked Cathi if she thought we were dealing with more than one entity.

"I don't know—I think there's someone else trying to come through."

"Okay, well, we can only talk to one of you at a time. Please, Mike, who's with you?"

No answer. Maybe Mike was done talking.

"Do you know Mr. Norris?" Cathi inquired of our mystery guest.

"*Yes,*" the Oracle responded. Now we were intrigued. Was this Don Norris or someone who knew him? We pushed for more information.

Cathi asked, "We know something terrible happened here a long time ago. It was very sad and we still have questions about it. Do you know what happened to Mr. Norris?"

"*Died.*"

"Yes, he died. How did Mr. Norris die?" I asked.

"*MURDER!!*" the answer screamed from the voice recorder.

This emotional response shocked us! Cathi looked at me, eyes wide and mouth open.

"Murder? Was Mr. Norris murdered? By whom?" She pushed a little too far.

"*AAAGGHH!!!*" The screaming response from an angry spirit confirmed our suspicions. We both believe Don Norris was indeed murdered, but we can't prove it. Was this his spirit crying out for justice?

After that, the Oracle went silent. The heavy, stagnant air thinned a bit and it became easier to breathe. Our new toy had worked like a dream. A terrifyingly wonderful dream. We thanked the spirits for talking to us, asked them to please forgive us if we had upset them, and, for God's sake, NOT to follow us home. We left.

Personal Experience—
Theresa: The Enigma of Mike

Cathi Weber and I have a spirit named Mike who follows us around. This is one of the dangers of our field: Spirits can and do attach themselves to the living, sometimes following them home. We believe we first encountered him during an investigation at the Ohio State Reformatory (OSR), and he's been with us ever since, appearing at investigations at Prospect Place, the Lake County Historical Society, Waverly Hills Sanatorium, and more recently Willoughby Coal.

We have consistently captured EVPs with the same voice claiming to be Mike. He knows us, knows who we are and what we do; he even knows our maiden names! This spirit scares me. He usually becomes very agitated whenever I am around and has sworn and cussed at me on several occasions. With Cathi, he is calmer, less threatening, but I have warned her to be careful with him, to not interact with him, especially at home.

Cathi thought something strange was afoot after the investigation at OSR: weird shadows darting around her kitchen, cold spots developing suddenly, and the intense feeling of being watched. But then she encountered a large black mass in human form in her house. The tall slender shadow man boldly passed by her, without any attempt at subtlety. Was this Mike? To find out, Cathi broke the golden rule of ghost hunters: She did an EVP session in her own home. She wasn't surprised when Mike came through on audio confirming her suspicions. She told Mike he must not hurt her and must stay away from her children and grandchildren.

As I was writing this in the summer of 2013, Cathi was visiting the zoo with her six-year-old granddaughter Emma. Cathi and I had been communicating throughout the day, something we do regularly, especially while I'm writing about our adventures.

My writing was interrupted by a frantic text from Cathi. She'd been standing with Emma at one of the animal exhibits when the little girl turned to her suddenly and asked, "Did you hear that?"

Cathi had heard nothing but animal noises and asked Emma what she was talking about.

Emma insisted, "That man's voice in my ear. You didn't hear him?"

"No, Emma, what man's voice? What did he say?" Cathi saw the sincerity in her eyes and heard the earnestness in her voice.

"He just said his name, right in my ear, 'Mike! Mike! Mike!'"

Cathi's heart sank as an unsettling mixture of anger and terror welled inside her. Could this be the same Mike?

"Are you sure you didn't hear him, Nana?" Emma asked.

Cathi could tell Emma had heard what she said she had heard, a man's voice saying "Mike!" three times. Cathi dropped the subject—she didn't want to frighten Emma—but she was livid. She called me immediately. I had literally just finished reviewing our audio recorder and writing up Mike's Willoughby Coal cameo.

A few days after the incident at the zoo, Cathi felt the presence of Mike in her home, but this time things felt different, wrong. As she settled into her bed for the night, she felt the bed start to shake, moving rapidly in an unnatural manner. The sensation was sustained, lasting for almost a full minute. She called out to her son, the only other person in the house, who was downstairs at the time. The moment he opened the door to her bedroom, the shaking stopped.

Cathi and I have decided it's time for Mike to go. We are exploring different avenues to help this spirit move on. We're not sure we have the power or the right to "get rid of" a ghost or spirit, but a boundary has been crossed and we refuse to be haunted or bullied by someone from the other side.

Last Stop Willoughby

Most horror fans are familiar with the seminal 1960s television series *The Twilight Zone* and its creator, Rod Serling, but relatively few are aware of the connection between the show and Willoughby, Ohio.

In one of the most memorable and haunting episodes in the classic series, an overworked, underappreciated, mentally exhausted New York City media buyer drifts into an idyllic dream of a simpler time in a quaint little town, Willoughby, that exists only in his dreams.

This Willoughby is a place lost in time where children run barefoot and horse-drawn carriages fill the streets. Everyone knows your name and greets you with a smile. In "A Stop at Willoughby," Serling paints a picture of a perfect, peaceful place that might represent heaven.

Slightly tongue-in-cheek, the real town of Willoughby, Ohio, celebrates this ideal, this identity, every year with an end-of-summer festival called *Last Stop Willoughby*.

CONCLUSION

Willoughby Coal is different from the other locations in this book. It's the only one that isn't using its paranormal reputation to promote business—its actual business has nothing to do with ghosts. It is still a coal company and a hardware store. Cathi and Theresa went looking for insight into a mysterious death, the loving bond between a dog and his master, and a rumored treasure hidden somewhere in the walls. But they found much more than ghost stories; they found a home. Willoughby Coal is the Haunted Housewives home base, a place where they share their world with others. By day, the historic building is a successful business, a staple in the community for over a century; by night, it's a playground for the many spirits that inhabit the store and property.

What You Need to Know Before You Go:

Willoughby Coal and Garden Center
3872 Erie St.
Willoughby, OH 44094

Contact Information:
(440) 942-34700
willoughbycoal.com

Willoughby is a picturesque Ohio treasure. The historic downtown area is an entertainment and shopping district, with charming boutiques, cozy cafés, and a wide range of dining options.

Willoughby Coal is located just east of the square, next to the Willoughby Area Welcome Center.

Besides the store's building supplies, drainage products, pavers, retaining wall systems, and garden supplies, there is a wide variety of unusual and interesting antiques on display. The friendly staff will be happy to share their ghost stories with you. To see this and all the historic and haunted sites in town, join the Haunted Housewives on the Willoughby Ghost Walk.

Additional Reading:
Haunted Willoughby, Ohio by Cathi Weber (History Press, 2010)

Lodging:

Red Roof Inn Cleveland East—Willoughby, (440) 946-9872
4166 State Route 306, Willoughby, OH 44094
redroof.com

Courtyard by Marriott Cleveland Willoughby, (866) 767-0278
35103 Maplegrove Rd., Willoughby, OH 44094
marriott.com/courtyard

Days Inn Willoughby/Cleveland, (866) 925-4159
4145 State Route 306, Willoughby, OH 44094
daysinn.com

Radisson Hotel & Suites Cleveland—Eastlake, (866) 538-6252
35000 Curtis Blvd., Eastlake, OH 44095
radisson.com

Homestead House Bed & Breakfast, (440) 946-1902
38111 W. Spaulding St., Willoughby, OH 44094
homesteadhousebb.com

The Villisca Ax Murder House

Villisca, Iowa

INTRODUCTION

By the turn of the twentieth century, small towns lined the railroads that traversed America. Villisca, Iowa, was one of these places, the epitome of "small-town America": safe, friendly, and community oriented—a good place to raise a family.

Local lore claims *Villisca* means "pretty place" or "pleasant view," but Native Americans of the Sauk and Fox tribes offer a more sinister etymology. Derived from the word *waliska*, its name means "evil spirit."

On the evening of June 9, 1912, the Moore family—Josiah (43), Sarah (39), Herman (11), Katherine (10), Boyd (8), and Paul (5)—and overnight guests Lena Stillinger (11) and her sister Ina (8) attended a highly anticipated children's program at the local Presbyterian church. The program ended late, after 9:30 P.M. The town of Villisca was dark. There was no moonlight, and a dispute between the municipal power company and city officials had resulted in the streetlights being turned off.

The Stillinger girls, afraid to walk alone through the darkened streets, telephoned home seeking permission to stay with the Moores. The family and their young guests made their way home and settled into bed sometime around 10 P.M. When the sun came up Monday morning, a neighbor doing her wash noticed how unusually still the Moore house was. By the time the clock struck 7 A.M., curiosity turned to concern and she telephoned Ross Moore, Josiah's brother.

Ross telephoned the house. Getting no answer, he called his brother's store to find he had not yet arrived at work. Growing more concerned by the minute, Ross made haste to the Moore house. Along with the neighbor, Ross circled the house, calling out to his brother's family, looking for any signs of life.

At 8:30 Ross pulled out his keys and opened the locked door. Once inside he made his way through the kitchen and parlor toward the downstairs bedroom. Almost immediately, he was confronted by the horrific sight of two bloody and lifeless figures lying in the small single bed in the downstairs sewing room.

Ross stopped and immediately called Villisca marshal Hank Horton, who arrived promptly to investigate. Once inside, Horton methodically went through the tiny house of horrors.

"There's someone murdered in every bed!" he exclaimed in disbelief.

The only clue as to what had befallen the eight victims was a bloody ax placed against the wall of the sewing room. Each victim had been bludgeoned with the blunt end of the ax until no face was recognizable. It was later discovered that at least one of the Moores had been struck with the sharp end as well. The bloodied faces of each victim, and, oddly, every mirror and window in the home, had been covered with items of clothing or blankets.

Word spread like wildfire through the close-knit community, and soon the house was overrun with police, neighbors, towns-folk, and curiosity seekers. Any hope of securing the crime scene was lost, and vital potential evidence was destroyed in the frenzy of activity.

An outraged and fearful public cried out for justice and a culprit. Authorities sent out posses and bloodhounds, looking for any "stranger" who might have committed such a monstrous crime. When no viable "outsider" suspect was found, it appeared the killer was one of Villisca's own. Accusations flew like daggers, and a frenzied terror overtook the community. As potential suspects came and went, authorities narrowed the list of suspects down to three.

At the top of the short list was F. F. Jones, a wealthy politician, banker, and business rival of Josiah Moore. Josiah had worked for Jones in his farm implement business but had quit to start his own venture, taking the lucrative John Deere account with him. Local rumors of an affair between Jones's daughter-in-law Dona and Josiah Moore were rife at the time, further adding to specu-lation of Jones's involvement.

The prevailing theory was that Jones had orchestrated the hit on Moore. A patsy named William "Blackie" Mansfield was targeted as the man hired by Jones to kill the Moores.

F. F. Jones and William Mansfield were indicted for the mur-ders in 1916, but the case was quickly dismissed.

The victims' families and half the town were convinced Jones had hired Mansfield to kill Josiah Moore and remained steadfast in their quest for justice. A private detective named James Wilk-erson led the charge against Jones, determined to close the case once and for all. Jones retaliated by suing Wilkerson for slander. Wilkerson's attorney argued that the slander case was not valid because his accusations were all true! They went to trial and instead of Wilkerson relenting, he turned the tide on his accuser, essentially trying Jones, now a state senator, again for murder. Neither charge made it past the grand jury.

The people of Villisca and the Moore and Stillinger families were devastated; it seemed the eight slain victims would never be avenged. But in 1917 another offering was made to the gods of justice in the form of Reverend Lyn George J. Kelly. Kelly, a visiting Presbyterian minister, had arrived in Villisca just days before the murders. Almost immediately, his odd behavior had raised eyebrows.

Kelly was a waif of a man, about 5'2", 119 pounds, schizophrenic, and a possible pedophile who had been arrested for sending obscene materials through the mail. He spent the better part of a year in a mental hospital in 1914. His proclivity for young girls and a witness's statement that he had known details of the Villisca crime before the bodies had been discovered led to a criminal investigation in 1917.

Kelly was an outsider, an Englishman, not of the Villisca community. While in custody, he supposedly confessed to the murders three times, each version being slightly different. It is likely these confessions were coerced or beaten out of him, yet vivid details painted a horrific picture, leading many to believe he was somehow involved in the massacre.

According to his confession, on the night of the murders Kelly hadn't been able to sleep, so he had gone for a walk. While walking he heard God's voice speaking to him, telling him to go forth and "slay utterly." A dark shadow appeared, leading him to the Moores' house where God spoke to him again: "Suffer the little children to come unto me." Kelly said he was in a trancelike state following the directions of the Lord, who led him to the ax by the shed. He picked it up as ordered, went inside, and killed Josiah and Sarah. The voice told him to do the same to the four sleeping children in the next room. Afterward, the voice said,

"There's still more to be done," and he descended the stairs into the sewing room and quickly killed Ina and Lena Stillinger.

Vivid confession notwithstanding, most doubted Kelly had actually committed the murders, stating the obvious fact that he lacked the physical attributes to do such a thing. The first of two trials ended in a hung jury, eleven-to-one for acquittal. The second trial led to an acquittal. Most believed Kelly was deeply mentally disturbed but doubted he actually committed the crimes.

No one else was ever tried for the murders.

The massacre faded into the memory of the town like the bloodstained walls in the Moore house, whitewashed again and again in an attempt to cover the past. The house remained vacant for a number of years before a series of families passed through. Occasionally an occupant reported something strange, but for the most part the house remained quiet, paranormally speaking.

In 1993, Darwin Linn bought the property with the aim of restoring it, choosing *not* to forget the horrors of 1912. Linn turned the home into a living museum, opening it up to the outside world for the first time in nearly 100 years. Soon visitors reported strange experiences. It was evident that the notorious Villisca Ax Murder House was haunted.

Several television programs have filmed episodes there, including *Scariest Places on Earth*, *Ghost Adventures*, and *My Ghost Story*, as well as an award-winning documentary, *Villisca: Living with a Mystery* by Kelly and Tammy Rundle, featuring commentary by Dr. Ed Epperly, aka "The Ax Man." Epperly, *the* expert on the Villisca murders and the history surrounding the case, admits that after decades of research he is still baffled by the events.

Reports of startling, sometimes terrifying experiences continue to pour out of the modest house. Dark ominous shadows, unusual cold spots, disembodied voices, a young girl's muffled cries, children's laughter, unseen hands rolling a ball, and doors that open and close by themselves are a few of the supernatural claims. Heartbreakingly, spirits of the murdered children seem to linger shyly in the shadows.

The reputation of the crudely but appropriately named Villisca Ax Murder House grows with each visit, each inquiry into its painful past. The deaths of eight innocents live on in the memories of the thousands of souls who make the pilgrimage to Iowa to pay their respects and commune with the spirits of the most haunted house in the United States.

Take the Haunted Tour—The Property

The small, nondescript, white two-story house sits in a quiet residential neighborhood. If not for the sign announcing *Villisca Ax Murder House* on the front lawn, passersby would hardly give it a second glance. The red trim accents on the house match the sign's letters, garishly painted to look like dripping blood.

Still standing is the red wooden barn that housed the Moores' horse and buggy team. Between the house and barn sits a utility shed where the killer(s) found the ax used in the grisly crime. Just yards away is a small well with an iron hand pump. From the side, two semicircular windows, reminiscent of the *Amityville Horror* house, peer out like eerie eyes. The small porch remains vacant and the front door is permanently locked.

The current owner, Martha Linn, wife of the late Darwin Linn, maintains the meticulously restored former Moore home, keeping the integrity of the era with original and authentic reproductions of the furnishings and décor.

Take the Haunted Tour—The Kitchen

Entry to the house is gained via a long wooden ramp at the back door that leads into a compact kitchen.

To the right of the door is a cupboard, its white painted exterior worn with age. The pantry, basically a walk-in closet with shelves and a work space, sits to the side. To the left is the sink with an old-fashioned hand pump poised to bring water into the home.

Directly across is the stove where a busy Sarah Moore prepared meals for her family. An empty teakettle awaits use that will never come. A coffee grinder and oil lamp adorn the top of the stove. In the corner is a round wooden washing machine. An antique telephone hangs on the wall above a small table fitted to the cramped space. An icebox sits on the adjacent screened-in porch, which once held a puzzling clue to the mysterious events of the night of the murders.

A trayless wooden high chair sits between the entrance to the living room and the stairs that lead to the second-floor bedrooms. The wooden floors are well worn and the green-and-white walls have seen better days. The kitchen is ordinary, unpretentious, and poetically beautiful: a snapshot in time. Its simplicity disguises the horrors unleashed there a hundred years ago.

Personal Experience—
Daniel Hooven: Initiation by Fire

It was November 11, 2011, and I was new to the Resident Undead team, new to the paranormal, and here I was at the most notorious haunted house in the country, the site of a grisly unsolved multiple murder. Joining me were team leader Adam Kimmell, Jim Leopardo, and Villisca local Johnny Houser. This was my very first ghost hunt, my initiation into the paranormal.

When we first arrived at the house I was surprised by how small it was—tiny, actually—and by the fact that it was located in a residential neighborhood. The only clue to its horrific history was the big white sign painted with dripping bloodred letters announcing *Villisca Ax Murder House*. Remove that and we could be anywhere in small-town America.

Inside, the house has been restored to its 1912 condition, with as much of its authenticity preserved as possible. I had the uncomfortable sense of being in someone's house . . . because I *was* in someone's house, even though that someone was dead. I felt intrusive, like an uninvited guest. Seeing a family's everyday objects, especially those of the children, was unsettling. This was going to be a long night.

After a very quick tour of the property and house, it was time to start our investigation. Adrenaline pumped through my body. I was ready. Adam had a plan of attack for the night and knew exactly what he wanted from us, but I needed a few lessons on equipment before we started.

I was on the first floor in the tiny kitchen, audio recorder in hand, trying to familiarize myself with the device. I hesitantly began my first EVP session. It was a moment I'll never forget. As I asked questions out loud, hoping to communicate with the spirits in the house, Adam suddenly jumped out of the pantry and scared the crap out of me! After the initial shock, we laughed it off and got back to business.

I had no idea how profound that moment was until Adam and I played back the recorder. We heard the distinct sound of a little girl's laughter! We had not heard anything at the time of recording, yet it was unmistakably there on playback. Was this laughter in response to the prank Adam had played on me?

I was stunned by the ghostly sound of a child—Lena, Ina, or Catherine—making her presence known to us in the house in which she had been murdered. My initiation into the paranormal world had begun!

Take the Haunted Tour—The Parlor (Living Room)

The wooden floor creaks as you enter the living room. Beige walls are accented with a dark brown trim. On the shaded windows, delicate white lace curtains filter the sunlight coming through, casting a soft glow over everything in the room. The black iron potbellied stove looks like a short-legged octopus, its longest tentacle reaching up to grab its prey on the floor above.

Black-and-white pictures of the Moore family hang on the walls to remind visitors whose home they're in. A pillowless brown leather sofa and a few small tables adorned with flowers, books, and various knickknacks add a homey touch. In the corner, an upright piano sits silent. Above it hangs a reproduction of Leonardo da Vinci's iconic painting *The Last Supper*. One can't help but wonder what the eight victims had for their last meal, oblivious to the doom that awaited them that sultry Iowa evening in June 1912.

Personal Experience—
Adam Kimmell (Lead Investigator, Resident Undead)

Our night in the Villisca Murder House was full of unexplained paranormal activity, some subtle, some not. Daniel and I captured an EVP of creepy childlike laughter in the kitchen and were ready to explore the rest of the house. About halfway through the evening, we gathered in the living room to try a few more experiments. I wanted to "amp up" the energy by bringing in someone who would be familiar to any spirits lingering in the house: Johnny Houser, a Villisca resident and house tour guide.

Tools of the Trade

Spirit Box: also known as a ghost box, Frank's Box, or a shack hack; a modified AM/FM transistor radio that continually scans the radio dial, stopping for a fraction of a second on each station. The white noise and audio remnants heard are thought to be manipulated by spirits in order to communicate with investigators.

The SB-7 is a similar device created by Gary Galka specifically for instrumental transcommunication (ITC), which is the use of a technological device as a tool for communicating with ghosts.

Johnny lived right next door and claimed that activity actually "spilled over" from the Moore house to his own. He was featured on the program *My Ghost Story: Caught on Camera* in April 2012, in which he told the harrowing tale of living next to the notorious Ax Murder House. His presence definitely had a noticeable effect. Suddenly, the sleepy house came alive with activity.

I brought out the spirit box, hoping to communicate with the spirits. Johnny sat on the stairs, I stood to his right while Dan filmed with the infrared (IR) camera.

I asked, "Can you give the names of who is here right now?"

The box answered, *"The same old reverend."*

I knew a Reverend Kelly was a suspect in the murder case and had even confessed to the crime at one point during the investigation. Guilty or not, I believe he either had some knowledge of the murders or stumbled upon the crime scene after the fact. I theorize that he was the one who covered the mirrors and put clothes over the victim's faces, realizing this was an act of evil.

We continued on with the spirit box session and were bombarded with responses! We heard my name, *"Adam,"* twice, and the names of Johnny, Jim, and Dan. A woman's voice said, "*Sarah*," as well as "*help*."

We also picked up some very unsettling responses such as, "*Satan*," "*hack it*," and "*confession*."

Dan and I were commenting on the response "*confession*," when the same chilling voice said, "*Better catch up with the Bible, gonna need it*."

The onslaught of messages continued; some of the other responses we captured were, "*Help me*," "*traumatic brain and skull*," "*get out*," and "*kill you*."

The entire session lasted only about five minutes, but this was an incredible amount of evidence that tied in directly to the house and the murders. I wholeheartedly believe there are many ghosts inside the house. Who they are remains a mystery. Although we heard a little girl's laughter, I don't believe the spirits of the murdered Moore and Stillinger children are still in the house. I don't want to believe that; it's too sad. There is a negative energy, possibly that of the murderer, or one of the murderers, lingering inside the house. This energy attracts more negative energy, like a magnet, drawing it into the space and holding it there.

As the night wore on, the rain outside became more intense. After exploring the upstairs rooms, Daniel and I returned to the living room, this time dressed in period attire, in an attempt to trigger more communication with the spirits in the house.

I began a real-time EVP session, short bursts of questions followed by immediate playback of the file. Instead of EVPs we heard what sounded like whispered conversation—the spirits seemed to be well aware of our presence and were discussing things among themselves.

Addressing the spirits, I said, "There's a thunderstorm outside. Is anyone scared?"

Immediately we heard two male voices carrying on a conversation. Although the first part was hard to make out, a second, clearer voice said, *"Why are they here?"*

Dan and I both heard the ghostly voices and pushed to hear more.

"We're hearing voices that shouldn't be here . . ."

I was interrupted by another voice: *"Where?"*

". . . which leads me to believe someone's here who shouldn't be here," I concluded.

These disembodied voices were audible, intelligent, and puzzled by our presence. Whom did we hear? Were these the voices of the killers? It's been theorized that there must have been two culprits, that one person alone could not have pulled off such a bloody and brutal crime by himself. Or had we captured a piece of conversation between two spirits that had nothing to do with the murders but were drawn to this nexus of energy created by the haunting?

Take the Haunted Tour—The Sewing Room
(Lena and Ina's Room)

Off the living room is one of three bedrooms in the house. Although originally for sewing, the room was used as a guest bedroom at times. The bright blue walls match the multicolored quilt atop the single bed in the corner. At the foot of the bed is a large wooden storage trunk just feet from the doorway. A turn-of-the-century sewing machine sits between the bed's white metal headboard and the dresser on the opposite wall.

The mirror on the dresser is covered with cloth, just as it was the night of the murders. Ina Stillinger's Bible, left atop the dresser, was used to identify the two "extra" victims found mutilated beyond recognition inside this tiny room. Lena's body was disturbingly positioned at the bottom of the bed, undergarments removed, face covered.

Next to the curtained doorway is another dresser, on it a plaque commemorating Lena and Ina Stillinger. Mementos are scattered about, serving as a grim reminder of the innocence lost that tragic night.

The ax used in the heinous crime was found leaning against the wall in this room as if the killer had casually set aside a broom after sweeping the floor. Oddly, a slab of uncut bacon wrapped in cloth, identical to one in the icebox, was found next to the ax. Was this mysterious clue left to confuse authorities, some sort of bizarre calling card, or a mocking gesture to the world, suggesting the victims were nothing but butchered meat?

According to the documentary *Villisca: Living with a Mystery*, FBI profilers have theorized that the bacon was used as some form of sexual aid in the presence of the half-naked body of Lena Stillinger. An oil lamp with the chimney removed placed at the foot of the bed adds credence to this appalling theory.

Theories abound, but evidence is fleeting. After over a hundred years, there are still more questions than answers.

Personal Experience—
Daniel Hooven

As part of my "baptism by fire" I was "quarantined," required to spend time alone in the downstairs bedroom. The space was extremely small, more like a large closet than a bedroom. I did my best to get comfortable, but I couldn't shake the image in my mind of two butchered children lying in the very spot I occupied. I sat back on the bed, took a deep breath, and prepared for an EVP session.

Nervously, I began my quarantine, hoping to contact any spirits in the room with me. I was about halfway through my session when I felt the room get colder, not a subtle chill but a definitive drop in temperature. My entire body was covered in goose bumps. Then, like something out of a movie, my breath became visible, as if I were outside in the middle of winter. With every exhale, my breath grew more frosty as all the warmth fled the room.

This freaked me out and I wanted to get the hell out of there! Luckily, Adam arrived to relieve me from frigid solitary in the creepy room. He also noticed how cold it was, and the two of us made a hasty exit.

When we reviewed the audio from my digital recorder, we heard a loud childlike shriek at the precise moment Adam had entered the room. I believe Adam startled the spirit with whom I was communicating. I don't think it was the ghost of Lena, Ina, or any of the Moore children. In fact I don't believe it was a child at all. I think it was a collection of negative energy manifesting itself, possibly impersonating a child.

Take the Haunted Tour—The Master Bedroom

To access the second floor you must use a narrow S-curved stairwell from the kitchen. The stairs creak noisily as you climb the tight space to the top. The aged, painted wooden steps are splintered and peeling, worn from the thousands of feet that have traveled the short distance from bottom to top and back again—although six pairs of feet never made the return trip down on their own.

The second-floor houses the master bedroom, the children's

room, and the "attic," an unfinished storage room. As soon as you reach the top of the stairs, you've entered the master bedroom. The foot of the bed becomes visible before you reach the landing. There are no doors into this room, no barrier to stop intruders.

Josiah and Sarah Moore closed their eyes for the last time that June night believing their four children were safely tucked in their beds, just a few feet away. Was the killer(s) hiding somewhere in the room? Investigators couldn't understand how anyone could have climbed the creaky stairs without waking the Moores. Some believed the killer hid in the closet, waiting for the family to fall asleep, but the closets were so packed with clothes it would have been nearly impossible to fit a full-size adult inside.

Josiah must have been the first victim, taken out quickly so the murderous rampage could continue unhindered. Did one blow suffice to kill him? Maybe, although each victim was bludgeoned multiple times with the blunt end of the ax. Forensic specialists discovered that Sarah Moore was hit with the sharp end as well, possibly after her death.

The master bedroom is a small utilitarian space, dark and eerie, and oozing with the memories of a horrible summer night.

Ghost Adventures—
EVPs and Empathy

The notoriety of the hauntings in Villisca captured the attention of Zak Bagans, who brought his crew to Iowa during season four of the Travel Channel's *Ghost Adventures* (episode thirteen). Guided by property owner Darwin Linn and local Johnny Houser, the Ghost Adventures Crew (GAC) spent the night locked down in the smallest location in which they've filmed.

The night did not disappoint, and the trio collected a bounty of evidence, including a number of EVPs and disturbing spirit box sessions. The ghosts were very cooperative, even providing the names *Lena, Paul, Herman,* and *Reverend Kelly.* While some of the evidence presented on the show is debatable, one very disturbing piece of audio sent shivers up and down our spines.

While investigating the upstairs with skeptic and former detective Roy Marshall, they captured an EVP that said, "*I . . . killed . . . six . . . kids.*"

The audio files were immediately processed by audio/video tech Billy Tolley and played for Villisca expert Johnny Houser. All present agreed the creepy male voice captured was confessing a deadly deed from beyond the grave, an obvious reference to the eight butchered victims, six of whom were children. The voice was not the childlike voice they had captured earlier downstairs but a more menacing and macabre one.

The evil was apparent to everyone present, and the poignancy of the tragedy visibly affected Bagans.

Take the Haunted Tour—The Attic:
"The Devil Lives in Here"

The attic, an unfinished room over the kitchen used for storage, can be accessed only through a tiny door in a closet off the master bedroom. The theory that the killer(s) hid in the attic before emerging in darkness to viciously kill eight people in the middle of the night seems unlikely. It is difficult for an adult to fit through this small doorway, and it would have been virtually impossible to pick through a cluttered and overcrowded attic quietly without awakening the family.

Personal Experience—
Adam Kimmell and Jim Leopardo (Member, Resident Undead)

After a long stormy night in small-town Iowa, we were ready to confront the Devil. The tiny house seemed infested with spirits, and a strong negative energy cowardly hid in the attic. This was our final stop.

We awkwardly made our way through the closet to the miniature door that leads to the dusty, cobweb-filled attic. The attic was much smaller than I imagined, and it was challenging to get the equipment set up the way we needed it. We brought in a couple of chairs from another room so we didn't have to sit on the splintering wood floor.

We hadn't completely set up of all our cameras when our recorders picked up several interesting EVPs, including a voice saying, "*BOO!*"

Was this the ghostly voice of a kid trying to scare us, or an attempt at ironic humor on the part of the entities surrounding us? I guess we'll never know.

Not aware of the EVPs, we continued with our work. We captured another voice, this one puzzled by what we were doing, "*You're still in the attic?*"

I asked if any spirits were hiding in the attic. Something responded, "*I'm here.*"

The sound of rain echoed from the roof in an eerie rhythmic barrage. Theoretically, the energy from a storm, especially a thunderstorm, can increase paranormal activity. But the volume of the rain was so loud I thought it would ruin our chances of capturing any audio evidence. With the storm growing outside, we retreated downstairs for a while. Once the rain stopped, we each took another turn up in the attic, in an effort to rattle the Devil's cage.

Jim Leopardo returned to the attic while the rest of the team did some experimenting in the living room. Jim broke out a device known as a PX box. Used in a similar way to the spirit box, the PX has a built-in vocabulary of several thousand words. Jim was able to get some incredible responses during his final session in the attic.

He settled into one of the folding chairs we had placed inside the cramped space. Almost immediately, the PX began to talk, spewing out a barrage of ghostly banter from a spirit who was eager to communicate.

"*Suffer.*"

"Who suffered? The family?" Jim questioned.

"*Three.*"

"Did you enjoy killing the Moore family?"

"*Thing, murder.*"

"Why did you come back here?"

"*Because.*"

"We don't understand why you'd come back to a place—" Jim's voice was cut off.

"*Proud.*"

"You're proud of what you did here?"

"*Like . . . comment, property, story.*" Word after word poured out of the box.

Amazed, Jim urged the spirit for more information: "Yeah, we want to put the story out of what really happened."

Jim told the entity that Dan and I would be coming back to talk as well. The chilling response was, "*Hurry, Reverend.*"

Jim asked if he enjoyed killing the kids the most, and the response was, "*Suffer, hide, paranormal.*"

"Yes, we're paranormal investigators. I don't know if you're the actual spirit of the person who killed them . . ."

"*Demon, homicidal, murder, murder.*"

Jim continued to talk, and the spirit continued to answer.

"Are you up here with me?"

"*Eight killed.*"

Dan relieved Jim and took his place in the attic, hoping for similar results. Unfortunately, the spirits were silent. No further messages came through.

I wanted to offer up something irresistible to the dark entity:

a chance to kill again. I began taunting, going so far as to "tempt" the evil presence with a sharpened ax rigged over my head. We devised a setup so that any slight touch would cause the blade to fall on me. Zak Bagans attempted a similar experiment when filming the *Ghost Adventures* Villisca episode and survived unscathed. I hoped for the same result.

I was in place under the ax when we all heard something odd. The strange noise, a guttural growl, grew louder each passing moment. These were not animal-nor human-made sounds, but something else, something inhuman. This was a terrifying moment, staring at the ax above my head while ghostly growls came out of the darkness!

No ghost took the bait—I kept my head.

We believe the growling to be a manifestation of evil, the negative energies inside the house. Maybe it was left behind or trapped by the murderer, or maybe it was lured in, attracted to the house, drawn to it like a magnet. Or it's possible one of the thousands of visitors unknowingly brought it in, and it's decided to stay.

Take the Haunted Tour—The Children's Room

Connected to the master bedroom is the slightly larger children's room. All four of the Moore children shared the room adjacent to their parents' bedroom. The first thing that catches a visitor's attention is the crib belonging to Paul Moore, the youngest of the victims, and then the three little beds, adding up to four young lives. They went to sleep one hot summer night, never to awake again in this world.

Actually, we *need* to think they never woke up during their ordeal. This may be why their spirits still haunt this house. They may not realize what happened to them at all. Or maybe the killer keeps their souls trapped in this purgatory forever, reliving the horrible night of their death over and over and over again.

Tools of the Trade

Infrared (IR) Camera: a specialized night-vision video camera that can record in 0 lux (total darkness) using the infrared light spectrum (not visible to the naked eye), essentially allowing the user to see in the dark.

Visitors report unusual paranormal phenomena in the children's room, including a closet door that opens and closes on its own and disembodied ghostly giggles. EVPs of children's voices are common, including ones using the names of the murdered victims.

Ghost Adventures—
This Door Remains Closed

The GAC captured a fascinating poltergeist or telekinetic phenomenon while investigating this area. In their usual style, the guys placed their signature X to mark the position of a static (stationary) camera. This allows several hot spots to be monitored while they investigate in other areas. While Zak, Nick, and Aaron reviewed audio files in the barn, the upstairs IR camera covering the children's room captured something startling.

With no living soul inside the house, an open closet door slammed shut forcefully! The remarkable footage clearly showed a wide-open door quickly and deliberately closing on its own. Could this have been a violent display of power by the spirit of an ax-wielding murderer, or a frightened child desperately seeking help?

CONCLUSION

Villisca is a small town with a big secret, one it would have preferred to bury as deeply as the eight bodies in the local graveyard. But without justice, there can be no peace, and the spirits of the innocent have waited over a hundred years for truth and restitution.

The killer was never caught, or at least never convicted, and no one was ever punished for butchering an entire family and two little girls who were in the wrong place at the wrong time. The energy of this atrocity fuels the paranormal phenomena inside the little white house.

The town of Villisca survived the fear that ensued following the murders. It survived being split in two by those who presumed one suspect's guilt over another's. The families suffered the pain and indignity of never knowing what really happened to their loved ones, and three men suffered the permanent stain of being accused of the crime when other options were right next door.

Authorities lost control of the crime scene. Forensics and proper evidence collection techniques were nonexistent or in their infancy. The town was so eager to place blame for the murders, they rushed to convict someone, anyone.

A more likely suspect than those charged was Henry Lee Moore (no relation to the murder victims), known as America's first serial killer. Moore spent time in a Kansas reformatory for forgery but was paroled in April 1911. Shortly afterward, the area was plagued by a series of bizarre murders, strikingly similar in nature.

In September 1911, two Colorado Springs families—neighbors—were brutally murdered with an ax. The bloody weapon was left at the scene. In October, another family of three was bludgeoned to death in Monmouth, Illinois. Two weeks later in Ellsworth, Kansas, a married couple and their three children were murdered with an ax while sleeping in their beds. Details of this crime scene were alarmingly similar to those in Villisca. A kerosene lantern, chimney removed, was found at the end of the bed, the wife's head severely mutilated and her body posed grotesquely in a sexual position. All of these murder locations were tied to each other via railroad, by which the killer likely made his escape.

Henry Lee Moore, who worked for the railroad, arrived in Columbia, Missouri, on December 17, 1912, the day before the murdered bodies of his mother and grandmother were discovered. In his hotel room, incriminating items including clippings of the previous murders and blood evidence were found. He also bragged to friends of how he had viewed mutilated bodies in the morgue. Moore was convicted in March 1913 of the murder of his mother and grandmother. The wave of bizarre, vicious ax murders ceased after that.

Was Henry Lee Moore overlooked as a suspect in the Villisca crimes? Were the wounded residents of Villisca so focused on their tiny portion of the world that they were blind to the bigger picture? Murder is nothing new, but a wave of seemingly random ax murders over such a short period of time is far outside the norm.

When Darwin Linn bought the property and began dredging up the past, the good people of Villisca were mortified. But it needed to be done; the secret was too big to hide under a cloak of ignorance and denial. When the renovations began, Linn stirred up more than just angry neighbors; he woke the spirits of the house, and not just the victims' but seemingly the murderer's as well.

Do the ghosts of six children still linger in limbo in the place of their deaths, or is something else residing there? The victims, completely unaware that they are indeed dead, may still be living their afterlife in the place they died. The viciousness of the attack left behind a permanent mark, a negative energy field that is palpable to visitors and investigators.

It is also possible that the number of people who've visited the house over the years have brought something with them, imprinting their fears, anxieties, excitement, and sadness into the structure itself. Has the house become a vortex, a magnet for energies of all kinds: good, bad, indifferent?

The small house of big evil has become infamous as the most haunted private residence in the United States. Thousands make the paranormal pilgrimage to Iowa to satisfy their curiosity and look for answers. It's not a matter of disrespect; it's a matter of acknowledging that such evil can and does exist, so you won't be caught off guard. You'll live each day as if it were your last, appreciate the moment, love a little harder, hug your children a little longer, lock your doors a little tighter, and sleep with one eye open.

What You Need to Know Before You Go:

Villisca Ax Murder House
508 E. 2nd St., Villisca, IA

Contact Information:
Call Martha Linn: (712) 621-1530
villiscaiowa.com
dmlinn@wildblue.net

The Villisca Ax Murder House is open March 1st to November 1st for daytime tours.
Daylight Tours: House is open daily from 1 P.M. to 4 P.M.
    Tuesday through Sunday; closed Mondays.
Overnight Investigations: House is open seven nights a week

year-round. Please check the calendar on the website or call
Martha Linn for availability.

Lodging:

If you make the journey to Villisca and stay overnight at the
infamous Ax Murder House, you probably won't get much sleep!
Here are a few options for hotels in the area:

Stanton Inn Motel, (712) 829-2585
620 Halland Ave., Stanton, IA 51573
stantoninnmotel.com

Super 8 Clarinda, (712) 542-6333
1203 N. 12th St., Clarinda, IA 51632
super8.com

Celebrity Inn, (712) 542-5178
1323 S. 16th St., Clarinda, IA 51632
thecelebrityinn.com

The Knickerbocker Hotel

Linesville, Pennsylvania

INTRODUCTION

Exactly halfway between New York City and Chicago, in the sleepy northwestern Pennsylvania town of Linesville, sits a beautifully refurbished and decorated three-story brick landmark, the Knickerbocker Hotel, which happens to be bursting at the seams with spirits. Those spirits—while sometimes moody, mischievous, even cranky—often seem as willing to entertain guests as were the original, living innkeepers during the building's heyday a century and more ago.

The original proprietors, Milo and Clara Arnold, built the establishment, originally called Arnold House, on land Mrs. Arnold inherited from her second husband (Milo was number three). On January 12, 1882, they held a gala ball to open this hotel, restaurant, entertainment lounge, and family residence. The twenty-room building has weathered the winds of change and stands proud and strong on its original foundation, with the past and present, the seen and unseen, inextricably intertwined.

The current owners, Peg and Myrle Knickerbocker, felt a calling to restore and decorate this gem as a tribute to the people, history, and style of its Gilded Age origins and have done so since they assumed full control of the property in 2005. Peg Knickerbocker changes the theme and décor of each room on a regular basis to keep visitors and ghosts on their toes. Every room is a moment caught in time.

Among the most prominent ghosts of the Knickerbocker Hotel are founding matriarch Clara Arnold, who died of tuberculosis at age thirty-seven just three years after the Arnold House opened; at least one small child variously seen in the basement and heard with stunning clarity on video; a roaming shadow figure caught on infrared video on the third-floor hallway and stairs; and a remarkably tangible former feline, seen, heard, and captured on video in the second-floor Cat Room.

Countless paranormal teams have reported and documented activity while investigating here, and the Knickerbockers have opened their doors to television shows including A&E's *Paranormal State* and the Biography Channel's *My Ghost Story*. Brian Cano, of Syfy's *Haunted Collector* fame, filmed a documentary here with his home team, SCARED!

Meticulous research, attention to historic detail, and the general positive vibes of the place make the Knick a must-see for any paranormal enthusiast.

Take the Haunted Tour—The Main Floor

From the hotel's austere exterior, it's difficult to imagine the size and the splendor of the Knickerbocker, but once inside, the welcoming charm of the hotel enfolds the visitor. The lounge area is elegant and comfortable, with ample room for a small gathering. Small tables and chairs are positioned about, and plush couches frame the subdued, rectangular space.

Adjacent to the lounge is a brightly lit room used for meetings, informal get-togethers, and dining. It is ideal for lectures and similar events and is typically the staging area for paranormal investigations held at the hotel. Captured evidence can be conveniently reviewed and shared via large flat-screen TVs with computer connections in the dining room and lounge, giving this area a modern feel in sharp contrast to the period rooms and hallways above.

Now You See It, Now You Don't

An odd sequence of events befell paranormal legend Lorraine Warren of *The Conjuring* fame during one of her many visits to the Knick, on the occasion of her eighty-first birthday.

Warren was sitting in the dining area at a small table with her purse at her feet listening to a paranormal lecture. When the speaker concluded, she reached down to retrieve something out of her bag, only to find it missing. Bewildered and upset, Lorraine asked Peg to help her find it.

Peg gave a little smile and helped her search for the purse, knowing it wouldn't be found through "normal" methods. Peg often refers to the Knickerbocker as if it were a living, breathing entity, with characteristics and quirks like the rest of us. When a purse, phone, pair of earrings, or set of keys seems to vanish into thin air, one must ask the building to "please give it back."

Dubious, but willing to try, Lorraine stood up and with open arms pleaded, "Building, please return the purse." The other guests found this amusing, but Peg assured them it would work. After the room was cleared as part of the process, Lorraine quickly returned with Peg, and to her astonishment, found the purse exactly at the spot from where it had gone missing.

Object manipulation of this type is indeed rare, and the ramifications fascinating: Where did the purse "go" in the interim? Was it actually somewhere else or was its presence somehow cloaked? Was this the action of a single spirit or some sort of group effort? The world can be a very strange place.

Theresa had a similar experience in the Angel Room on the third floor, which we will recount later.

Grand Opening Reenactment

In September 2011, the Knickerbockers held an event reenacting the original 1882 grand opening of the Arnold House. Using a contemporary newspaper account as their guide, participants relived the day the hotel first threw open its doors, beginning its strange journey through time. The guests all dressed in period attire, and each had a part to play. Peg was chef and served a lovely dinner to the guests, Myrle entertained the crowd with piano music popular in the 1880s, and their friend Mark Painter portrayed Milo Arnold, original proprietor of the hotel.

It was a grand party, much like the one held over 130 years ago. Everyone stayed in character throughout the night, enjoying food and music authentic to the era. After serving the guests in the lounge, the "staff" sat down for their meal in the dining room.

Eventually "Milo" stood up and addressed his guests, thanking them for coming to the grand opening celebration. As he spoke, the party guests stared in awe at what was conjuring behind him. "Milo" turned as well, just in time to see a wavelike body, like a heat mirage, emerge from the east wall and sweep across the room to the west.

Before anyone could speak, a man dressed exactly like faux Milo stepped out of the wall into the room, took a quick look around, and then stepped back into the wall and disappeared!

Stunned by what they had seen, the partygoers bolted from the lounge to the dining room to report what had just happened.

Peg was shocked when she heard their tale, especially since her group, the ones portraying hotel staff, had seen the same man peeking in at them through the door just moments before. It seems as though Milo Arnold crashed his own party.

Personal Experience—
Peg Knickerbocker (Owner, Knickerbocker Hotel) and Clara Hyder (Sister): Impatient Bathroom Specter

A woman and her grandson from Mentor, Ohio, were in town in September 2012. It was around 4:30 P.M. on Sunday and everything was closed. The woman knocked and asked if her young grandson could use the bathroom. I was out, but my sister Clara Hyder, who was visiting, said, "Of course."

The woman took her grandson into the bathroom, and when she came out she said, "I'm sorry if we made the woman in the bathroom mad, but my grandson really had to go."

"Who was she?" my sister asked the grandmother.

"She was a short woman with short dark hair that cupped her face, black cat-rimmed glasses, and wearing a little brown outfit. She stood right there, tapping her foot with her arms crossed. I said 'Ma'am, I'm sorry, but my grandson will be done in a minute.' Then she left."

My sister told the stunned woman, "That's wonderful, because only you, me, and your grandson have been in the building."

Take the Haunted Tour—The Kitchen

Today, guests enter the building through the east side entrance, which opens to the aforementioned lounge area to the left, with the bar on the right and a central reception area straight ahead. One can almost picture Victorian- and Edwardian-era crowds, dressed in their finest, gathering for cocktails at the bar before sashaying off to the opera via the hotel's private entrance on the second floor.

Farther to the right, behind the bar, is the kitchen—a moderately large, workable space that was the heart of the hotel during its glory days, serving not just guests but family and staff as well.

My Ghost Story—
A Lighter Shade of Shadow

The Knickerbocker was featured on season four, episode nine of *My Ghost Story*, which first aired June 9, 2012. In the episode, Peg says that she wasn't aware of the building's haunted nature before she and Myrle purchased the Knickerbocker. But when they started renovating the second and third floors, it soon became evident that the hotel had come with some extra guests.

Peg was at the sink washing up dishes after an event. She suddenly felt as if she weren't alone. She glanced up toward the back kitchen door. When she looked up at the door there was a shadow person, standing, looking at her from the doorway. She was shocked. She thought, "I need to get out of here," so she did just that.

This wouldn't be the last time Peg saw the shadow man. Like a silent sentinel, this mysterious figure has appeared over and over again—always quiet, always vigilant, keeping a watchful eye on the hotel.

Others have reported seeing a shadow man as well, but for them, his presence has been a little more chilling.

While touring the Knickerbocker with Peg, guest investigator Megan Newell also encountered a shadow man in the same area. When she walked past the kitchen she saw a shadow that ran past the back of the kitchen. She was petrified. She had never seen anything like it.

Visitors have reported a shadow person in several other areas of the hotel, including the stairways and the basement. The *My Ghost Story* episode included a stunning photograph of a shadow man in the Angel Room on the third floor. This is near the same area where staggering video of a very active shadow person was captured by the Paranormal and Supernatural Seekers group in 2009.

This shadow person may be a single entity or one of many. With the menagerie of ghostly entities at the Knickerbocker, it's hard to know for certain.

Take the Haunted Tour—The Basement

Hidden below the main floor of the Knickerbocker is a place of literal and perhaps spiritual darkness. Underneath the liveliness and comfort of the lounge and dining rooms, a locked door opens to a narrow staircase that descends to a dirt-floor basement, the one area of the building that actually looks and feels creepy.

The basement features everything you might imagine in the cellar of a haunted house: dirt floors, low ceilings, storage areas that hold nothing but cobwebs, bricks, and damp wood. There are pipes that run along the ceiling; furnaces and water heaters that linger in the shadows, unnoticed except for their constant hum; and the incongruous pulse of dim computer lights, sending out the building's streaming video signal to the world.

Personal Experience—
Theresa

My fellow Haunted Housewives and I were invited in June 2011 to a premiere party for Zak Bagan's ghost hunt competition series *Paranormal Challenge* by our friends Adam Kimmell and Daniel Hooven, whose Resident Undead team was one of two competing in the inaugural episode.

Our own episode of *Paranormal Challenge* was scheduled to air later in the season, and we were dying to see what a finished product looked like. The Knickerbocker was a perfect place for a premiere party: lots of televisions, an inviting gathering area for speechifying, a gracious host, and a genuine haunted venue to investigate after the program!

Resident Undead front man Adam Kimmell is a natural with crowds. He is warm and welcoming, with a charismatic personality that draws you in and makes you want to follow him. Daniel Hooven was relatively new to the paranormal, having been with the team less than a year, but he had experienced enough in that time to make him well seasoned in the field.

About twenty others joined in the festivities that night, all eager to see Resident Undead do their thing on TV. The crowd watched the show unfold and cheered joyfully as Resident Undead came out victorious!

After the show was over, about a third of the crowd drifted cheerfully out into the night and about a dozen remained as we moved on to the next portion of the evening. Among the participants were experienced investigators, true believers, and a few skeptics thrown in for good measure.

Peg Knickerbocker regaled us with a brief history of the Knick and some of her most riveting haunted experiences. Then we broke into small groups and took turns rotating to different areas of the hotel to investigate. The time came for my group to head to the basement. I was apprehensive about this, not because I feared the ghosts said to be down there, but because I am somewhat claustrophobic, which is not a fortuitous trait for a paranormal investigator.

Dread pulsed through me and my heart beat faster as we made our way down the creaky wooden stairs into the thick, inky blackness.

Senses tingling, I made my way through the gloom across

two-by-fours laid out as a makeshift walkway. I had to duck several times to avoid smacking my head into pipes that hung low from the ceiling. The only light visible was the eerie electronic glow of the computers tucked away to our right, about halfway toward the back of the basement.

Time to get to work. We pulled out our handheld digital voice recorders and began an EVP session. As a rule I do not believe in provoking spirits. I think it's rude and disrespectful. But there are certain occasions when I will bend this rule. I have a great dislike for anyone, living or dead, who treats women poorly, and a spirit with whom we hoped to communicate had a nasty reputation for misogyny.

Cathi sensed this man's angry presence all around us and felt something touch the back of her head. Cathi is a bit vertically challenged, so we ruled out the ceiling pipes as the culprit.

We asked any present spirits to identify themselves. "What is your name? What business do you have in this place?"

Our first attempt yielded only a few muffled responses, so I got a little more personal.

"Do you have a problem talking to all women, or is it just us you're angry with? Are you afraid to talk to us?" I taunted the spirit.

This time when we played back our recording we got his message loud and clear.

"*You . . . fucking . . . bitch!*" Hmm, sounded like we struck a nerve.

I was eager to leave the area and return to the upper floors after this. When we compared notes with some of the other teams, it seemed we weren't the first group to encounter this guy that night.

Then it was time for everyone to meet in the basement for one final group session. Maybe there would be safety in numbers.

Recorder in hand, Adam began a group demonstration of

ITC—instrumental transcommunication—basically, talking to the dead by use of a digital recorder and "real-time" EVP.

He explained the process. He would ask a series of questions, leaving ample silence between each, hoping to catch a response from any ghosts that might be present. The recorder was voice activated, so if the group didn't make any sounds, there would be nothing but Adam's voice on the recording during playback. Simple. Logical.

Adam asked for a volunteer. One young lady offered up her boyfriend, whom she had dragged to the event unwillingly. He was a skeptic bordering on nonbeliever and thought the whole exercise was rather pointless. Adam exclaimed confidently to the group that he would prove the dead can speak, that we can communicate with ghosts. His bravado was astonishing, even to his teammates, who all hoped he would make good on his word.

With the volunteer by his side, Adam began his session.

A few basic questions: "Is anyone here with us?" "What's your name?" "Can you give us a sign of your presence?"

Straight out of the Ghost Hunting 101 playbook.

Then Adam announced the clincher. He asked the volunteer, someone he had never met before, to say his first and his last name.

"Randy Caldwell," the man answered.

"Okay, now I want any spirits here with us to say this man's name. First and last. Please, nice and clear, say, 'Randy Caldwell.'"

Adam knew what was on the line. It was evident by the small beads of sweat forming on his brow and the nervous smile on his face.

"This is it; this will prove that this stuff is real."

He asked for silence and told everyone to have their recorders ready. He played back the recorder, holding it up high for everyone to hear.

A question. A muffled response. Another question. Another unintelligible response.

Then the mother lode.

"Please, nice and clear, say 'Randy Caldwell,'" instructed Adam's voice on the recorder.

"*Randy . . . Caldwell*," came the response.

A collective gasp went out from the group, along with a few choice expletives.

Daniel said, "Play it again, play it back one more time!"

One and all clearly heard, "*Randy . . . Caldwell*."

An intelligent, deliberate response from an unseen entity captured on the recorder in front of a room full of witnesses in real time. There was no tampering with the recorder, nothing set up in advance. The man whose name was called was not in on any kind of scam. He was a skeptical man dragged to some silly ghost hunt event and asked to participate in a parlor trick.

"So what do you think now, Randy Caldwell? Do you believe in ghosts?"

A dumbfounded, bewildered Randy shook his head and said, "Well, I believe now."

Skeptics may be able to dismiss one person's account, find a reasonable explanation for an event reported by two, but this event was witnessed and documented by a dozen people.

A few people made a quick exit after this, having had enough paranormal activity for one night. The basement took on an

Tools of the Trade

Real-Time EVP: immediate playback of recordings during an EVP session, allowing a conversation-style communication between investigators and entities.

extra creepy feel at this point. We all knew we were not alone. There was at least one spirit down there with us—one who knew how to manipulate an audio recorder and speak to the living.

Take the Haunted Tour—The Stairways:
The Ups and Downs of a Haunted Hotel

A recurring visitor claim at the Knickerbocker is the sensation of being pushed when on the stairs. This is a tough claim for an investigator to tackle, as it is nearly impossible to document a "push." *Paranormal State*'s Ryan Buell and his team attributed the sensation to old, creaky, wooden steps contributing to a sense of imbalance in the unsuspecting, while filming an episode of his show at the Knick.

Personal Experience—
Theresa

During an investigation, I ran upstairs to retrieve a tape from the stationary infrared camera I had set up outside a third-floor guest room. Eager to join my companions on the main floor, I grabbed the tape and quickly made my way to the landing. I paused momentarily, noticing a strange burst of cold air on my neck. I tried to brush off the uneasiness that washed over me as I headed back down the stairs.

At first I thought I was hearing noises carried up from my friends downstairs. By the time I reached the second stairwell, I couldn't ignore what was happening. It sounded like a muffled conversation or possibly an unfamiliar language. I slowed my pace and strained to listen.

The voices grew more distinct and much closer. It was as if

they were standing directly behind me. I could "feel" their presence as well as hear them talk: two voices, locked in conversation. I fought the urge to run, fearing I would fall.

"*Should we go?*" a female voice whispered.

"*No, stay,*" came the ghostly reply.

I bounded down the stairs two at a time until I reached the bottom.

THIRD-FLOOR HALLWAY AND STAIRS: SHADOW PLAY

The Paranormal and Supernatural Seekers team from Trumbull County, Ohio, held an investigation at the Knickerbocker on the night of October 9, 2009. The team, led by Cindyjo Dailey, Danielle Dilisio, and tech whiz Steve Dailey, captured something on video that is nothing short of astonishing.

The team set up a series of infrared cameras in various hot spots of the hotel. Each camera was connected to a central DVR system. One camera was stationed by the south wall of the third-floor hallway, facing north toward the stairwell. The camera had a view of the top of the staircase, the banister around and above it, and the dark north hallway beyond. A separate IR camera was trained on the camera that recorded the fateful video.

The day after the investigation, during the routine—and frankly, tedious—review of hours of the DVR footage gathered by each camera, Steve noticed movement so distinct and purposeful, he assumed it had to be an investigator.

"At first I thought it must be one of the team; it had to be a person," Steve told us.

"But I checked the DVR and everyone was accounted for. You could see where the rest of the team was on the other cameras."

For the first seven seconds of the video, the world as we know it prevails: No living thing is present and nothing moves. Then, just after the seven-second mark, we see the quick, faint flash of an investigator's camera from the darkness of the north hallway beyond the stairs.

A second or so after the flash—almost as if frightened or startled by it, as Steve noted in a conversation about the video—we see movement from the north hallway toward the stairs, toward the recording camera. Remember, there is no source of visible light (other than the momentary flash) in the area.

At first, it's a barely perceptible darkening of the darkness in the hallway, but then the darkness congeals and sharpens strikingly into a humanlike form that descends a few stairs, its "head" still visible just above the banister, its "body" below it with the balusters between it and the camera. Then with inhuman fluidity and speed, it turns to its left, glides toward the wall, and disappears.

This would be remarkable enough, but there's more. Between the eleven-second and fifteen-second marks, the figure reappears out of the same spot in the wall into which it had vanished and moves back up the stairs much more slowly and laboriously than it had previously moved, as if walking up the stairs one step at a time and with what appears to be the flourish of a cape or Victorian dress off to its right, before disappearing once again into the darkness of the hallway beyond.

But there's *still* more. The figure appears *again* from the hallway at the sixteen-second mark and descends rapidly, though with a walking rather than gliding motion, down the stairs and out of sight.

All told, the shadow figure is seen for a full eight seconds—eight of the strangest and most compelling seconds we have ever witnessed.

Steve and the crew tried to debunk the footage by recreating the shadow and its movements themselves. If a person was moving in the north hallway, could they cast that kind of shadow movement? First, there is no light source. Steve assured us that at the time of the recording, "No lights were on at all—we were completely in the dark."

Second, even if there *were* a light source coming from the north, how would you account for the clear movement up and down the stairs?

If the light source were from below on the second floor (perhaps car lights shining through the window on the south wall), you could create some form of up-and-down shadow movement on the stairs, but there would have to be a *person* to create it, and that person would have to actually *be* on the stairs.

And there wasn't one.

In addition, the shadow is humanlike in form, but the gliding movements are too rapid and smooth to be human, and humans don't often vanish into walls.

Other investigators have tried in vain to explain this video by either debunking or re-creating it. To date, no one has even come close. In addition to being posted on the Knickerbocker website, the video was also included in the *My Ghost Story* Knickerbocker episode. If you can come up with a natural explanation, we'd like to hear it.

Take the Haunted Tour—The Cat Room: Maybe They Really Do Have Nine Lives

The two-room suite in the southeast corner of the second floor is the Cat Room. There is a large bed, a dresser, and a single wooden chair in the first room. The adjoining room can fit two single beds, a couch, or whatever suits Peg's fancy at any given time. Its décor has changed many times, but one thing remains constant: This room is the favorite hangout of the Knickerbocker's most popular spirit, the Ghost Cat.

The single chair has been placed in the room specifically for the comfort of the phantom feline. A startling photograph of the Ghost Cat is proudly displayed on the dresser. Although the image is a relatively low-resolution screenshot of the live feed sent in by a viewer, it clearly shows a translucent cat curled up comfortably in the chair. One can even make out its markings: orange on top, white below. The Ghost Cat not only has been seen, but has been heard on numerous occasions.

Personal Experience—
Theresa

Cathi Weber and I were conducting an EVP session in the room across the hall when we heard cat noises.

At first we thought the sound was coming from outside. Worried about a poor stray caught out in the February cold, we searched in vain for the source of the sound. There was no way the cat was outside the window, as we were on the second floor. Others with us that evening captured meowing and purring on their audio recorders as well.

The appearance of animal spirits raises many interesting questions about what happens to our beloved pets after they die. Do they have personalities that survive bodily death? Are they aware they are dead? Is it their intent to remain here? As humans, we have knowledge of the paranormal; we may even be able to *choose* to remain earthbound or return as spirits. But how does that apply to an animal?

The ghost kitty at the Knickerbocker is not a residual spirit. It *can* and *does* interact with the living on a regular basis.

Paranormal Activities

Residual Spirit (Residual Haunting): the energy imprint of a spirit or event that replays, often at regular intervals, like a recording throughout time. Energy absorbed by surrounding inanimate objects can sometimes be released in this form of physical manifestation. The event replays as if on a loop; the apparitions never vary in their behavior. Residual spirits cannot interact with the living and are unaware of changes in their environment. They are not thought to be ghosts in the traditional sense.

Personal Experience—
Chris Mancuso (Paranormal Investigator, Co-Founder of SCARED!)

Brian Cano of *Haunted Collector* fame has been a guest at the Knickerbocker on several occasions. In 2009, Brian and his SCARED! team partner Chris Mancuso stopped by the Knickerbocker for a brief visit on their way to a convention.

Peg graciously opened the hotel for them and invited them to spend the night. Chris had heard much about the insane volume of paranormal activity in the building but had yet to experience anything for himself.

In fact, at that point in his career, Chris, then an eight-year veteran of the field, had had only one previous undeniable paranormal experience. He was pretty much a hard-core skeptic.

Exhausted from a long day's travels, Brian and Chris decided to turn in for the night. "It was twelve thirty or one o'clock in the morning, we were tired, we picked out our rooms. Mine was on the second floor toward the front. Brian had the room right across the hall, and Peg had her apartment," Chris recalls.

"So we went to bed. I put my pajamas on. I shut the door, and as I shut the light I heard a voice in my ear saying, '*We're right here!*'"

Chris was stunned and momentarily paralyzed. As luck would have it, he didn't have any equipment running to capture the disembodied voice. After all, they weren't there for an investigation.

Being in a state of shock and not wanting to wake anyone up, Chris took the only logical course of action. "I tiptoed back to my bed and pulled the covers over my head—if I can't see them, they can't see me!"

Well played, Chris Mancuso, well played.

Until that evening, Chris had considered himself very much a skeptic: years of paranormal investigating and only one personal experience. His unforgettable night at the Knickerbocker definitely moved him closer to the believers' side of things.

Brian and Chris were so impressed with the Knick that they chose it as the subject of a future SCARED! documentary. Brian wants to focus heavily on the history in this film, believing that it's the key to much of the paranormal activity happening inside the Knick.

Take the Haunted Tour—The Opera Room: The Supernatural Superhighway

Once *the* place to see and be seen, the Arnold House was conveniently located adjacent to Stratton's Opera Hall, even offering direct access through a private doorway on the second floor. The Arnolds' well-to-do guests—including traveling politicians, captains of industry, and Hollywood royalty—appreciated this amenity, which afforded them the opportunity to make appropriately grand entrances to the opera, their finery unspoiled by the rabble or inclement weather.

Today the entrance is bricked up; there is no access to the drugstore that has rather prosaically taken the place of the Opera Hall. The Knickerbockers have turned this former foyer in front of the blocked entrance into a guest room, but the arched doorway, although bricked, can still be seen.

The room is one of the smallest on the second floor, but it is also one of the most intriguing. A framed vintage photograph of an opera performer is on proud display, along with assorted other bric-a-brac of the time. The bed is soft and inviting, as are—truth be told—all beds at the Knick.

In the Opera Room, the theory that doorways can sometimes act as gateways between our realm and the next seems to be borne out. Many visitors, including Theresa, have reported strange voices and disembodied laughter, backed with anomalous readings on K2 meters and EMF detectors. The well-groomed ghosts of the Arnold House apparently still patronize the doorway to the Stratton, long after the final curtain call.

Take the Haunted Tour—The Angel Room

The most popular room in the Knickerbocker is the Angel Room. Located in the northwest corner of the third floor, it offers space

---

Tools of the Trade

K2 Meters and EMF (electromagnetic field) Detectors: handheld devices that detect natural and man-made electromagnetism in the environment. Electrical conduits, wires, and outlets; appliances; and metal pipes all give off alternating-current (AC) electromagnetic fields. Other types of meters (Trifield meters and gaussmeters) detect naturally occurring direct-current (DC) fields found in the environment.

and solitude to those who spend time here. There is an antique bureau, a mirrored vanity, a wooden bench for laying out one's evening wear or jacket, and a dining table set for two. Lovely and evocative antiques are displayed throughout.

Personal Experience—
Theresa: I Always Feel like Somebody's Watching Me

During my first visit to the Knickerbocker in 2011 I was instantly attracted to the Angel Room, but I also had a sense that I was invading someone else's space. I felt as out of place as the infra-red cameras set up in the room for the webcam, which in this room carries audio as well as video.

After almost seven hours of investigating with a group of a dozen friends, I was ready to call it a night. I removed my pearl earrings and placed them on the pillow next to me. The earrings were a gift from my daughter, and very special to both of us.

I had been asleep for only a couple of hours when my friends called me downstairs for breakfast. I jumped up, collected myself and my equipment, and turned to head out of the room. I realized I didn't have my earrings and went back to the bed to retrieve them.

They were nowhere to be found.

I assumed they had fallen off the bed and probably landed on the floor. Or maybe they had slipped under the covers, even though I had only lain on top of them. Perhaps they were caught in my hair or still in my ears.

None of the above.

After a quick but thorough search, I headed down to my friends, explaining the delay. I recruited everyone, including Peg, to help me search for the missing jewelry. We looked every-where, even going so far as to take the blankets and sheets off the bed. We removed the mattress; we searched inside drawers.

Armed with flashlights and determination, we scanned every nook and cranny of the Angel Room, to no avail. Peg asked if I was ready to accept the fact that the building had taken them. Desperate and tired, I conceded defeat.

"You know what you have to do, Theresa," Peg said with a knowing grin.

With a sigh of resignation I said, "Building, please give them back. Those earrings are very special to me, and my nine-year-old daughter would be very disappointed if I lost them."

As per the dictates of the ritual, we vacated the room for a moment and then returned. It took less than a minute before someone spotted the earrings, placed neatly together on the wood plank behind the headboard of the bed we had dismantled moments before.

The building had, in fact, "given them back." I have twelve witnesses to the fact that the earrings had vanished only to reappear minutes later in a spot where we had just searched! There were even people watching and listening to the live streaming video who concurred that no one had come into the room while I slept, no one had touched the earrings, and no one had placed them back after our thorough search.

I cannot explain the depth of wonder I felt. The unseen world of ghosts and spirits can physically interact with us, not just by shadows and sound, but by object manipulation and intelligent intent.

I'm just relieved that the spirits of the Knickerbocker are kind enough to return the items they "borrow" from visitors. I feel privileged that I was able to experience such an unusual and fascinating phenomenon.

"I Don't Want You to Go"

On December 3, 2009, Peg invited a small group of friends over to the hotel for the evening with the hope of introducing them to some of the Knickerbocker's resident spirits. The group gathered for an EVP session in the Angel Room on the third floor. The session was recorded individually by several of the people present, as well as by the streaming camera's audio and video.

After a forty-minute period of questions and attempts to communicate met with little concrete activity, Peg figured the spirits might be a bit "camera shy," hesitant to come out with so many strangers around. She thought if everyone left the room, they could slowly come back in one by one, letting the spirits gradually adjust to the presence of the investigators.

On the video you see and hear Peg gently explaining to the spirits what they are doing, and as the group rises and begins to leave, Peg says, "We're going to each take a turn . . ."

A pleading child's voice replies, "*I don't want you to go . . .*"

Some EVPs have an inhuman, even metallic timbre to them, but this voice is so human, so clear and immediate you assume it had to come from one of the group. But it didn't.

None of the five living participants heard the voice at the time. It was, however, captured on one other video camera and two of the four audio recorders. The fact that not every recorder picked up this EVP strengthens its validity. If the voice had been a living person, a natural sound in the room, all recording devices would have captured it more or less equally.

It was also a shockingly intelligent and intimate response to what was happening at the moment, and it was directed toward Peg, someone with whom the spirits were very familiar.

According to Peg, this is the clearest EVP ever captured at the Knickerbocker, and it's one of the most compelling we've ever heard—the plaintive cry of a lonely ghost child.

Take the Haunted Tour—The Third-Floor Common Area: The Woman in White

The hallway of the third floor is divided in half—on the north side of the floor are the two Children's Rooms, the Angel Room, a communal bathroom, and the hallway between them, creating something of a suite.

In addition to the wildly active shadow figure captured on video by the Paranormal and Supernatural Seekers team, this hallway is the domain of the Woman in White. Her ghostly appearances have been reported by guests and the owners of the Knickerbocker.

Psychic C. J. Sellers, featured on the Knickerbocker episode of *Paranormal State*, picked up on a female presence upstairs in a white gown, with the name Katie or Katherine or the like. Unbeknownst to C. J., Peg told Ryan Buell of a Katie Hickey who lived and worked at the Arnold House in the 1880s and who nursed Clara Arnold on her deathbed.

"This Place Is Going to Kill Tata"

From the third floor to the stairwells, a disembodied woman's voice has sent chills down many a visitor's back.

Reports concur that it is a muffled sound, hard to decipher, spoken by a female who seems to be speaking in another language. At times the voice seems like it is right behind you; other times it's just out of range.

Katrina Weidman of *Paranormal State* got a taste of this foreign phantom.

She heard something, a voice uttering a short sentence, she informed her teammates in the episode.

Katrina and team member Eilfie Music tried to communicate with the spirit, asking if there was a woman who wished to speak with them.

A startled Katrina heard the same voice again, right in her ear.

Ryan joined the ladies on the third floor to see if he could also hear this audio anomaly.

He invited any spirits to come forward and communicate with them quickly, as time was short.

As if on cue Katrina heard the voice again, a woman.

The team picked up a female voice on their recorders. Upon playback it seemed muffled, but Katrina was adamant that what she had heard was a quieter version of what she had heard the night before.

Peg Knickerbocker's sister Kathy also saw and heard a female apparition in this area, face covered by a veil, wandering about. According to Kathy, the apparition spoke, "but in a foreign language—I couldn't understand her."

Agnes Tomczak lived and worked at the Knickerbocker decades ago with her husband and her children. Polish immigrants, the Tomczaks were hardworking, family-oriented people. Agnes—known as "Tata" by her loved ones—spent long hours inside the hotel cooking, cleaning, taking care of guests, whatever work there was to be done. Her dedication was admirable, but it took a toll on her health. Her children began to worry about her.

"This place is going to kill Tata," her daughter said on several occasions. *Paranormal State*'s team captured that exact phrase in Polish on their digital recorder.

During a visit in 2011, Kayla Paden and her fiancé, Richard, encountered the startling spirit of a Woman in White right outside the Angel Room. Theresa was at the bottom of the stairs on the second floor when she heard their screams. She nearly ran into them as they retreated from the area, and she made her way toward them to see what had happened.

They were "newbies" to paranormal investigating, and seeing a full-bodied apparition terrified them.

"She just appeared out of nowhere, all in white," Kayla reported.

"She looked right at us, turned, and disappeared!" added Richard.

"Congratulations," Theresa told them, trying not to let her investigator envy show through. "Some of us go a lifetime without ever seeing a full-fledged ghost!"

They took little comfort in her words and quickly darted downstairs to a "safer," more brightly lit area of the hotel.

CONCLUSION

The Knickerbocker can be compared to a storybook, with each of its rooms representing a chapter, each chapter with its own unique characters. Each character has a common denominator, a connection to the building itself. When you enter the Knickerbocker you become part of the story, and the characters may reveal themselves in fascinating and sometimes frightening ways.

Theresa has had a number of ghostly encounters at the Knick. She has witnessed many bizarre things unfold before her during these visits. She believes each of these encounters has been with a different spirit, and that is what she finds so intriguing about the place.

There are haunted houses and then there are *haunted* houses. If you're lucky, you might find one or two ghosts during a hunt. At some larger venues you may find more. But the Knickerbocker seems to be rife with paranormal entities at a ratio far greater than just about anywhere else.

Sometimes a place is destined to be haunted due to tragic and traumatic history surrounding it, such as Waverly Hills Sanatorium, where thousands of lives were cut short by disease and despair. These emotions provide ingredients for a supernatural soup. Occasionally, in a place like the Stanley Hotel, it is the land itself that appears to power the haunting, the geography literally fueling paranormal activity like a battery.

Clara Arnold, for whom the hotel was a short-lived dream, was very likely a Spiritualist, someone who adamantly believed in spirit communication through a living agent, embracing it as religious dogma. Those who knew Clara considered her a staunch supporter of the movement fomenting in nearby Cassadaga, New York, at that time. Her dying words, "I am only going to sleep," are very much in the Spiritualist tradition. Perhaps her belief, and perhaps participation, in the fascinating world of afterlife communication created a foundation for the events that have continued to unfold long after she left this earthly plane.

We can only venture to guess what Clara did behind closed doors, but it seems possible her Spiritualist beliefs have something to do with the haunted happenings at the Knickerbocker. She is likely the original ghost, the first and the most permanent entity reported at the hotel, joined by a profusion of other former residents.

Peg and Myrle Knickerbocker have become much more than just property owners; they have taken on the responsibility of being caretakers of the past, preserving and celebrating the lives of the dead. There is an old legend that a haunting will cease when the dead are forgotten. If no living soul says your name, you simply fade away into obscurity. If this is true, then the spirits at the Knickerbocker will remain, never forgotten and always respected, under the watchful and loving eyes of Peg and Myrle Knickerbocker and those worthy of being guests at one of America's most haunted hotels.

Postscript

There's one more amazing aspect of the Knickerbocker that we've never heard attributed to any other building. Like some kind of historical or metaphysical boomerang, things always seem to come back. It's not just spirits who return to the place they held so dear in life, but *objects* make their way back as well.

Over the years the Knickerbocker has gone through a multitude of changes: owners, renovations, redecorations, repairs—old and worn furnishings and displays have been replaced as needed by each of the proprietors. This is typical for any business or home over time, of course.

Fortunately for the Knickerbocker, its current owners have worked enthusiastically to restore the building to its former glory. Peg tries to have each guest room represent a different ten-year period from the hotel's glory years. She is always on the lookout for period items and furniture to include in her displays.

Just days before our most recent visit to the Knick in January 2013, Peg came across some historical documents that listed the hotel's inventory when it changed hands in 1932 upon the death of then-owner Joseph McGuire. She had these papers with her as she was giving us a tour of some of her more recent décor changes.

Theresa was admiring the new addition of an old steamer trunk and its vintage contents—leather shoes; nylons; fur wraps with legs, tails, face, and all—tucked neatly inside its drawers. Then Peg pulled out the 1932 inventory of the very same room: one bed, one chest of drawers, one floor lamp (all of which were in the room now), and one steamer trunk with *identical* items inside.

In the hallway were a sofa, framed photographs, and a vacuum cleaner, again all of which were listed on this document. But it didn't end there. In almost every room was the same number of chairs, tables, rugs, couches, or lamps. Somehow, the hotel had called these things back, reconstituting itself. It's as if the building is not only full of spirits, but the hotel itself *is* a spirit.

What You Need to Know Before You Go:

The Knickerbocker
115 W. Erie St., Linesville, PA 16424

Contact Information:
(814) 818-0055
knickerbockerlinesville.com
contact@knickerbockerlinesville.com

For rental rates and availability, please contact Peg
Knickerbocker. For a calendar of events, check the
website.

The Knickerbocker is located in Linesville, a small town on
the border of Ohio and Pennsylvania. Although the building is
sometimes referred to as a hotel, it does not offer overnight
lodging for guests. Peg and Myrle Knickerbocker run the building
as a gathering place, an event facility, and a place for paranormal
exploration.

Please refer to the Knickerbocker website for more
information and to view the videos mentioned in this
chapter.

The Knickerbocker is wired for Internet video and audio and
streams live to thirty-seven countries around the clock. The
thousands who watch the live camera feeds have reported
amazing real-time activity that would have otherwise gone
unnoticed.

Lodging:
Hotel Conneaut, (814) 213-0120
12241 Lake St., Conneaut Lake, PA 16316
(Rumor has it that this hotel is also haunted.)

Hampton Inn, (814) 807-1446
11446 N. Dawn Dr., Meadville, PA 16335
hamptoninn3.hilton.com/en/index.html

Quality Inn, (866) 611-6770
17259 Conneaut Lake Rd., Meadville, PA 16335
qualityinn.com

Econo Lodge, (866) 611-6770
11237 Shaw Ave., Meadville, PA 16335
econolodge.com

The *Queen Mary*

Long Beach, California

INTRODUCTION

Of the famously haunted locations in the United States, the RMS *Queen Mary* is the most iconic and instantly recognizable. From its maiden voyage in 1936 to its retirement in 1967, this stately embodiment of elegant travel has seen life and death come and go with the tides.

When she first got her sea legs, the *Queen Mary*, flagship of the Cunard Line, was the fastest, most luxurious (and just short of the largest) ship to sail the Atlantic. The first-class accommodations may have been named for a queen, but they were fit for a king, and celebrities such as Clark Gable, Greta Garbo, and Winston Churchill were but a few of her A-list clientele. Though it was still the Depression, there was no lack of excess and opulence at the top, and luxury cruises were the only civilized way to travel between the Old and New Worlds.

But those days came to a screeching halt with the outbreak of

World War II in 1939. The *Queen Mary*—along with sister ship, the *Queen Elizabeth*—was called into service, and she answered. She was converted into a transport ship for Allied troops. Six miles of carpet, 220 cases of china, crystal and silver service, and tapestries and paintings were removed and stored in warehouses for the duration of the war. She doubled her capacity from 2,410 to 5,500 (and eventually much more) and received a new, stealthy paint job that earned her the nickname "The Grey Ghost."

During the course of the war she ferried over 800,000 troops to Europe. She set the record for most people aboard a floating vessel, 16,683, which still stands to this day. The *Queen Mary*'s contribution to the war was unmistakable but not without its share of tragedy.

In October 1942 the *Queen Mary* was carrying ten thousand troops across the Atlantic. It was procedure for the large vessel to travel in a zigzag pattern, an evasive maneuver that lessened the likelihood of detection by German U-boats. Her escort was the HMS *Curacoa*, a much smaller, less powerful ship that provided antiaircraft cover for the Grey Ghost. The *Curacoa*'s engines strained to keep up with the *Queen Mary* and her captain made a fateful error, running straight instead of zigzagging.

The *Queen Mary*, humming along at a speed of twenty-eight knots, sped toward the *Curacoa*, which had no chance of avoiding the impending collision. The *Curacoa* was literally cut in two. Because of the threat of U-boat attack, strict orders prevented the *Queen Mary* from stopping or attempting any sort of rescue mission. The screams of the dying rang across the water as the Grey Ghost continued on her journey. The *Curacoa* sank in less than six minutes, taking all but 99 of the 338 crew with her. The *Queen Mary* suffered minor damages compared to the complete devastation of her escort.

After the war, the Grey Ghost returned to her role as luxury ship, but the age of the airplane had arrived. Air travel gained popularity and affordability, and by the 1960s the *Queen Mary* was operating at a loss. After a thousand trips carrying over 2.1 million passengers, she was retired in 1967.

The grand dame was given new life as a hotel, museum, and tourist attraction after being permanently docked in Long Beach, California, and it was then that staff and visitors began to report unusual sounds and ghostly apparitions in nearly every part of her. With at least forty-nine reported deaths aboard the *Queen Mary*, it's no wonder she plays host to so many spirits.

Agonized screams and the sound of tearing metal have been reported in the boiler room. Many believe these to be from the spirits of the doomed men of the *Curacoa*. Another more frightening apparition nicknamed "Half Hatch Harry" has been spotted near watertight door #13, where an eighteen-year-old sailor was crushed and literally severed in two by the thick heavy door in which he was trapped. Was it a routine drill or an ill-fated game of chicken that took this young man's life?

Another of the ship's prominent spirits is that of a young girl who plays an endless game of hide-and-seek around the empty first-class pool. Her tiny wet footprints have been reported coming out of the pool dressing room, thought to be some kind of spiritual vortex.

Paranormal investigators flock to Long Beach hoping to catch a glimpse of one of these resident ghosts. *Ghost Hunters*'s Jason Hawes and Grant Wilson brought their team to the ship for an episode of their show. Although they uncovered an obvious hoax attempt, they couldn't deny the energy and activity that surrounded them during their stay.

Fact or Faked star Bill Murphy brought his squad to the *Queen Mary* as well and agreed that there is something otherworldly going on in the dark recesses of the ship. Murphy produced a documentary about the hauntings on board that examines many different facets of this remarkable national treasure.

Personal Experience—
Theresa: All Aboard

In April 2012, Cathi Weber and I visited the famous *Queen Mary*. We were in Los Angeles to film our episode of *My Ghost Story*, and Long Beach was just a short drive from our hotel. There was no way we were going to leave Southern California without investigating the most haunted ship in the world.

The classic beauty of this grand ship is stunning. I felt small in its shadow as the black, white, and red paint of the ship's exterior glistened in the bright California sun. We climbed the gangplank to the promenade deck, filled with anticipation and awe. I wondered how such a huge ship could stay afloat in the water—what a marvelous feat of engineering!

Silently I wished we were setting sail on a long ocean voyage, or at least spending a few leisurely nights at the hotel, but a day of exploration would have to do. Our timing was perfect; there were only a handful of guests on board, and a cheerful staff member was happy to help us investigate the ship at our leisure.

Take the Haunted Tour—The First Class Swimming Pool (R Deck)

As we descended into the belly of the massive steel-hulled vessel, we were surprised at how easy it is to get turned around. If not for our guide, we'd have been terribly lost. The deeper we went, the darker it became. The creep factor had escalated by the time we reached our first destination, the First Class Swimming Pool.

I'd never seen anything like it. Although empty of water, the pool is quite a sight to behold. Balconies inlaid with turquoise accents crown two of the marble walls that surround the pool deck, while an Art Deco picture of beautiful swans is embedded in a third. Round ornate light fixtures cast a golden glow over the entire area, bringing out the blues of the pool and the richness of the polished stone. A smooth metal sliding board is still intact but looks out of place, stopping abruptly in midair about eight feet above the bottom of the empty pool. Only the defunct heating pipes that run horizontally along the sides and the grated drain in the pool bottom show true signs of age.

It seemed as if the place would instantly come to life if only water were added, like the regeneration of a dehydrated flower.

The first-class pool is the domain of arguably the ship's most famous spirit. According to the legend related by our guide, many years ago, during the *Queen Mary*'s golden age, a little girl named Jackie, around seven or eight years old, wandered into the pool area unsupervised. She either tried to swim on her own or slipped into the water and drowned.

Since then, visitors and crew have reported strange happenings in the area, including the sound of splashing water coming from the empty pool, and a child's laughter echoing in the emptiness. Several people have reported following small wet footprints from the edge of the pool only to have them disappear abruptly at the women's dressing room door. Investigators have captured numerous EVPs, and visitors have spotted the wispy apparition of a petite figure skipping along the pool deck, thought to be little Jackie.

But the legend differs from official reports. Ship records show there were several deaths aboard the vessel, but no drownings in the First Class Swimming Pool. Paranormal investigators and *Queen Mary* crew members believe it is Jackie who haunts the first-class pool, although they believe she drowned in the second-class area.

Maybe she's trying to climb the social ladder in the afterlife, or maybe she knows she has a better chance of being heard in the more traveled part of the ship.

Cathi and I took our time examining the exterior of the pool deck, listening intently for any strange noises or girlish laughter. Since Cathi, the guide, and I were the only three living people in the area, it wasn't difficult to control the scene. I pulled out my voice recorder and started an EVP session. Instead of the usual "give us a sign of your presence," I used a more personal approach.

"Hello there! Does anybody want to play? Would you like to go swimming?"

Cathi joined in, "I taught my daughter and granddaughter how to swim. Can I teach you as well?"

No response. I tried again, "I have a little girl. She is ten years old. Her name is Karen and she loves to swim. What's your name?"

Upon playback there was the clear sound of a little girl's laughter—our tactics had worked! Connecting with the spirit of the girl as women, as mothers, had worked. Our guide was unfazed by our audio evidence; apparently this type of thing happens there quite often.

After a successful session by the pool deck, our guide told us of the bizarre paranormal activity reported in the women's dressing room. Psychics have claimed there is a vortex inside, a place of great spiritual energy where spirits cross back and forth between our world and the next. This we *had* to see!

The dressing room features a series of tiny stalls that provided privacy for those changing before they took a dip in the pool. Although the smell of chlorine no longer permeates the room, something else filled the air. It wasn't so much a smell as it was a heaviness, an electricity. I'd never placed much faith in the notion of spirit vortexes, but every molecule in my body reacted to some invisible force in the narrow space between the rows of changing stalls in the little room.

Cathi pulled out the EMF detector and I the thermometer. There *was* something strange going on: The EMF was off the chart and we located a four-foot radius cold spot where the temperature was only 55°F, as compared to 68°F throughout the rest of the room.

Cathi checked and double-checked our instruments, which appeared to be working fine. I tried another EVP session. Standing right in the center of the vortex, I asked if we were communicating with the little girl we had heard outside.

"If you're the one we heard laughing by the pool, can you let us know?"

At that moment I felt something cold—like an icy dead hand reaching up from the depths—grab my ankle. Tiny invisible fingers curled around my leg, gripping it tightly before letting go. I jumped, let out a squeal, and pointed frantically down. Cathi quickly aimed her flashlight at my feet, which revealed nothing.

"Did you just touch Theresa? Can you talk to us or let us see you?" Cathi asked.

Suddenly, Cathi jumped also. "I just felt something on my leg!" she cried.

I reciprocated with my flashlight, shining it toward her feet. To my surprise, there were four incipient red scratch marks on her ankle. Cathi scampered out of the vortex and examined her legs. Within seconds the marks began to fade. By the time we had our cameras ready, the marks were almost completely gone.

The EMF meter buzzed erratically for a few seconds and then went still. The cold spot and the static in the air dissipated—the room "normalized." In the distance we heard a barely audible giggle coming from the pool deck. Then an eerie quiet fell upon us, melancholy and peaceful. Our encounter was over. Time to move on.

Take the Haunted Tour—The Queen's Salon

The most visually striking area of the majestic ship is the Queen's Salon, once the First Class Dining Room. This lavish room is

4,600 square feet of burnished opulence, adorned in yellows and bronze, rich imported woods, floors of polished marble, a parquet dance floor, and a trio of golden onyx fireplaces. The Art Deco extravagance of the *Queen Mary* is celebrated in grand style in the salon, leaving the very notion of "excess" an understatement.

Among the more interesting features of the room are a performance stage lined with heavy gold drapes, and intricately carved motifs of a bygone era. The pièce de résistance is an elaborate, stylized map of the ship's ocean crossing from the United States to England and back, complete with a tiny moving crystal ship that tracked the position of the *Queen Mary* on each voyage.

Guests could follow the progress of their journey as they dined on gourmet fare, although few were in a hurry to actually arrive at their destination. The skyscrapers of New York City flank the left side of the map, while the ancient cities of old Europe flank the right. A glowing sun shines its rays across the gentle waves while a crescent moon and twinkling stars hang high above.

The haunted reputation of the Queen's Salon includes numerous reports of paranormal activity. Most notably, another Woman in White resides here, her wispy apparition seen gliding gracefully across the floor, a long white gown covering her slim form as she dances to a song heard only in the afterlife. Presumed to be the ghost of a first-class passenger from decades past, she is content to carry on her afterlife in this beautiful place completely oblivious to the living souls around her. She is most likely a residual haunting, a repeating energy loop blissfully unaware of her surroundings.

A similar ghost has been spotted in other areas of the ship, although it is unclear if the sightings are of the same spirit. A woman in a long white dress has been seen descending a set of stairs in the cargo hold, an odd place for a passenger to be. One possible explanation is that the spirit is "attached" to something stored there, such as an antique piece of furniture or a more personal item that held great significance to her.

Personal Experience—
Theresa

Cathi and I were giddy with our luck the day we explored the *Queen Mary*. Our guide was more than willing to grant us access to areas normally off-limits to tourists, including the Queen's Salon, which is now reserved for private parties and functions. I imagined the rich and famous of another era mingling merrily, cocktails in hand, a gourmet four-course dinner soon to be served by an attentive staff.

I was drawn to the amazing map-art piece on the wall. Our guide told us how the miniature moving ship tracked the *Queen Mary* on voyages across the sea, and then granted us time alone in the salon while she waited outside, making sure we were undisturbed. We walked slowly around the room taking in every bit of ornate detail, mouths agape in awe.

I pictured the room set up very differently during the war, converted to a mess hall, stripped of its opulence in favor of efficiency and practicality—the menu quite different as well!

"Ooops, we're busted. Someone's in here," Cathi said.

"Huh? Where?" I asked, disappointed we might have to leave.

"Right over there . . . I . . . I . . . there was someone in uniform over by the wall," she gestured, puzzled.

As Cathi lifted her hand to point to the person, I saw him too, very briefly. A large older gentleman, in what I thought was a military or captain's uniform, turned quickly away from my gaze. He was solid like a living person; not transparent like a ghost. I didn't see his face, only his form, which was unmistakable. He tipped his cap as he turned away, further blocking his face from our view. Then he disappeared. He didn't walk away, he just *vanished*! Cathi and I turned to each other in unison, shocked by what we had just witnessed.

We stood glued in place for a few moments but snapped out of it quickly. "Let's go see," I said.

We ran over to the spot where the apparition had stood. No one was there. Could he have left through a door of some kind? There was no door, nook, or cranny into which a living person could have ducked. We looked all around the room but found nothing.

"Let's go talk to the guide. Someone *had* to be in here!" I exclaimed.

We met up with our guide and asked if anyone had joined us in the salon. She assured us we had been the only ones inside. No one was supposed to be in the area, including us. We described the man we had seen. The uniform we described was not one that current staff of the *Queen Mary* wear.

I had never heard of a male apparition in the Queen's Salon, but we learned quickly to expect the unexpected aboard America's most haunted ship!

Take the Haunted Tour—The Engine Room

Deep in the belly of the *Queen Mary* sits the heart of the ship: the engine room. Once a loud, hot, bustling place, the engine room is now a maze of silent machinery and cold metal. The labyrinth of steel passageways remains much as it was during the *Queen Mary*'s sailing days. Each sound reverberates endlessly off the hard surfaces. A dull blanket of white and gray paint covers the engine room, in stark contrast to the vibrant color palette of the ship's public areas.

Few passengers ever saw this part of the ship; only crew and staff had reason to be here. But this hidden world holds its own stories and secrets.

The most famous tale from the engine room is of an eighteen-year-old crewman named John Pedder who tried to slip through watertight door #13 as it closed during a fire drill in 1966. It's possible he was engaged in a game of "chicken" with another crewman, taking turns running back and forth through the door, trying to be the last one through before it slammed shut, but that might be legend.

Either way, young John rather calamitously miscalculated and became jammed in the thick metal door as it closed. He was mortally wounded, some say severed in two. In death he was assigned the rather cavalier nickname "Half Hatch Harry," likely because it has a better ring than "Grievously Jammed John," or something similar.

Personal Experience—
Theresa

As the mother of a young sailor, I know that sometimes testosterone-filled young men have something to prove to each other, especially on long, tedious voyages. Cathi and I examined the doorway trying to decide if we believed the famous tale. As I stared intently at the narrow door, I noticed a translucent mist forming into a humanoid shape, with a distinctive head and shoulders. I couldn't decide if it was condensation, some sort of fog, or something truly paranormal. I mentioned the mist to Cathi, but it disappeared as quickly as it had formed. We approached the door with trepidation but found nothing unusual and no explanation for the ghostly mist—no condensation, no moisture, nothing.

Suddenly, we both felt a cold chill spring out of nowhere, and I couldn't shake the feeling of being watched. Our silent consternation was shattered by an odd noise, a strange mechanical hum, growing louder and morphing from machinelike into a melodious, almost musical tone.

Then I jumped, startled by a wailing moan from just behind me, thick with pain and anguish—the sound of death. Cathi pulled out her camera and I fumbled in my bag for my audio recorder, hands slightly shaking. Something was "off" about these sounds—were we being toyed with?

"That's got to be the machines, right?" Cathi asked.

"Yeah . . . maybe . . . but none of these are working," I answered.

"Hello? Is someone trying to get our attention? It's working, we're listening. Can you do that again?" Cathi asked.

The ghastly moaning sound continued.

"It's got to be the boat rocking in the water—it has to be!" I said a bit too loudly, trying to convince myself.

Before Cathi had time to answer, another sound got our attention. This one chilled us to the bone. We stared at each other in disbelief at the distinct sound of a man laughing "*Ha ha ha*" in a tone so disturbing we had no doubt it was meant to scare us. If this was Half Hatch Harry, he wanted the last laugh.

In the 13Pictures documentary *The Queen Mary: A Floating Phenomenon*, Bill Murphy toured the ship with guide and psychic Erika Frost. On more than one occasion, they both heard an eerie moan in various areas of the ship. The tone and tempo of the noise changed, making the mystery of its origin even more fascinating. At one point while they were in the cargo hold, the moaning sounded strangely similar to a conversation.

Bill pointed out that every time he started to speak, the creepy sound would begin again. This pattern repeated several times during filming. After watching the documentary, I recognized the moaning as something very similar to what Cathi and I heard in the engine room. I can't rule out the possibility that the source of the sound was something natural aboard or outside the ship, but an uneasy feeling stirred in my gut when I heard the haunting sound again in the film.

Take the Haunted Tour—B Deck, Room B-340

B Deck once housed the third-class cabins and is used today by guests of the *Queen Mary* hotel. These aren't the biggest or most luxurious of the rooms, but they are comfortable nonetheless. A trip down the deck's long passageways of glossy wood paneling and carpets of burgundy-and-gold flowers includes an interesting visual phenomenon: Instead of a straight corridor, the ship has a curved, banana-like structure intended to add stability to the large vessel. The unusual shape can cause a slight funhouse-type effect, possibly adding to the paranormal vibe on the deck.

Of the twelve decks of the *Queen Mary*, B Deck is known as the most haunted of them all. One particular room takes the top prize, and for good reason. It is by far the most "occupied" unoccupied room on the ship.

The *Queen Mary* has 314 staterooms, eight full suites, and five mini-suites. Several of these are considered haunted. But the one with the most notorious reputation is room B-340, which isn't available to overnight guests. Anyone interested in the spirits of the ship is welcome to explore this room, which is featured on the popular Ghosts & Legends tour. Originally the space encompassed three third-class staterooms, but it has been remodeled to become one large room.

Even with its expanded dimensions, the room is quite small and sparsely outfitted with a simple single bed, modest dresser, chair, and small round table holding a basic lamp. A modern shower and bath were installed during remodeling, but third-class passengers had to share washroom facilities. Two small round portholes offer an outside view, although it is difficult to see very far.

According to our guide, room B-340 was once available to overnight guests, but persistent complaints about paranormal activity such as strange noises, ghostly footsteps, and peculiar plumbing problems (faucets turning off and on by themselves, toilets flushing on their own) forced management to shut it down. Why this particular room is so haunted is a bit of a mystery. One theory revolves around a man named Walter J. Adamson, a third-class passenger who was found dead of unknown causes in room B-226 during one of the ship's early transatlantic crossings. When the ship was remodeled, room B-226 was folded into what we know today as room B-340.

One of the stories we heard (apparently originating from a psychic's impression) told of a war bride traveling from Europe to be reunited with her American soldier husband. She was pregnant and alone at the time, leaving behind everything she knew to start a new life in the United States. Alone and scared, she was afraid to venture out of the room. The journey was long and tiresome. The woman went into labor before the ship reached the shore. Her pregnancy was fraught with complications, and without proper medical assistance or a midwife, the woman and her baby died.

In another, slightly different account, the woman, a war bride with a newborn baby, was traveling from Europe to meet the father of her child, an American serviceman. She was confined to the room, unable or unwilling to leave the security of the tiny space. Frustrated and lonely, she spent her days fussing about the cabin and tending to the baby. Once she arrived, her dreams were shattered when her "husband" (they may not have been legally married) refused her and the child and sent them away. It is her frustrated spirit that causes poltergeist-type activity in the room, including throwing hangers and turning the faucets off and on.

B-340 was the center of a very controversial episode of Syfy's *Ghost Hunters* that aired on October 5, 2005. During an investigation of the *Queen Mary* by The Atlantic Paranormal Society (TAPS), the team set up a stationary camera in room B-340 hoping to catch an apparition or some of the other unusual phenomena reported there. When Steve Gonsalves and Dave Tango returned to the cabin to change the tape on the camera, they found that the bed had been "messed up," although it had been neatly made when the investigation began.

The two immediately reviewed the camera footage and were shocked to find the comforter on the bed clearly moving, as if an invisible force were manipulating it! This piece of footage was so incredible, the team immediately turned their focus on the area.

After a brief investigation of the room, they found it was possible for someone to hide behind a utility closet door that accessed the room from the hall and sneak in outside camera view. A person could have reached the camera undetected, stopped it momentarily, then mussed the blankets before turning the camera back on.

This theory was confirmed when an eagle-eyed Dave Tango noticed a jump in the video, indicating the tape had indeed been stopped and restarted. A very disappointed Jason Hawes and Grant Wilson were heartbroken by this find, admitting it put a damper on the entire case, leaving all experiences and evidence suspect.

Jason and Grant were invited back to the *Queen Mary* for the documentary *The Queen Mary: A Floating Phenomenon* by 13Pictures founder Bill Murphy, who, along with guide Erika Frost, explained the hoax theory in greater detail.

The TAPS founders agreed that no one could be positively blamed for the deceptive act; they couldn't prove who did it or why. Grant added that it was unnecessary to perpetrate such a hoax, as the hauntings on the great ship speak for themselves without need of unethical "help" from anyone. Erika, who was disappointed by the original incident, admitted that much good had come in the aftermath of the incident. Tighter security measures were put in place and a twenty-four-hour live webcam was installed in the room to preclude further tampering.

A paranormal team called Beyond Investigation Magazine (BIM) led by Patrick Wheelock investigated the incident in B-340 and pointed out some interesting and overlooked facts about the *Ghost Hunters* episode and the hoaxed video in question.

During the original airing of the episode, Jason and Grant verbally "suggested" that only a person of small stature could have sneaked into the utility closet or unnoticed third door, manipulated the camera, and messed up the bedclothes. In reality, any reasonably-sized person could fit through the small door and remain out of camera range.

The BIM investigation with the same make and model Hi8 camera also proved that any attempt at manually stopping or pausing the camera would cause the video to "jump" and produce an audible beep. But the remote provided with that particular model could be used to pause and restart the tape and give the effect shown on the episode. Who had access to a remote for the camera? The camera's owner. Who owned the camera? TAPS.

Other details surfaced in the aftermath that potentially point a finger at a TAPS member, although these could not be verified to our satisfaction. It is for the public to decide what happened that night.

Patrick Wheelock also researched some of the more common claims of paranormal activity from B-340 and came up with some interesting findings. The last time the room was occupied by a guest was during its final ocean voyage in 1967. The claims that hotel guests were so scared of the activity in the room that they left during the night or asked to be moved are unfounded, as the room was never available for overnight stays. The hotel opened in 1972 but did not originally include B Deck. B Deck was opened in the 1980s but not B-340.

How then do you explain the many and persistent reports of activity in this room? For one thing, who's to say that ghosts must remain where they died? Just because no one passed away in B-340 doesn't mean there are no ghosts there. Also, B-340 was converted from three separate rooms. Maybe someone *did* pass away in one of those earlier cabins, such as Walter Adamson, mentioned previously.

Personal Experience—
Theresa: Cabin Fever

Our guide explained the unusual shape of room B-340, how it had been expanded from three separate cabins. She then recounted the tales of the rejected war bride and other paranormal reports from B-340. All had an air of sadness about them, to say the least. I wasn't sure if any of these stories were based in fact or just colorful tales of woe that added to the ghostly reputation of the room.

There *were* hundreds of war brides who traveled on the ship, and some were certainly pregnant or had babies with them. A long ocean voyage would have been difficult for anyone in a "delicate" condition, and I'm certain some men were less than honorable with women they had met overseas.

It didn't take long to investigate the room; Cathi took one side, I took the other. I examined the sink in the bathroom, hoping to find a reason for the water turning off and on by itself, but found nothing. We examined the bed as well, not sure what we were looking for. While taking photographs around the room, I heard what sounded like a baby crying.

"Did you hear that? Sounded like a baby," I said.

"No, where from?" Cathi asked.

Before I could answer I heard it again, this time it sounded closer.

"There! There it is again!" I was certain about it this time. As a mother, I am in tune to a baby's cries, no matter whose child it may be.

Cathi was puzzled, "Theresa, I'm not hearing it. Maybe you just *think* you heard it because you're homesick."

"No, no, I'm sure. I heard a cry. A baby's cry." I wasn't *that* homesick.

Once more the sorrowful sound hit my ears; once more no one else heard it. I thought maybe the cry was coming from outside in the hall, possibly a visitor or tourist, but it was loud. And close. Why was I the only one who could hear it? Was I having some sort of auditory hallucination?

I tried to capture the sound on my audio recorder, but the crying had stopped. I was exhilarated and disappointed at the same time, wishing I had caught it on tape or that my partner had heard it as well. Unfortunately all I was left with was an interesting personal experience and a sudden urge to call home.

Personal Experience—
Eric Olsen

I owned and operated one of the larger mobile DJ companies in Southern California back in the 1980s, Olsen Entertainment. We had every manner of customer from weddings and corporate events to showbiz parties and nightclubs. But our highest volume and most regular work was for various college groups, especially fraternities and sororities at USC and UCLA.

And, my friends, they had parties.

Augmenting the usual kegs-and-debauchery affairs they had at their houses on campus, the groups also had periodic formal dinner-dances at prestigious locales around SoCal, including the *Queen Mary*.

One such evening in the late 1980s, I pulled my little red truck up to the grand behemoth and began the laborious process of unloading all my DJ equipment and records out of the truck, onto a hand truck, and then to the service entrance. *All* equipment must go *only* in the service entrance in the interest of decorum.

On the ship, map in hand, I wound my way hither and yon to the designated elevator with the goal of reaching the Promenade Deck and the Queen's Salon, where the soiree was to unfold. I maneuvered the hand truck and myself into the narrow confines of the elevator, contorted around the piled equipment, and pushed the up button. The doors narrowly cleared and the elevator jolted into action.

Perspiring and slightly winded, I became alarmed as the walls seemed to close in on me, what little air there was in the coffin-like confines vanishing. I am not particularly claustrophobic, but it was all I could do to fend off panic. Then, to top it off, hot breath blew on the back of my neck and a rough, diffuse voice whispered, *"Tight quarters."*

My head slammed into the back wall of the elevator as I jerked around in response. Then the elevator doors opened with a cheerful *ding* and the real world seemed to return.

I was a little on edge the rest of the evening.

CONCLUSION

Few locations are as iconic and as easily recognizable as the RMS *Queen Mary*. Once the pride of the Cunard Line and among the most majestic ships ever to sail the seas, the *Queen Mary* was the epitome of luxury and elegance. When called into service during World War II, she answered and ferried thousands of troops to and fro, taking them courageously to the front line and gratefully home again.

Among the hordes that flock to her decks now are paranormal

enthusiasts and ghost hunters of every flavor. They come searching for adventure, a glimpse into the past, a peek into the world of wealth and privilege aboard the world's largest supernatural floating phenomenon.

The *Queen Mary* lives up to her reputation as one of the most haunted locations in the world. All ghost hunters worth their sea salt have heard of the *Queen Mary* and placed her high on their "must see" list. The attention has helped provide needed revenue to the ship—the daily ghost tours offered on board complement the more traditional exhibits, tours, and happenings.

Those who seek to interact with the spirits call out to them, enticing them to communicate, opening the door and inviting them to come through. The combined intent of the living, the residual essence of the dead, and environmental factors such as the steady lapping of gentle waves against the steel hull of the ship all fuel paranormal activity.

But the grand ship is once again in danger, not from a Nazi U-boat or enemy plane, but from a decline in tourism and a faltering economy. The cost of maintaining the massive hotel and entertainment venue is extraordinary, and this may be the one enemy she cannot evade. The hotel's many staterooms and enormous halls sit empty too often, occupied only by the ghosts who never check out.

It would be a terrible loss if the reign of the *Queen Mary* were to end. A piece of world history would be gone forever. Who would tell her stories? Who would talk to her dead? Who would admire her magnificence? We hope those questions never have to be answered.

What You Need to Know Before You Go:

The *Queen Mary*
1126 Queens Highway, Long Beach, CA 90802

Contact Information:
queenmary.com
info: (877) 342-0738
hotel: (877) 342-0742

The *Queen Mary* is permanently docked in Long Beach, California, with breathtaking views of the harbor. The ship operates as a hotel, an event center, and a tourist attraction. An overnight stay is the best way to see the many different amenities the ship has to offer. Besides the hotel, the *Queen Mary* offers a number of different tours and exhibits to suit any taste, including special seasonal shows and events. Dining is available at the ship's many restaurants, cafés, and bars, and the marketplace is a menagerie of quaint stores and boutiques. The experience is something that should be savored and not rushed.

Tours:
A variety of tour options are available, but the best way to explore the ship is with one of the Passports. Discounts are available for seniors, AAA members, and the military.

Queen Mary Passport: Includes Ship Walk Tour with audio headset, Ghosts & Legends show, *Queen Mary* Story, Museum & Historic Exhibits.

First Class Passport: Includes Self-Guided Audio Tour, Ghosts & Legends show, choice of The Glory Days Tour or Her Finest Hour Tour, Foxtrot-class Submarine Tour.

Royal Passport: Includes Self-Guided Audio Tour and Diana: Legacy of a Princess, a Royal Exhibition.

The Haunted Encounters Passport: Includes Haunted Encounters Tour, Self-Guided Ship Walk Tour, Ghosts & Legends show, and Ghost Plaque Scavenger Hunt.

During October, the *Queen Mary* presents **"Dark Harbor,"** a Halloween attraction.

Don't forget to visit the **Scorpion Submarine**, a unique attraction right next to the *Queen Mary*. This authentic Russian sub is open daily from 10 A.M. to 6 P.M.

Lodging:

A variety of guest rooms and suites are available on the *Queen Mary*. Staying aboard is the most highly recommended way to fully experience this historic treasure. Please call for details.

Westin Long Beach, (562) 436-3000, (888) 627-8403
333 E. Ocean Blvd., Long Beach, CA 90802
westinlongbeachhotel.com

Renaissance Long Beach Hotel, (562) 437-5900
111 E. Ocean Blvd., Long Beach, CA 90802
marriott.com

Courtyard by Marriott, (562) 435-8511, (866) 440-3390
500 E. 1st St., Long Beach, CA 90802
marriott.com

Travelodge Long Beach Convention Center, (562) 435-2471
80 Atlantic Ave., Long Beach, CA 90802
travelodgelongbeach.com

Trans-Allegheny Lunatic Asylum

Weston, West Virginia

INTRODUCTION

Trans-Allegheny Lunatic Asylum (TALA), previously known as the Weston State Hospital or the West Virginia Hospital for the Insane, would be intimidating even without the ghosts. Its monumental main structure, the largest hand-cut stone masonry building in North America, divides 242,000 square feet over four floors, is a staggering 1,296 feet long, and is outfitted with 921 windows and 906 doors. A two-hundred-foot-tall clock tower stretches up from the center like a hand reaching to God. The walls are two and a half feet thick, dense enough to muffle the screams of even the most tormented soul, alive or dead.

In the wake of a reformist wave propelled across the land by remarkable mental health crusader Dorothea Dix, the Virginia General Assembly allocated the princely sum of $125,000 to build the Trans-Allegheny Lunatic Asylum in the early 1850s, purchasing 269 acres along the West Fork River opposite down-town Weston.

Dr. Thomas Kirkbride, whose thinking dominated the physical design of asylums and care for the mentally ill in the United States for half a century, was hired as advisor. Renowned architect Richard Swoden Andrews designed the Gothic/Tudor blue sandstone structure following the "Kirkbride Plan": long wings in a "shallow V" formation, arranged "en echelon" (staggered), so all patients had access to unobstructed sunlight and fresh air. The building itself was meant to be "a special apparatus for the care of lunacy," supported by "highly improved and tastefully ornamented" grounds.

Kirkbride, a humanist and the first doctor in the United States to recognize mental illness as a disease that could potentially be cured, believed that those afflicted were "not disabled from appreciating books . . . nor from enjoying many intellectual and physical comforts," and with institutionalization central to his plan, he sought to create an egalitarian environment where patients would be treated with dignity, compassion, and respect.

Construction began in 1858 on the main structure, known as the Kirkbride Building, but came to a screeching halt when the Civil War broke out in April 1861. Border state Virginia was deeply divided culturally and economically. Most people in the western part of the state were Appalachian mountain folk, not plantation owners, who had little need of slaves and were generally unable to afford them anyway.

In June 1861, Virginia officially seceded from the Union, throwing itself into the bloody struggle. West Virginia then seceded from Virginia, remaining with the Union. The war literally marched into Weston on June 30, 1861, when the 7th Ohio Infantry, led by Colonel Erastus Bernard Tyler, swept into town, ostensibly to round up Confederate sympathizers. But Tyler's underlying motive was revealed when he sent the trusted Captain

List and two armed soldiers to the Weston branch of the Exchange Bank of Virginia, where they seized $27,000 (over $500,000 today) in gold coins being stored in the bank vault for the purpose of covering asylum construction costs.

Banker Robert McClandish, summoned to open the vault, couldn't dissuade Captain List from his appointed mission, but did negotiate to retain $2,371.23 already owed to creditors. The bulk of the cache was sent to Wheeling, where it helped fund establishment of the new state of West Virginia.

The 7th Ohio then tromped over to the partially constructed asylum and established Camp Tyler, a Union post strategically located near several important roadways. The completed southern wing of the asylum provided barracks, and the main foundation served as a stable for horses.

Confederate raids in 1862 and 1863 temporarily disrupted Union control, and in 1864 raiders confiscated $5,287.85 from beleaguered banker McClandish and stripped the asylum of all food and clothing intended for its first batch of patients.

The hospital admitted its first patients in 1864, though construction continued until 1881. With the war over in 1865 and the soldiers gone, building on the asylum boomed, saving the Weston area from postwar economic depression. The asylum would remain the economic heart of Weston until it closed 130 years later.

With understanding of mental illness still in its infancy, a bewildering array of maladies and complaints were treated at the asylum between 1864 and 1889, including "masturbation, laziness, fits, desertion of husband, superstition," and the dreaded "menstrual derangement."

As responsibility for the unproductive, noncompliant, mentally impaired, and genuinely mentally ill shifted from families and private organizations to the state, asylums like TALA became dumping grounds for the damaged and unwanted. Originally designed to house 250 with privacy and comfort, the hospital held 717 patients by 1880, 1,661 in 1938, over 1,800 in 1949, and a dangerously overcrowded 2,600 in the 1950s.

In keeping with the Kirkbride ideal of self-sufficiency, and to keep up with a growing population, more buildings began to sprout up within the property, including a greenhouse that supplied fresh produce, a geriatrics center for the elderly and those with dementia and Alzheimer's, a large kitchen facility and cafeteria, a building for the court-ordered criminally insane, and a state-of-the-art medical center complete with morgue and autopsy room.

TALA also had a separate tuberculosis building. Because of the contagious nature of the disease, it was necessary to keep these patients isolated from the general population. This building differed in design from the others with its open-aired wings and screened-in sunporches. Today, this building remains relatively intact and hosts the local Halloween haunted house attraction each fall.

The growing community of the Trans-Allegheny Lunatic Asylum encompassed more than just the land on which it sat. TALA was the main employer for the city of Weston. It was a symbiotic relationship, with the hospital dependent on the city for its supplies and employees, and the town economically tethered to the hospital. Everyone benefited from this relationship except for patients, who, crammed into an overcrowded, understaffed, underfunded facility, cried out for help, and in some cases justice. Death was no stranger to TALA, and several murders were committed inside its walls.

The deteriorating hospital, designated in 1990 as a National Historic Landmark, became unsupportable and mercifully closed its doors in 1994. The facility sat abandoned for years, a deteriorating eyesore in the community whose economy had revolved around it for so long.

Finally, the West Virginia Department of Health and Human Resources put TALA up for auction in 2007. Contractor Joe Jordan made the winning bid of $1.5 million with the intention of revitalizing the property while preserving as much of the history as possible, but a series of fires and code violations thwarted his plans for a successful historical facility.

Those who spent time in the building regularly reported seeing apparitions of nurses, doctors, and patients roaming the staggered corridors and hearing anguished cries echoing through the hallways.

Taking a cue from shuttered institutional facilities like the Ohio State Reformatory and Waverly Hills Sanatorium, Jordan began offering historic tours and overnight ghost hunts, folding revenue back into the facility for repairs and restoration. As its reputation quickly spread, TALA attracted the attention of the media. The TAPS team from *Ghost Hunters* filmed and investigated TALA in 2008, and *Ghost Adventures* followed in 2009 with a live televised seven-hour investigation on Halloween Eve.

Both teams believed the building to be haunted, and there have been countless subsequent reports of ghostly activity at TALA by visitors and staff. Thousands of suffering souls entered the hospital, seeking refuge or salvation; others were dumped there, thrown away like unwanted trash. With such a thick mixture of energy and emotion, it's no wonder TALA offers a rich potpourri of paranormal phenomena.

The lonely spirit of a young girl named Lily wanders the halls, looking for a playmate. She makes herself known to visitors in several ways, including interacting with a menagerie of toys set out in the room dedicated to her memory. But Lily isn't the only child at TALA—ghosts of many of the hospital's younger residents haunt the upper floors, sometimes following visitors throughout the building, even following them home.

The Civil War left more than scars behind in Weston. Tortured moans of the wounded, heavy-booted footfalls, misty forms, and ominous shadows permeate the Civil War section of the building.

Nor are the upper floors as vacant as they seem. The spirits of at least two vicious murderers remain, trapped in an earthly purgatory for their crimes. Slewfoot, a cunning psychotic, murderously lashed out in a lavatory; the phantom of an even more depraved, unnamed multimurderer haunts the dungeonlike seclusion cells.

Some of the most despondent asylum patients thought suicide a way out, but they too remain stuck indefinitely between this world and the next. Their desperation seeps from the walls like water from broken pipes.

Guides and visitors feel that some spirits come and go, perhaps using the facility as a doorway; some stop by for a short while before passing on to other destinations, while others cannot or will not move on, embedded in the very foundation of the asylum.

A still controversial treatment was used extensively at the hospital. The "ice-pick" (transorbital) lobotomy was a crude procedure in which a sharp one- or two-pronged device was driven through the orbital socket of the eye and into the brain with a sharp blow, causing permanent damage thought to relieve some of the patient's more severe symptoms.

In 1952, one doctor performed 228 such lobotomies during a two-week period in West Virginia. The aptly named "Operation Ice Pick" became part of the grisly legacy of Dr. Walter Freeman, TALA's most notorious doctor.

Take the Haunted Tour—The First Floor

Mirror-imaged north and south sides of a building flanking a central core may seem a simple layout, but miles of darkened corridors and floor after floor of similar wards can make TALA difficult to navigate.

To the left (south) of the main entrance are Ward One, Ward Four, and the Civil War section. To the right (north) are Ward A, Ward D, and the Arts and Crafts Wing. There is also a subfloor under Arts and Crafts. The first floor is the largest of the four, the additional space coming from the Civil War and the Arts and Crafts sections, with long narrow appendages jutting out like bony fingers from a cold stone hand.

WARDS ONE AND FOUR

The central staging room for tours and investigations is situated in the core section of the main building, affording easy access to all wards. From here visitors travel brightly lit corridors to the first notable portion of the asylum, Ward One. The long, wide hallways are adorned with decorative archways, like vertebrae in a spine.

Sunny yellow walls and ample natural lighting reflect the pleasant atmosphere that Kirkbride envisioned when designing the hospital. The walls are covered with a multitude of black-and-white photographs of varying sizes and colorful hand-painted artwork reflecting life inside the asylum over the decades.

LILY'S ROOM

"I'm not sure where it all started, but . . . Lily talks," explained Zach McCormick, four-year TALA tour guide and paranormal enthusiast.

The most popular area on the first floor is Lily's Room, located in the eastern corner of Ward Four, a "step" between Ward One and the older Civil War section. The staff has turned this room into a sort of shrine to their resident spirit, honoring her life and memory.

Legend has it that Lily was a little girl who spent all or most of her short, sad life inside the walls of TALA. Some believe she was dropped off at the hospital, like an unwanted stray, by parents who couldn't or wouldn't care for her. Another story has it that she was born at the hospital shortly after her mother was committed, taken in and cared for by hospital staff until she died tragically of pneumonia at age nine. After her death, her spirit remained inside TALA, the only home she had ever known.

The most active of all the ghosts in the hospital, Lily likes to play games with visitors and has become especially close to some of the current guides. Her room is a cheery yellow, one of the brightest in the building, although the peeling walls and broken window glass remind you that no living soul occupies this space, and the iron bars on the windows are a stark reminder of the bygone realities of asylum life.

The room is stocked with a variety of toys, including a pink-and-white music box with a miniature ballerina turning pointe to a tinkling lullaby when the box is opened. The music box sometimes decides to play on its own.

Other items, such as baby dolls and plastic bouncy balls, are scattered about the room. These toys, set out as an invitation to play, have been known to move by themselves or in response to commands. Lily will, on occasion, roll the ball back and forth with visitors in an eerie game of catch. Lily seems to delight in these ghostly playdates, and visitors often hear her giggles—equal parts sweet and spine-tingling—echoing down the halls.

TALA guides have developed a special protective bond with the girl's spirit, demanding that she be treated with kindness and respect. Lily remembers and favors frequent visitors, interacting with them in specific ways. Paranormal investigator Aaron Sulser has investigated the asylum a dozen times. He claims one of Lily's favorite games involves the music box and flashlights.

During a recent session Aaron asked Lily if she remembered him, and if so, to please make herself known. He placed flashlights in different areas of the room, set up so that a slight twist on the top would turn them on or off. Aaron wound the music box and began asking questions. A flashlight turned on, indicating Lily was there. As the music slowed the flashlight dimmed, only to return to full brightness when the music box was wound again. This occurred several times throughout the session. When Aaron asked if Lily was making it happen, he got a positive response. The correlation between the music box and the flashlight was so consistent, Aaron had no doubt Lily was manipulating it.

Lily's Story—Fact or Fiction?

Lily's life story is ambiguous at best. Where did the "facts" of the Lily stories come from?

According to an April 2010 episode of *Ghost Stories*, a paranormal investigation series that aired on the Travel Channel, psychic Tammy Wilson first discovered the spirit of a small child named Lily on a tour of the asylum. The girl was about nine years old, wearing a white dress. Her mother, first name starting with the letter *E*, an only child of a prominent family from England, was brought to the hospital already pregnant. E was told her parents were killed in an accident and couldn't come back for her. She had to remain at the asylum, where she gave birth. Both mother and daughter lived the remainder of their days at TALA.

According to the producers of *Ghost Stories*, patient records from the 1920s showed that a woman, first name beginning with *E*, was admitted to the hospital while pregnant and later gave birth, possibly to a girl, possibly Lily.

The show also interviewed local historian Shelley Bailey, who claimed to have encountered Lily several times, leaving small gifts for her such as toys and a box of Cracker Jack, which moved on its own. She heard the distinct sounds of a box opening and crunching coming from the same area. A captured EVP politely said, "Thank you for the snacks." Shelley and her companions claimed they played a game of catch with Lily, using a plastic ball that bounced back and forth for almost forty-five minutes.

Another interesting account (in which her name was spelled *Lilly*) first appeared on the Internet in October 2009.

In 1863, a woman named Gladys Ravensfield, abandoned by her husband, was admitted to the hospital after being savagely and repeatedly raped by a group of soldiers. Gladys not only was traumatized by the assault, but also found herself pregnant. Taken to TALA, she slipped deeper into madness, rocking robotically back and forth for hours. Gladys gave birth to an infant girl who survived only a short while.

In this version, the staff at the hospital felt that the spirit of both mother and daughter never left. Lily, the name given to the child, actually grew up there, even if only in spirit form. She plays games with guests and has a fondness for sweets. Lily's tiny hand reaches out for someone to hold. Her mother's benighted spirit is locked forever in a state of shock and despair.

What's fascinating about this version of Lily's story is how quickly it spread and was taken as fact. The author, Stephen Wagner, About.com's Paranormal Phenomena guide, created it for an Internet promotion that invited bloggers to create a short *fictional* story about a ghost or event that occurred at TALA to help promote the *Ghost Adventures* live seven-hour TV event, which aired on October 30, 2009. However, the story spread across the Internet as a "historical account," a graphic reminder that just because something is posted on the Internet (or shown on reality television) doesn't mean it is true. Accounts should be confirmed from multiple sources—ideally from the original source—before a story is taken at face value. Ironically, though a wonderful research tool, the Internet has also facilitated the spread of false rumors and tales.

Another Lily tale asserts that she was indeed born at the hospital, to a mother who couldn't care for her. Beloved by the staff, Lily lived her short life inside the walls of TALA until her death at age nine from complications of pneumonia. Many similar stories circulate within the paranormal community, with wavering details but consistent basics.

Where is the truth, if any, in Lily's story? Are there slivers of fact intermingled with these elaborate accounts? Did she die there? Did she ever live there?

Myth or mystery, what does remain is the evidence, the accounts, the EVPs all suggesting that a small female child who goes by the name Lily roams the halls of the Trans-Allegheny Lunatic Asylum, making her shy and yet playful self known to visitors who come to meet her. Lily speaks, and as long as she has something to say, we will listen, regardless of her terrestrial origins.

THE CIVIL WAR SECTION

On the first floor, at the southwest corner of the building, is the oldest, least modernized section of TALA, first put to use during its stint as a Civil War camp. Many have reported sightings of Civil War soldiers, and their moans and cries echo off the dank walls in a symphony of sadness. Disheveled silhouettes of young wounded men hobble about the ward, seeking aid from passersby.

The original kitchen of the asylum is inside the Civil War area. Extending out from the middle of a larger horizontal section, the kitchen is one of three "fingerlike" rooms, narrow and dark. Remnants of its active days are still visible: Rusted pipes travel horizontally across the high ceiling, and the floor is riddled with holes from heavy industrial equipment that once crowded the area.

It's not difficult to imagine a busy staff toiling in stifling heat to keep the hungry hordes of patients and staff fed. Broken windows line the walls on each side, letting in daylight that reveals the decay of the room. Shattered glass and debris hazardously riddle the floor. The rhythmic *drip, drip, drip* of a leaking ceiling resonates throughout the room.

Personal Experience—
Theresa: Committed

I was drawn to the Trans-Allegheny Lunatic Asylum not only because of the many ghost stories, but also because of its central place in the history of mental health care and of the Civil War. I have loved ones who have dealt with varying degrees of mental illness, which made this a personal as well as professional journey. As difficult as it is today to deal with a mental or emotional disorder, we are far better off than our ancestors, whose dark days were indistinguishable from nightmares.

In March 2012 I had the opportunity to investigate the old hospital with my fellow Haunted Housewives and a few additional *Paranormal Challenge* alumni, including Aaron Sulser, Darcy Hunley, Jordan Murphy, and Daniel Hooven. After our brief but intense reality television experience, many former *Paranormal Challenge* contestants bonded and became an extended paranormal family. Before we split off into separate groups, the first-timers were given a guided tour by one of TALA's best guides, Zach McCormick.

We had barely left the first-floor staging area when I started feeling sick to my stomach and couldn't figure out why. I tried not to think about it, concentrating instead on Zach's oration on the history of the main floor. As we continued our walk, beads of sweat formed on my brow. I felt hot, flushed, with the back of my shirt drenched with perspiration, even though the temperature inside the building was quite cool.

I felt overwhelmed by the unsettling sensation of someone standing right behind me—hot breath on my neck sent a parade of goose bumps down my spine. I stopped and whipped around to face whoever was in my "space," but found no one.

My odd behavior attracted Cathi's attention, who asked me

what was wrong. I told her it was nothing. She didn't buy it, but she didn't push.

As the historical rundown continued, the wide-open room took on a heavy, smothering vibe. I heard strange voices whispering incoherently, moving in closer and closer. I wanted to run!

I seemed to be the only one experiencing this, as everyone else was smiling, listening to our guide's stories. Everyone but Cathi, that is.

"Theresa, what the hell is wrong with you? You look—I hate to say it—like you've seen a ghost!" She wasn't joking.

"I don't know . . . something just doesn't feel right. I feel a little sick, and I thought I heard something," I confessed.

"Like, whispers? Coming from everywhere?" she said.

Surprised but relieved, I answered. "*Yes!* And they're getting closer!"

"Well, shake it off. We have four more floors to get through."

Thanks for the advice, Captain Obvious.

I consider myself a "seasoned" investigator. I don't jump to conclusions, back down from a challenge, or scare very easily. But during our initial tour of TALA, I felt my sense of well-being bombarded with negative forces beyond my control.

I was shaken. I was SCARED!

After about an hour, our initial tour was finished. I *had* to get the hell out of the building and collect myself before I could return to investigate. I was tempted to get in the car and go back to the hotel, just throw in the towel and retreat to somewhere safe. But I pulled myself together, splashed some cold water on my face, said my prayers, did a protection ritual, and joined my teammates inside.

Cathi met me on the way back in. She was having similar thoughts, even considering waiting in the car until morning, but we decided to push our apprehensions aside and continue on with the investigation.

We headed back to the "most haunted" (and creepiest) area of the asylum, the Civil War section. In the corner of the large main room is a large antique carriage that resembles a Victorian hearse. It was strange to see this old buggy parked inside the otherwise empty space, as if awaiting the return of its final passengers.

We set up our recorders and our spirit box, hoping to communicate with the spirit of the soldier we had heard about from veteran TALA investigators. The modified radio was incredibly loud and echoed off the walls, assaulting our ears. We asked a series of relevant questions, but the radio's non-stop spew of noise yielded nothing useful. Well, almost nothing.

"Do you stay in this area? Were you a soldier? Do you need medical assistance?" I asked.

Random radio gibberish.

"Do you like it when people come visit you?" Cathi asked. "Can you see us? Do you know why we're here? How many of us are in this room with you?"

More gibberish.

"My name is Cathi, this is Darla, this is Theresa. Can you name one of us or please introduce yourself?"

Then, finally, one clear response came over the ghost box: "*THERESA.*"

I was stunned by this response, so I asked for clarification.

"Did you just say 'Theresa'? My name is Theresa."

"*THERESA,*" it said again. Goose bumps surged and my knees buckled.

"Who are we talking to? Can you tell us your name?" Cathi asked.

"*Mary.*"

"Are we talking to Mary?" I asked.

"*Yes, Mary.*"

"Do you know who Mary Ryan is?" Mary Ryan was a hospital employee who devoted her life to helping patients. Her ghost is thought to linger in the Civil War section of TALA.

No response.

Being in close proximity to the kitchen, we asked, "What's on the menu for today? What's for dinner?"

"*Nothing.*" That was the last clear message from the spirit box on the first floor, but that was enough. After several more minutes of silence, we journeyed on.

Personal Experience—
Aaron Sulser (Paranormal Investigator, Dark Alley Paranormal)

In April 2011 I attended a public paranormal event at TALA, featuring paranormal celebrity guests Steve Gonsalves and Dave Tango from *Ghost Hunters*. There were plenty of people around that night but the place is so big, it was easy to find yourself alone at any given time.

I broke off from the pack to do some exploring. I had one other person with me and we wanted to check out the Civil War section, so I took him down to the old kitchen area that juts out from the main ward, the oldest and creepiest part of TALA. Every time I've been back there I've either heard something or seen something that sent shivers up my spine.

As the two of us slowly made our way back, deeper into the darkness of the old kitchen, a strange noise, as if someone were shuffling near the doorway, caused me to turn around. As I strained to focus my eyes in the darkness, an image began to manifest in the frame of the doorway: four feet tall, stocky, with some sort of hood or cloak on its head. The first thing that came to mind was the classic image of the Grim Reaper, but the misty form was white, not the dark color you'd expect of the Angel of Death.

I was mesmerized and terrified at the same time. I didn't move a muscle, didn't even breathe, just stood silently watching this *thing* even though my every instinct was to run! That's the curse of being a ghost hunter, I guess. I chose fight instead of flight.

The person with me was not so steady on his feet and immediately wanted to get the hell out of there. As soon as he reacted to the misty form, it began to dissipate. I didn't have time to get my camera, so I missed a great opportunity to document some fantastic evidence.

Personal Experience—
Zach McCormick (Tour Guide, Photographer)

I've had my share of strange experiences at TALA: unexplained lights, ghostly footsteps, eerie voices, the unshakeable feeling of being watched. TALA has it all! But one of the scariest things I've ever encountered actually happened *outside* the building.

It was fall 2009, Aaron Sulser's first time visiting TALA. He was with one of his friends, Austin Rausch. By the time the sun set, we were the only three people left in the building. Or so we thought. We had a sequence of strange events happen throughout the night, one bizarre thing after another, which is typical when you're alone at TALA. It's like they *know* when they have you outnumbered or something.

It was getting pretty late; we were on the first floor checking out Wards A and D after investigating the Arts and Crafts Wing. We kept hearing this strange knocking sound.

Tap tap tap tap.

We followed it through the corridors but never seemed to get any closer.

As soon as we thought we had found the source, the knocking started up somewhere else, taking us deeper and deeper into the opposite side of the building. It was like we were being led. We ended up in the area just outside Lily's room near the Civil War section.

Tap tap tap tap.

The sound bounced all around the room, but we couldn't figure out where the hell it was coming from. Eventually it stopped and we gave up looking for it. We were deliberately led there. Why? I don't know.

Since we were near the back of the building, I asked Aaron and Austin if they wanted to see the cool-looking stone gargoyle faces carved on the façade of the building. The three of us went outside and walked down the sidewalk to where the gargoyles were, when all of a sudden, we heard this really loud banging.

Tho-thunk! Tho-thunk! Tho-thunk!

We turned and saw a huge black mass pulsating on the sidewalk a few yards in front of us. The dark figure lunged forward and came barreling toward us! This thing literally chased us back toward the door. Aaron ran in, Austin ran in, and then I ran in, bolting the door behind me! Whatever that thing was, it came right for us, and I wanted to make sure it stayed outside.

I made sure all the other entrances were secure. I couldn't see anyone outside, and no one else was in the building. It really gave us quite a scare! I'd never had anything like that happen before, in the building or out.

Later the same night, the three of us were investigating the fourth floor when again, we heard this crazy, super loud banging.

Boom! Boom! Boom!

This time it was coming from the huge, heavy double doors of the main entrance in the front of the building. The sound was so loud it carried up the stairwell, echoing all the way to where we were sitting, three floors above. I was freaked out but ran downstairs to make sure it wasn't someone trying to get in or playing a trick on us.

Of course it didn't make me feel any better when I discovered no one was at the door! I checked the entire area, looked all over the yard, but found nothing that could or would have made that sound.

I think the ghosts of TALA like to freak people out, especially when there isn't a large group. Many nights I've been set up with a tour somewhere on the first or second floor, knowing no one else was in the building, and played the "shave and a haircut" knocking game with the spirits. And they answer *"bang bang,"* slamming the metal doors of the seclusion cells on the fourth floor or something similar, in rhythm.

My theory is the spirits at TALA are very aware of what the ghost hunters are doing, what they're looking for, and they choose to communicate *on their terms.* Maybe they get bored hearing the same questions asked over and over again. I mean, seriously, how many times would you want to be asked, "What's your name? Did you die here? Can you give us a sign of your presence?"

The more personal you get with the ghosts, the less they want to cooperate. They seem to have more fun playing games and messing with people. I've learned that creativity is the key to a successful investigation at TALA.

People should also be aware that the ghosts of TALA tend to follow you home. Just recently I was alone in my house after a night at TALA, walking down the hallway toward my bedroom, when I heard very clearly in my ear, *"Hey, Zach, did I scare ya?"*

I stopped immediately and looked around for someone even though I *knew* I was alone! That was pretty freaky, and yes, it *did* scare me.

I've had all sorts of strange things happen since I started at TALA. Things will disappear or go missing only to show up in odd places later. One of my gloves disappeared one night. I searched my car, looked everywhere for it with no luck. I thought I'd left it behind at a restaurant, even went back looking for it, but it wasn't there either. Eventually I gave up looking and pitched the other glove out. That same day I found the missing glove, sitting on the driver's seat of my car, plain as day.

Another time, a button off my favorite jacket fell off while I was working at TALA. I didn't notice when it happened, just noticed later it was gone. I was bummed but didn't really think much of it. Weeks later, as I went into my house I felt something hit me on top of my head, like it had literally fallen from the sky. I picked it up and was shocked to find that it was the missing button! I know the spirits from TALA are responsible for weird stuff like that. How else can you explain it?

Take the Haunted Tour—The Second Floor

The center stairs lead from the main floor up to the doctors' spacious and comfortable apartments. Wards radiate out from the center of the hospital. Like a Native American totem symbol of a thunderbird, the shape, originally meant to be comforting, takes on an ominous feel. Paint sloughs off the walls in swaths like a snake shedding its skin, exposing a pain-ridden past buried under layers of misery. Moonlight illuminates flying dust particles, creating small storms of fake orbs—self-deceptive fodder for the overeager ghost hunter. Stagnant, stale air loiters oppressively.

At first glance the second floor is almost visually void, in striking contrast to the first floor with its bright yellow walls and restored sitting rooms. Even the damp and clammy Civil War section, with its rusting pipes and dripping water, feels more alive than the second floor. Sound doesn't carry far on the second floor, suppressed by the deadness of the air.

Emerging from the center stairs, to the right are Wards B and E, relatively quiet from the paranormal perspective, identical rooms that held a stream of unfortunate residents for over a hundred years. Standing still in the hallway between Wards B and E, one can sense the ghostly caterwauling of tortured souls locked away inside their rooms and inside their minds. Residual activity is prevalent in this area of the asylum, but the other side of the second floor has a more sinister history.

WARD TWO: HANGING AND STABBING

There are two areas of particularly nefarious interest on the second floor of the asylum. The first is room 408, also known as the Double Suicide Room, where two patients were found dead with sheets tied around their necks, hanging from ceiling pipes. Suicide was sometimes seen as the best option by the most troubled residents, but two together was highly unusual and doubly disturbing.

Nearby is the Stabbing Bathroom, named after a reportedly brutal murder that occurred inside. A sociopathic patient called Slewfoot had been in and out of institutions his whole life. He could make himself seem sane as necessary, which led to a job in Dietary, where he had access to silverware. One day he ran into a new patient in a bathroom in Ward Two, a man with an alcohol problem who needed to dry out a bit.

Slewfoot, in a deranged state, attacked and attempted to rape the man. But the would-be victim fought back. Slewfoot dashed from the bathroom and retrieved a stolen kitchen knife from his room. He returned to the scene of the crime and maniacally stabbed the man seventeen times in front of the urinals. The victim dragged himself toward the nurses' station at the center of the building but bled to death on the way.

Paranormal reports from Ward Two include bone-chilling EVPs, wicked whispers, and a menacing presence skulking in the darkness. Many investigators have felt threatened by a shadowy figure perceived to be Slewfoot in the old bathroom, perhaps waiting to pounce on his next victim.

Potential threats like this are an excellent reminder that ghost hunters must be alert and have their wits about them at all times. Do not investigate "under the influence."

WARD FIVE, THE CHILDREN'S WARD: A PLAYDATE WITH TERROR

At the left end of the second floor is Ward Five, the Children's Ward, which housed young people who ended up at the asylum. Staff attempted to make the rooms as bright and cheery as possible, hoping to alleviate the depressing circumstances these children had to endure.

The only thing that kept these youngsters apart from the adult insanity of Ward Two was a locked door. Security at the hospital grew to be a critical issue along with overcrowding. Besides treating the children's mental and physical problems, protecting them from predators and pedophiles was an ongoing priority for their keepers.

The sounds of children's laughter and running feet cascading down the corridors are commonly reported in the vicinity. Playful shadows spy around darkened corners, and visitors report hearing soft crying coming from vacant patient rooms. These impish ghosts have been known to follow people from one section to another, tugging pleadingly on coattails and heartstrings.

Personal Experience—
Aaron Sulser

It's always hard to be away from your family when you ghost hunt, but even more so when you have young kids. I've never felt completely comfortable being in the Children's Ward, but this particular night, something was really wrong.

I was standing with Zach McCormick in the hall just outside the doorway that leads into Ward Five. As we approached the ward, I felt overcome by this sick feeling in my stomach, and my head started spinning like a top. My body was just wrecked by

Paranormal Activities

Orbs: balls or spheres of light of various sizes and colors captured on film or video, or, far less often, seen with the naked eye, thought by some to be disembodied ghosts or spirits. Debate over the orb phenomenon skyrocketed after the advent of digital photography. In most cases, photographed "orbs" are the reflection or refraction of light as it hits moisture in the air, or particles of dust. Flying insects can also generate "orbs" when photographed or videotaped from certain angles. The debate over the authenticity of spirit orbs has divided the paranormal field for decades. Believers say that an orb is genuine if it is solid in color and reflects its own light. Most orbs can be explained naturally.

this sudden change—it overwhelmed me and caught me completely off-guard.

I barely made it into the ward, steadying myself against the wall as we entered. I asked Zach what type of activity had been going on up here lately, not letting him know I was sick. To my surprise, Zach told me that a week before he had been overcome with a physical sickness in the exact same spot where I was now standing. He was surprised when I told him I was experiencing something similar. We thought it best we get the hell out of there.

WARDS B AND E

The two wards located in the northern corridor of the second floor, Wards B and E, have layouts identical to the wards above and below and are mirror images of Wards Two and Five. These areas were packed to the gills with patients as hospital capacity reached critical mass.

Personal Experience—
Theresa: The Parent Trap

After spending time in the Children's Ward and Ward Two, darkened as they were by the double suicide and stabbing murder, I was anxious to get to a "lighter" portion of the asylum. Walking past the doctors' apartments, my heart went out to those who had dedicated themselves to making life better for the mentally ill at TALA and places like it.

Thoughts of the evil, or at least severely misguided, Dr. Walter Freeman, who performed "ice-pick lobotomies," filled my mind. Like a scene from a Vincent Price horror film, I imagined men and women lined up like animals at a slaughterhouse, waiting their turns with the doctor and his instrument of terror. No compassion, no emotion, just procedure after procedure, damaging brain after brain, life after life.

I hurried into Ward B, but things didn't improve. Overwhelming sadness and remorse bombarded me. I fought the urge to cry, trying hard to keep it together. A mixture of empathic thoughts from both patients and doctors invaded my body.

I can't be sure if what I felt was some sort of psychic residue left over from the spirits or if I was actually sick, but my experience was not uncommon. Aaron Sulser recalls a similar experience from the same area.

Personal Experience—
Aaron Sulser

The night the *Paranormal Challenge* teams got together to do a private investigation of TALA in March 2012, I had a weird experience in Ward B.

When I investigate, I always talk about my three daughters,

letting the ghosts know I'm a dad with young kids at home, so they can feel comfortable talking with me. The spirits of those children are starved for the parent-child connection. They must be incredibly lonely and scared.

Out of nowhere, I felt an overwhelming sense of sadness, as if I were picking up something empathically. It was like a horrible case of separation anxiety, how a parent feels leaving their kids, knowing they won't be together for a while. I'd never had such a feeling of dread, at least not during an investigation. We had just left the Children's Ward, so I thought some spirits might have followed me, attached themselves to me, someone they could trust, someone who wouldn't hurt them. My emotions were running high and my body felt like it wasn't my own. I have never experienced that anywhere else.

I have no other explanation for what happened on Ward B, other than it was spirits from the Children's Ward imprinting their emotions empathically and physically attaching themselves to me. Parents can sense when their child is hurt, and I felt the emotional pain these spirits were in.

I continued my trek through the second floor, and the emotional turmoil eventually dissipated. I stayed away from that area for the rest of the night.

Take the Haunted Tour—The Third Floor

As one ascends the central staircase, Wards Six and Three are on the left, and the notorious Wards C and F on the right of the third floor.

Nurses' apartments, not nearly as comfortable and spacious as the doctors' quarters one floor below, were set up on the third floor. Amenities offered the overworked staff did not include soundproofing their rooms. The tunnel-like structure of the halls amplified the constant roar of madness, which became deafening when the facility swelled to ten times its original 250-person capacity.

In order to protect themselves from the most unruly patients, the nurses and other staff padlocked their doors, becoming prisoners of the facility along with those for whom they cared.

During 1949, when the hospital was at its maximum capacity, overcrowding and understaffing led to numerous problems, including deteriorating living quarters and facilities and an extremely low staff-to-patient ratio. One inspection found that there was one toilet and one attendant for every fifty-seven patients. The bathrooms were flooded with feces-infested water and redolent of the most horrendous filth imaginable. Of course, many of the hospital's patients hadn't much use of a bathroom anyway—they had no control of their bodily functions.

In the women's ward, conditions were not much better. Because of the overcrowding in the patient rooms, the women spent the day in the hallways, rocking or sitting restrained in chairs, or pacing endlessly up and down the long corridors. Filth and urine stained the floors to the point where it was dangerous to be without shoes, as most patients were.

Today the smell of death and disinfectant is gone, but it is not difficult to imagine the conditions as they were some sixty years ago. The energy of those patients, who lived in conditions unfit for animals, lingers on.

THE AUDITORIUM

The auditorium was a place of great joy for residents of the asylum—at least some of them. Many festive events, including plays and musical performances, were held there, lending cheer to an otherwise grim hospital environment. At one point the auditorium was rented out to schools and other groups in the Weston area for proms and cotillions, benefiting TALA financially and creating a sense of commonality and goodwill between the institution and the community.

Today, the two-story open stage area is not accessible to visitors. Some claim to hear the faint sound of laughter and applause rising up to the balcony from the empty seats on the main floor, and see strange orbs of light dance along the walls, as if choreographed by an unseen intelligence.

WARDS THREE AND SIX

Veteran guide Zach McCormick has confronted paranormal activity in all areas of TALA, but some of the most playful spirits hang out in Ward Three.

Personal Experience—
Zach McCormick

It was a quiet Friday night in June 2012. I was giving a tour to a small group of seven women—well, three women and four girls about thirteen or fourteen years old, who were extremely excited to be at TALA. Two of the women, sisters, were annoyed by these young girls and had absolutely no patience for their tomfoolery. I couldn't really say anything. The girls weren't doing anything wrong, just being kids.

Eventually the girls went home and I was left with a group of three, including the sisters who just wouldn't lighten up. I did my best to get them to smile, not wanting anyone to leave unhappy. It was getting late, about 4:25 A.M. I had to run down to the break room to grab some batteries and a flashlight.

I came up the through the main stairwell and crept quietly past the nurses' station toward Ward Three, where my group was waiting. I wanted to do something to lighten the mood, so as I got closer to the women I jumped out to scare them, held my hands up and made a silly noise: "*Boogedy boogedy!*"

Well, that made them all laugh and everyone went home happy.

The next night, I had a private tour in the same area. As we were going through the nurses' area I noticed that a door that had been open and unlocked for the past two years was now somehow jammed shut. I couldn't get it open no matter what I did. As I was fighting with this door, this one girl in the group start acting really fidgety—she was quietly freaking out, pacing back and forth.

"What's wrong?" I asked. "Did you see something?"

"No no no, I'm fine, I'm fine!" she answered, obviously lying.

"What happened? Something happened!" I insisted.

"No, nothing happened. Well, maybe I heard something," she finally answered.

I tried to get her to tell me what had spooked her, but it was like pulling teeth! She seemed kind of embarrassed. Finally she came clean.

"I swear to God, it sounded like someone said 'Boogedy boogedy' right in my ear! I know that sounds stupid, but that's what I heard!" Her face was bright red; she was embarrassed and confused.

I could not believe it! She had no idea what had happened the night before. I hadn't told anyone—it wasn't a big deal, until now. This poor girl wasn't any more comforted when I told her about the previous night. She'd heard the mimicking voice in the exact same area I had been the night before.

Doppelganger? Prankster? I don't know, but the spirits at TALA get a real kick out of jokes like that!

WARD C: VIOLENT FEMALES

Separating the violent females from the violent males was a daunting task for the staff at TALA. Their carnal desires were at times out of control, and attempts to connect with the opposite sex sometimes led to security problems. Only a locked door separated Wards C and F, and patients were known to wait in ambush for that door to open, granting them access to the other side.

There are also rooms on the third floor that no patient ever hoped to see: the seclusion rooms. When patients became violent or too difficult to deal with, the staff would take them to these cell-like rooms. The iron doors have a medieval feel to them, heavy and cold, requiring significant force to open and close. Metal rings protruding from the stone walls were used to secure the restraints or shackles of those placed inside.

If the doctors, nurses, or handlers felt a shower was necessary, the unfortunate soul was stripped naked, hands bound overhead, and hosed down.

These doors make a distinct sound when opened and closed. The doors, too heavy to be moved by wind, are known to slam shut by themselves even when no one is on the floor, the deafening noise echoing throughout the facility, sending shivers up the spine of anyone within earshot.

WARD F: VIOLENT MALES
The Bedpost Murder

The most horrific death recorded at the asylum was the infamous "Bedpost Murder" that occurred—where else?—in Ward F. They didn't call them "Violent Males" for nothing. There is little documentation on this event, but at least one former hospital employee claims it is absolutely true. Another official Weston State Hospital report claims the incident happened in the 1970s and was so traumatic that even some of the staff had a difficult time dealing with it. According to Kathy Turner, who was featured on the program *Ghost Stories*, three patients were involved: Charlie, Joe, and an unnamed man.

Charlie had been the unfortunate recipient of one of the hospital's notorious lobotomies. His new condition left him with some repetitive mannerisms that were irksome to Joe and his nameless co-conspirator. They decided to put an end to the annoyance by putting an end to Charlie. They crafted a rope from bedsheets, tied them around Charlie's neck, and hanged him from the pipes along the ceiling. But their plan didn't work as expected and poor Charlie remained alive!

Trying another tactic, the two men took him down, laid him on the floor, and placed the post of a metal bed frame on his head. They then jumped up and down on the mattress, driving the metal post into the Charlie's skull.

Personal Experience—
Cathi Weber

Like Theresa, I got some weird vibes on our introductory tour of the hospital. Each floor, though physically very similar, seemed to have its own distinct personality, from playful and endearing to dark and disturbing.

We had just come up from the second floor after investigating the Double Suicide Room and the Stabbing Bathroom. I was still trying to get the visual images of the three gruesome deaths out of my brain. We came up through the center stairwell, past the nurses' apartments, heading toward Ward F. I was standing with another investigator, Darcy Hunley, listening to the gruesome story of the Bedpost Murder in the Violent Males Ward.

Suddenly, I felt compelled to turn around and look back toward the end of the hallway we had just come up. There was just a tinge of visible light coming from the stairs, but something dark caught my attention. At the very end of the hall—probably a hundred feet from me—I saw a tremendously long, thin shadow figure, about nine feet tall, slide across the wall at super speed. It was very fast and darker than the dark, but clearly humanoid in shape.

Paranormal Activities

Doppelganger: a German word connoting "body double" or "ghost double." A doppelganger is the apparition—in spirit or solid form—of one's own personal twin or double. It is basically the "ghost" of a living person. Seeing someone's double is thought to be a generalized harbinger of doom; running into one's own doppelganger portends impending death as the double seeks to "take over" its subject in a body-snatching sort of way.

Darcy and I looked at each other, gasped, and said, "Did you see that?" at the same time. We both described the same tall figure moving at an incredible speed in the same direction. No one else had noticed it; they were too absorbed in the story.

I ran toward the shadow—apprehensively, of course—but found nothing that would have created a shadow of that shape. My heart raced and my adrenaline pumped; I had no explanation for what we had just witnessed.

Take the Haunted Tour—The Fourth Floor: Wards T and V

The few notable physical differences in the many wards of TALA are evident on the fourth floor. On the opposite side of the building, away from the newer Drug and Alcohol Wards of S and R, sit Wards T and V. In the asylum's heyday, this space was used as a dormitory for the workers who kept the hospital up and running.

The rooms were a bit more pleasant than the regular patient rooms, outfitted with wooden floors, which made them more homey and offered a bit of insulation from the ubiquitous cries of madness reverberating throughout the hospital.

Today, the wooden floors resonate with the phantom footsteps of wandering apparitions. A large industrial fan sits defunct at the end of Ward T. Some investigators use it as a communication tool, asking the blades to turn left or right indicating *yes* or *no* answers. The imposing hunk of metal looks cold and menacing, even without any eerie phantasmal movement.

Personal Experience—
Theresa: You Light Up My Life . . . NOT!

During our investigation, the Housewives and our guide, Zach, steadily and systematically made our way up through each ward until we reached the fourth floor. We settled in to do some experiments near the haunted fan in Ward T. Unfortunately, it wasn't in the mood to move for us. Not easily deterred, we tried something else.

Zach set up five flashlights in a cross formation in the middle of the hallway. The flashlight technique is controversial, with detractors claiming that poor handling and natural physics cause the light to turn off and on, not ghosts. Sure, I'll buy that a flashlight can "naturally" turn off and on because of temperature fluctuations, poor handling, batteries, or vibrations—that's not hard to believe. But when you have multiple flashlights turning on and off on command, I tend to lean toward the paranormal.

Zach asked the spirits to light up specific flashlights in response to his questioning.

"Are you a patient here? If yes, turn on the flashlight on the right, please."

The far-right flashlight turned on.

"Thank you. Can you turn it off now?"

The light went off.

"Are you a female? If you are, can you turn on the flashlight in the middle of the floor, please? The one that's on the chair."

We watched in amazement as the flashlight on the chair lit up. Zach wanted to be sure and asked the light to blink twice. The flashlight blinked. Twice.

We were all stunned and impressed, wanting to get in on the action.

"Was your room on this ward?" Cathi asked. No lights.

"Did you stay on a different ward?" she asked again. This time the flashlight on the right turned on again. "Thank you."

"If you followed us from another part of the building, can you let us know by turning on the flashlight farthest away from me?" Cathi asked.

On cue, the far flashlight turned on.

I was standing there, mouth agape. Zach wasn't even fazed by this, accustomed as he was to spirit interaction using this technique.

He asked the spirit, "Do you know who I am? If you recognize me, turn all the flashlights on, one by one."

One by one the flashlight on the left, the one on the chair, the one to the far back, the one closest to the group, and the one on the right all turned on and then off.

My turn to get in on the action!

"Were you put here against your will? Turn the flashlight to the right on for yes, please."

Nothing.

Hmm, maybe too personal? "Are you alone in the building?"

All remained dark.

"Are you upset that we keep asking questions? You can turn *any* of the lights on, please." I was starting to feel like I was talking to myself.

No lights lit up.

Cathi asked, "Are you still here?"

The flashlight on the right turned on and off.

Really?

"Can you please talk to us again?" Zach asked, and the right flashlight blinked again.

"Is there someone here you don't like?" The light blinked again.

"Okay, I'll have everyone say their name. If there is someone you *don't* like, turn the far left light on when they announce their name," Zach said.

"Zach." Nothing.

"Darla." Nothing.

"Cathi." Nothing.

"Theresa." The far left flashlight turned on full force.

Now I really felt unwelcome. My companions found this hilarious and laughed uproariously.

"Wow, really? You don't like me?" I asked. The light blinked again as if to say, "Screw you!"

That was enough for me. Defeated, I sat there sulking silently until we left the ward.

Personal Experience—
Austin Rausch (Paranormal Investigator)

One early fall evening in 2012, Aaron Sulser brought a few friends, including teammate Austin Rausch, for an overnight investigation of TALA. They had the place to themselves and didn't have to worry about a bunch of people interfering with their work. Aaron describes Austin as "a quiet guy, an intelligent guy—usually very steady and levelheaded. He doesn't get riled up easily."

Aaron was standing against the wall in Ward T on the fourth floor with another of his teammates, and Austin was in the middle of the hallway facing the opposite direction toward Ward V.

Everything was quiet. The calm of the moment was broken as a gasp escaped Austin's mouth. Aaron immediately turned toward Austin, who was staring intently at something in the distance.

"I'll never know who he was or why he was there, but I'll never forget his face. The fourth floor of the asylum is notorious for pranks and misdirection, and I was fortunate enough to experience them both. It's not uncommon to see shadows move from one door to another. I had to strain my eyes to see the shadow in the distance," Austin told us.

"Out of nowhere, a man appeared not two feet in front of me. It was more a face than a full-bodied apparition, I couldn't see the entire form. He was elderly, with balding white hair and thick glasses, which seemed to be from another generation. I imagine it was a residual entity because it did not seem to notice my presence. And he was only there for a moment, like a still from a movie. There one second, gone the next."

The apparition never looked at him; it didn't seem to notice him at all. It was suddenly right in front of him one second, then continued to walk past him the next. This behavior is typical of a residual haunting, but there was something odd about its appearance that led Rausch to believe there was some sort of intelligence behind it. The face looked familiar.

Austin described the face as glowing with an eerie orangish hue. Hands still trembling from the encounter, he used his iPad to draw a detailed picture of the man. The face he drew had an uncanny resemblance to one of the other investigators, Jeff, but it obviously was *not* him, or any living person, for that matter. The overall "feeling" was that it was someone or *something* trying to look like Jeff.

Later that evening, an investigator named Jen was on the first floor with Jeff—the real Jeff. Jen was making her way toward the Civil War section when, in the distance, she spotted someone she thought was Jeff walking down the main stairwell. She clearly saw an older man, balding, same general body type, glasses. She was startled because she believed Jeff was behind her. Jen quickly turned around and confirmed that he was indeed behind her.

Startled, she looked again in front and the man had disappeared.

Aaron and his teammates believe the incidents were connected. They theorize that Jen and Austin had encountered a doppelganger, or spirit double. The entity, for whatever reason, decided to momentarily take the form of Jeff. Maybe this was done to confuse them; maybe it was the spirit's way of communicating in an unforgettable manner.

Doppelgangers are an unusual and unsettling form of spirit activity, showing intelligence, ingenuity, and intent.

This type of experience is common at TALA. Guides and guests see and hear friends and fellow workers in one part of the asylum only to discover they were actually in another. Guides at Louisville's Waverly Hills Sanatorium claim to encounter these ghostly "doubles" frequently as well.

WARDS S AND R: DEAD MAN'S PARTY

The opposite side of the fourth floor, Wards S and R, housed the alcohol and drug patients. As the medical world began to recognize addiction as a mental disease, TALA was flooded with new patients.

Besides psychological counseling, addicts received medical care as they went through various stages of treatment and withdrawal. Those going through withdrawal suffered nausea, joint pain, headaches, dizziness, and sundry other unpleasant symptoms as the toxins worked their way out of the body.

The staff and guides at TALA report all manner of unusual activity in this part of the building. Lights blink on and off down the dark corridors, footsteps echo off the narrow halls, and an assortment of voices chatter collectively when no one is around. Witnesses say it feels like "a party's going on" all around them.

During their visit, the Haunted Housewives all heard conversation and laughter coming from just beyond the threshold of the doorway between Ward S and Ward R. Thinking their friends had made their way up to the fourth floor, they gave a verbal welcome, but no one appeared or replied.

Personal Experience—
Cathi Weber

We employed every technique we knew to try to get the spirits to interact with us on the fourth floor of the asylum. My initial fear of the building had gone, and the flashlight session was actually kind of funny. Poor Theresa, she just isn't welcome in some of the places we investigate!

We ventured over to the other end of the floor, Ward R. Things were quiet; the air was still. All the ambient noises we had heard on previous wards seemed to have stopped. No owls, no cars, no crickets—just silence.

Theresa was trying to entice any available ghosts to communicate with us, but they too were silent.

Theresa's voice cut through the quiet. "Uh, guys, I just felt a cold chill on my neck!"

Darla checked the thermometer, "It's actually a little warmer now than it was over in T. I've got sixty-six degrees."

Suddenly, I felt something on my legs, like bugs. I immediately jumped and shined my flashlight at my feet. Nothing!

"If you're doing that, it's not scaring me. Bugs don't bother me," I said out loud.

As soon as I finished the sentence, I too felt a cold breath on my neck. "Theresa, I felt it too! Hand me the thermometer."

Room temperature had climbed two degrees, so we couldn't figure out where the cold was coming from. A quick but thorough survey of the area revealed no broken windows or blowing vents.

Then I felt a caress on my neck, as if someone were gently rubbing it. It wasn't unpleasant, but it was definitely unexpected.

"Hey guys, I just felt something on my neck!" I said.

Theresa came over with her flashlight to see if anything was on my hair or collar.

"*Oh my God*, Cathi! There are three scratches on your neck— I think they're bleeding!"

Theresa took a picture with her camera and showed it to me. Right under the nape of my neck, under my hair, were three deep vertical marks, about three inches in length. I wiped my neck, and there was indeed a little blood. Small but substantial beads of blood formed on each scratch. As soon as I wiped them away, more formed in their place. Something had just clawed me!

The strange thing is I hadn't felt any sort of pain at the time— it had actually felt rather pleasant. Once I saw the blood, my neck began to sting, a mild but steady burning sensation.

There's a theory suggesting that a sequence of three scratches, a claw mark, is somehow demonic, like an unholy trinity. I'll admit it was frickin' scary to see blood on my neck! What else do ghosts have the power to do if they can break the skin and draw blood? It definitely made me think more about the dangers of the paranormal.

CONCLUSION

That the mentally ill could be cured was an alien notion before reformers like Dorothea Dix and Dr. Thomas Kirkbride came along. Separating the criminal from the crazy was a giant step forward for the mentally ill and an affirmation of their humanity. As awareness grew, so did the need for special facilities, or asylums, and over the decades demand outstripped supply.

In spite of the best intentions, overcrowding and indifference created new horrors for the afflicted, and places like TALA became fortresses of pain, dumping grounds for the marginal of society and the mentally ill alike. Eventually, the development of new treatments and drugs mitigated the need for residential hospitals, rendering most large state hospitals like TALA obsolete.

TALA has all the ingredients of a "super haunt": large, isolated grounds; an imposing, institutional edifice; a fragmented history with gruesome murders, suicides, mad scientists, and doomed children; even a looming Quasimodo-type clock tower!

The reality of the past, for good and for ill, has left a film, a residue of energy that time cannot erase. The Civil War, a conflict that nearly severed our country, left behind deep scars and restless spirits, adding the volatile emotions of war to those of the mentally ill and their caregivers. An amalgamation of despair, madness, and cruelty, leavened with compassion and empathy, coats the very foundation of TALA, calling forth both innocent and iniquitous spirits, who, for whatever reason, remain in our dimension.

What You Need to Know Before You Go:

The Trans-Allegheny Lunatic Asylum
71 Asylum Drive, Weston, WV 26452

Contact Information:
(304) 269-5070
trans-alleghenylunaticasylum.com
info@trans-alleghenylunaticasylum.com

The Trans-Allegheny Lunatic Asylum, formerly the Weston State Hospital, is more than just a haunted attraction, it's a living piece of history. There is more to this facility than just ghosts.

Some of the other community activities held on the property are **Civil War Weekend, Dinner Theater, Fall Festival, The Asylum Ball** (costume party), and the ever popular **Haunted House.**

There are historic and/or paranormal tours appropriate for every age and comfort level, and photographic opportunities for both the amateur and professional shutterbug.

The property consists of more than just the main hospital; the grounds and several other buildings are worthy of historic and paranormal exploration.

Please check the website or call the business office for more details.

Daily Heritage Tours

Tuesday through Friday and Sunday, 12 P.M. to 6 P.M.

Saturday, 10 A.M. to 8 P.M.

Monday by appointment only

Private paranormal or historic tour (daytime) or photography tour dates: call the office at (304) 269-5070

Ghost Hunts/Tours (offered year-round)

Medical/Forensics/Geriatrics (8 hours) 3 buildings: 9 P.M. to 5 A.M.

Public Ghost Hunts (8 hours): 9 P.M. to 5 A.M.

October Hunts (6.5 hours): 11:30 P.M. to 6 A.M.

Private Ghost Hunts (8 hours): Minimum 10 people

Two-Hour Paranormal Tours (4 hot spots): 10:30 P.M. to 12:30 A.M.

Daytime Tours (1.5 hours): Saturday and Sunday, 1 P.M. and 4 P.M.

Flashlight Tours (30 minutes): ½ historic, ½ paranormal

Historic Tours

1st Floor (plus 1st floor of Medical Center): 45 minutes

All 4 Floors (plus 1st floor of Medical Center): 90 minutes

Civil War Tour (walking tour includes asylum grounds):
    75 minutes

Cemetery/Farm Tour (open-air wagon ride includes all three
    cemeteries): Saturday and Sunday, 12:30 P.M. and 3 P.M.

Lodging:

Holiday Inn Express & Suites, (877) 859-5095 (special rates for
    TALA guests)

215 Staunton Drive, Weston, WV 26452

ihg.com/holidayinnexpress

Super 8 Weston, (304) 269-1086

100 Market Place Mall, Suite 12, Weston, WV 26452

super8.com

Comfort Inn Weston, (304) 269-7000

2906 U.S. Highway 33 East, Weston, WV 26452

comfortinn.com

Relax Inn and Getaway (Bed and Breakfast), (304) 269-2345 or
    (304) 269-2288

509 Relax Inn Dr., Weston, WV 26452

relaxinnandgetaway.com

Bobby Mackey's Music World

Wilder, Kentucky

INTRODUCTION

In the small blue-collar town of Wilder, Kentucky, just south of Newport and across the mighty Ohio river from Cincinnati, sits one of the most fascinating establishments in the United States, Bobby Mackey's Music World. Nestled along the east bank of the north-flowing Licking River, the iconic destination at 44 Licking Pike has something for everyone: classic country music, cold beer and hard liquor, a mechanical bull, cowboys and cowgirls, ghosts and demons, perhaps even a portal to hell.

Like we said, something for *everyone*.

What makes Mackey's so intriguing is the juxtaposition of light and dark, day and night, good and evil. It is a place filled with laughter and gaiety, happiness and music—the kind of place people go to have a good time. But Bobby Mackey's is haunted, and not just garden-variety haunted: Along with a number of more-or-less benign spirits, dark things linger in the shadows, revealing themselves occasionally in shocking, even dangerous ways.

The building's history is one of blood, murder, suicide, gangsters, gambling, showgirls, rumored Satanism, and colorful characters galore—each with a fascinating story to tell. The ground Mackey's sits upon was contested by Native Americans for centuries. Access to the river and the fertile land it nourished was a privilege hard fought between the Cherokee and Shawnee tribes.

White settlers arrived in the 1700s and the area came to be called Leitch's Station, after Major David Leitch, who was given land for his service in the American Revolutionary War. The *Wilder* name dates to a railroad station built by the Louisville, Cincinnati and Lexington Railway in the mid-1800s and named after a company executive. The railroad facilitated the spread of farming and manufacturing, and the region prospered and grew.

A slaughterhouse was built on the site in the 1850s, where uncountable thousands of animals were "processed," untold gallons of blood drained along with the life force from their bodies. Before the EPA and government waste disposal regulations, all this material was simply funneled through a sluice dug from the building down to the river, which ran a very creepy red each time there was a dump from the slaughterhouse.

The slaughterhouse shut down in the mid-1890s, but the land and the water seemed to have developed an unquenchable thirst for blood.

In 1896, a lovely and vivacious young woman named Pearl Bryan, twenty-two and pregnant, was brutally murdered and decapitated near the site. Legend has it that the pair convicted of her murder—Bryan's boyfriend, Scott Jackson, and his accomplice, Alonzo Walling—threw her head into the sluice as a sacrifice to Satan, opening a "portal to hell" that now sits uneasily in the basement of Bobby Mackey's.

Hey, stranger things have happened.

The derelict slaughterhouse was torn down, and a roadhouse that was built on the spot became a speakeasy during Prohibition, 1919–1933. In the later 1930s, E. A. "Buck" Brady, an alumnus of the infamous George Remus bootlegging operation, built a sleek red-and-white showpiece adorned with marble floors and crystal chandeliers called the Primrose. The club proudly featured a five-star restaurant and five floor shows a night. The Primrose was a place of celebration and life with music and dancing, food and drink.

The Primrose was so successful that it drew business away from the nearby Beverly Hills Country Club, owned by a Newport crime group, the Cleveland Syndicate, who sent in enforcer Red Masterson to "persuade" Brady to sell. Brady decided to be proactive and ambushed Masterson in a parking lot, shooting but not killing him. Masterson recovered; Brady was tried for attempted murder, convicted of a much lesser crime when Masterson wouldn't testify against him, and realized the writing was on the wall. The Cleveland Syndicate took control in 1947 and opened the Latin Quarter Supper Club, as Brady retired to Florida.

The Latin Quarter was even more successful than the Primrose, an entertainment mecca that rivaled the finest establishments in the country. An illegal casino business ran profitably along with the fine dining and dancing. It was during this time that another legendary tragedy befell the building. The beautiful and talented Johanna, a popular club dancer, fell in love with crooner Robert Randall, who was smitten by her exotic charms.

The romance blossomed, much to the dismay of Johanna's gangster father, who forbade the couple from seeing each other. When they refused to give up their relationship, Johanna's father had Randall killed. More blood offerings to the darkness at the club. The enraged and heartbroken Johanna tried to poison her father as revenge for her lover's death and then poisoned herself in her dressing room in the basement of the Latin Quarter.

This tragedy, if it actually happened, didn't deter the success of the club. The mob's reign lasted until 1961, when authorities finally clamped down on organized crime in the area, destroying gambling equipment and shutting the club down for good.

After that, a series of seedy bars sat on the site, all magnets of sin and violence, before it metastasized into a biker bar named the Hard Rock Cafe (most definitely not affiliated with the international chain), in the early 1970s, but a series of shootings and general disreputability eventually closed it down.

Regional country music star Bobby Mackey bought the place in the spring of 1978 with the intent of opening up a live music venue, a place for classic country entertainment, a place where he could perform whenever he wanted in a roomy but intimate atmosphere, up close and personal with the fans. It was a place he could literally call his own. But even before the doors opened to the public, paranormal activity began.

Janet Mackey, Bobby's first wife, knew immediately that something wasn't right about the building. She was attacked by an unseen force inside the club. Handyman Carl Lawson was a target as well, apparently possessed by an entity intent on destroying him. The apparition of a mysterious but helpful Woman in White appeared outside the club, and another was reported inside.

A mysterious cowboy lurks in the basement, shadowy silhouettes peek out from hidden rooms, disembodied cries shatter the silence—anomalous happenings abound in every corner of the club. But it is the malevolent forces that are the most worrisome: the ones that pick up grown men and fling them like rag dolls across the room, scratch and push, possess and oppress.

Bobby Mackey's Music World is rife with spirits—some say as many as forty—and no amount of cleansing or blessing will

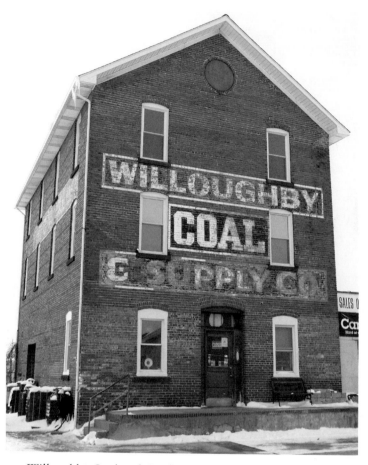

Willoughby Coal and Garden Center in Willoughby, Ohio
Michelle Murphy

EMF (electromagnetic field) detector: a basic ghost-hunting tool   *Theresa Argie*

The Villisca Ax Murder House, in which eight people were murdered
Seth Alne

Bedroom belonging to the four murdered Moore children
Seth Alne

The Knickerbocker Hotel in Linesville, Pennsylvania
Tom Deighton

Dramatic footage
of shadow play
has been caught by
infrared camera at the
Knickerbocker Hotel.
Theresa Argie

Hauntings on the high seas: the *Queen Mary*
Courtesy of the Queen Mary

Wet footprints have been spotted near the *Queen Mary*'s
empty First Class Swimming Pool.
Courtesy of the Queen Mary

The Trans-Allegheny
Lunatic Asylum in
Weston, West Virigina
Zach McCormick

The Asylum closed in 1994, but residents still roam its halls.
Zach McCormick

Bobby Mackey's Music World in Wilder, Kentucky, may look like a regular honky-tonk, but it is home to numerous spirits.

Theresa Argie

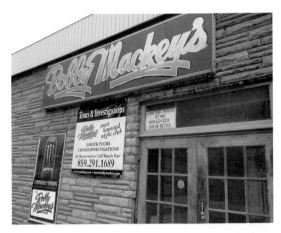

Above: The Stanley Hotel in Estes Park, Colorado, inspired the setting of Stephen King's *The Shining.*

Courtesy of the Stanley Hotel

Right: Room 217 at the Stanley Hotel

Courtesy of the Stanley Hotel

Did the Lemp family, builders of this mansion in St. Louis, Missouri, suffer from a curse?

Theresa Argie

Waverly Hills Sanatorium in Louisville, Kentucky

Allan G. E. Schmidt

Historians estimate that more than 5,500 patients died of tuberculosis at Waverly Hills.

Allan G. E. Schmidt

The Ohio State Reformatory in Mansfield, Ohio—
the most haunted location in America.
Michelle Murphy

In 1990, the Ohio State Reformatory was closed due to
"brutalizing and inhumane conditions."
Michelle Murphy

chase off the vast amount of paranormal energy that has taken root in the land and building. So come for the music, the fun, the good times, the ghosts, but be warned: This is one place where reality exceeds reputation among America's Most Haunted.

Take the Haunted Tour—The Main Floor

Bobby Mackey's Music World is not just a bar, it's a honky-tonk. What makes it different from a regular country-and-western drinking establishment—besides the ghosts—are the special features not found in other clubs, most notably the fully equipped stage. Drum set, guitar stands, amps, mics, colorful lights, and humongous banners adorn the stage. Spotlights shine down on Bobby Mackey himself, who graces the stage every weekend, as he's done for thirty-five years, drawing fans from all over the tri-state area and world at large.

In front of the stage is a parquet dance floor, ready for boot-scootin', heel-smackin', foot-stompin' fun. This isn't just a place for live music, it's a place for dancing and revelry of all kinds.

To the left of the stage is a small DJ booth where Wanda Kay Stephenson spins tunes and regulates club activities. Wanda Kay is a lovely woman who's been working at Bobby Mackey's for ten years as the club disc jockey and social chairman. She is nearly as much a part of the club's history as Bobby Mackey himself. Her warmth and charm light up the room, masking a secret. Over the past several years she has taken on another role: resident ghost hunter, in charge of all the paranormal tours and investigations that happen daily at the club.

A diverse collection of artifacts from the club's days as the Latin Quarter and the Primrose are displayed proudly in glass cases and on the walls. Although the furniture and the décor have changed over the years, the bones remain, and with a little imagination one can visualize the dancers and hear the performers who entertained the crowds with their supper club stylings. To-day the music is different, the dress code has changed, but the energy remains, contributing to the haunted history of the club.

To the rear of the dance floor are dozens of small tables and chairs, plenty of room to accommodate crowds of all sizes. The room extends back to the side wall of the building, ending at a slightly raised platform or mezzanine, which was the kitchen during the supper club era. A production booth, substantially larger than Wanda Kay's, functions as control center for stage lights and audio.

No honky-tonk would be complete without a fabulous bar, and Mackey's has it. The long, smooth wooden bar separates the performance area from the entryway, gift shop, and ghost tour waiting area. High-backed swivel chairs line the bar, waiting to nestle guests comfortably as they enjoy a frosty one. Take a seat, any seat, but one: Bobby Mackey's wife has her own spot, marked *Reserved for Denise Mackey*.

On the stage side of the bar, busy servers order and retrieve cocktails for thirsty revelers. Incongruous to us Ohio residents are the many ashtrays set about the club. People light up every-where, cigarettes dangling from their mouths and hands. In some Kentucky counties you can still smoke in bars, an activity forced outdoors across our home state of Ohio several years ago.

Our visit in July 2013 was like a flashback in time, which only added to the sense of spooky dislocation we felt at the world-famous haunted honky-tonk.

The wall to the immediate right of the entrance hallway, par-allel to the bar, opens into a smallish room with pool table, couch, and gift shop with two large display cases: one with Bobby Mackey's Music World souvenir T-shirts, CDs, and assorted branded items, the other filled with vintage trinkets and photo-graphs from the Latin Quarter. There are menus, ashtrays, glass-ware, bingo cards, and poker chips from the old casino. Posters

Paranormal Activities

Possession: the complete or partial overtaking of someone by an unseen, possibly demonic force. Those affected by an "evil" or demonic entity often exhibit bizarre and self-destructive behavior such as severe alcohol and drug abuse, criminal activity, and drastic mood swings. Sometimes possession is an attempt by the spirit to achieve some goal using the living person as an agent. The intent is not necessarily to harm the agent, just an unavoidable side effect. Milder forms of possession include oppression, where the subject is affected but to a lesser degree, and attachments, in which an unseen spirit will latch on to the subject and integrate itself into their everyday life.

and pictures line the walls, featuring cancan dancers and Ricky Ricardo–type singers frozen in their carefree smiles and razor-sharp fashions.

The casino days were anxious; operating a business outside the law was fraught with perils, and getting caught was only one of them. A locked door with sliding peephole separated the legal and illegal activities—if you knew the secret, a doorman buzzed you into a world of danger and excitement where fortunes were won and lost and blood sometimes flowed like wine for those who pressed their luck too far.

If you were granted access to the casino hall, you found slot machines, roulette wheels, and card tables everywhere. Carefree partiers ate, drank, and were merry on the stage side, while gamblers sweated out tense moments under the watchful gaze of thugs and gangsters on the other.

No self-respecting gambling joint would have been complete without a secret passage or two, and this place had them. One led to the small apartment/office upstairs and the doorway to the street, the other to the basement. These afforded a hasty and clandestine exit when the authorities or other trouble came knocking.

Today a mechanical bull sits majestically in the middle of what was once the gambling hall, in its own mini-arena, surrounded by inflatable pads that cushion the bodies if not the pride of riders tossed to and fro.

Vastly improved hydraulic mechanics in today's bull make for a safer and more finely calibrated ride, but that wasn't always the case. Sitting forlornly and a bit ominously in the northeast corner of the room is the original mechanical bull Bobby Mackey bought directly from his famous singing/saloon-owning counterpart, Mickey Gilley, just after *Urban Cowboy* finished shooting in 1979.

The original machines—built for real rodeo training, not tenderfoot amusement—were neither gentle nor calibrated, and bodies went flying with alarming force onto the makeshift padding of old mattresses. More blood, more pain, more violent energy added to the supernatural stew at Bobby Mackey's.

As the years passed, reports of paranormal activity multiplied. One anomaly that became almost commonplace in the bar was a jukebox that played itself, even when it was unplugged! And the song that it played, "The Anniversary Waltz," wasn't in the box at all.

A few witnesses have interacted with the shadow of a beautiful young woman whose description matches that of a 1940s Latin Quarter dancer, the fabled Johanna. Handyman Carl Lawson discovered a diary and a love poem presumably written by Johanna in a hidden room. In it she proclaimed her love for Randall and her unwillingness to live without him. It is said she haunts Bobby Mackey's because it is where she found true happiness, albeit temporarily. Some say the spirit of Johanna believes

Bobby Mackey *is* Robert Randall (quite literally he is "Robert Randall Mackey") and she will forever stay at the club as long as he is around.

Though investigators have yet to find any historical basis for the Johanna legend as it is told, there *was* a Mrs. Johanna Ragan who poisoned herself in the building in 1914.

Many years ago, not long after Bobby Mackey's grand opening, Larry Hornsby, a local police officer, was called late one night to the scene of a fatal traffic accident outside the club. Two people were killed in a head-on collision. The scene was very bloody and the officer searched for something to cover the mangled bodies with once they'd been removed from the vehicle. A young woman in a white dress appeared from inside the bar and silently handed the officer a tablecloth, which Hornsby draped over the crash victims. She then turned and walked back into the bar before Hornsby could say anything to her.

After the ambulance had come and removed the bodies, the officer wanted to thank the woman for the tablecloth and her gesture of compassion, but when he got to the door of the bar he found it locked. In fact, all the doors were locked and the bar was completely empty and dark. No one was inside Bobby Mackey's. Where had the woman gone? The officer of the law testified to the veracity of the story in the 2006 episode of *A Haunting* titled "Gateway to Hell."

Personal Experience—
George Lopez (Paranormal Investigator, Radio Personality)

In June 2010, Jeff Soethen, Tyler Daniels, and I did back-to-back investigations at the two most haunted spots in Kentucky: Waverly Hills Sanatorium and Bobby Mackey's Music World. The places couldn't be more different from each other in size, history, and the hauntings themselves. I'd heard the rumors and seen all the

TV shows. Honestly, I had my doubts, but I entered the club with an open mind and left with a certainty that will never leave me.

The place is much bigger than I'd expected. I'd never been in a genuine honky-tonk, so I was intrigued with the entire setup. The stage was very *Urban Cowboy* and the long bar was appropriate. The place had an energy about it, a tingling in the air that was almost audible. It seemed that something was lying dormant, waiting for a spark. The smell of stale beer and cigarettes was fitting, almost welcoming, giving the place a sense of *life*.

I knew most of the paranormal activity happened in the basement, but our host Wanda Kay assured us that no area of the club was immune—shit happened *everywhere*. Up and down were the only choices, so we started up. I wanted to ease into it slowly. Jeff, Tyler, and I had heard all the reports: shadow people, strange mists, disembodied voices, tons of EVPs. We were the only people in the place, so we had a genuine opportunity to capture some evidence.

We had just finished the preliminary pleasantries with Wanda Kay and were discussing our plan of action. We walked past the bar toward the game room when we saw the most amazing ball of light slide across the room!

"HOLY SHIT!" Jeff and I said in unison.

A white orb of energy the size of a beach ball passed right in front of our eyes. It went over the riding bull and moved toward the side of the stage, crossing our line of sight to the wall at the front of the building. This was a visual anomaly unlike anything I'd ever seen before. Orbs in photographs are highly debatable and almost always explainable as misidentified or natural phenomena. But this was something special. And two of us witnessed it with our own eyes!

Unfortunately, we'd just arrived at the club and hadn't set up any of our equipment, so we didn't capture it on camera, but we did gain a personal experience we'd never forget. As the night continued we saw a number of other balls of light skating along the front wall of the building. We tried to debunk the orbs by recreating the phenomenon, but nothing we did even came close.

I concluded that there was paranormal energy centrally focused in that area. A constant K2 reading confirmed that something odd was happening. The energy seemed to move with purpose and intent, as if it wanted us to notice it, perhaps a relatively docile, benevolent spirit that wanted to announce it was there. It was more fascinating than frightening.

The investigator in me noticed that it would have been almost impossible to capture any audio evidence in the bar area because of the constant hum of the coolers, the noise from the video games, and the buzz from other electronics that couldn't be turned off. But the visual phenomenon was undeniable.

I'm not a psychic, but next I had an experience that can only be described as a psychic one, and I believe it is connected to the balls of light we saw. I was sitting at one of the tables in front of the stage when I got a vision in my mind's eye of a pretty young woman in a long white dress with beautiful dark hair. Was this the ethereal Woman in White? Could it be Johanna? Are they one and the same?

She walked behind me before circling around to my right-hand side until she was directly in front of me. As she approached I was overwhelmed with a profound sense of sadness that washed over me like a warm wave. My eyes began to tear up and I fought the urge to cry. The emotion came not from inside me, but more as a reflection from her. She was communicating with me empathically. I felt a kindred connection with the woman in white as if our souls were in tune. I felt the emotion that was so evident on her delicate face.

This was a powerful experience, an undeniable one. She said nothing but spoke volumes with her eyes. I don't know why she approached me, but I believe she was the famous Johanna whose sad story is legendary at Bobby Mackey's, immortalized forever in song. I also feel she may be the one responsible for creating the balls of white light, trying to get my attention before fully revealing herself to me.

This experience was meant just for me, something only I could see with my mind's eye. I told Wanda Kay about it, and she too believes the woman in white was Johanna. Others have seen her, but she is choosy about to whom she reveals herself. I felt very lucky that I was among those chosen few.

In addition, we had shadow figures break the pattern of the laser grid we set up to cover the area near the restrooms. They were fleeting but unexplainable. We also felt an incredible heaviness in the seating area behind the production booth of the main floor. We couldn't find any natural or mechanical explanation for what we felt, but no one could deny how uncomfortable and thick the atmosphere was in that area.

Personal Experience—
Wanda Kay (Club DJ, Author, Paranormal Investigator): Phone Call from Hell

I have worked at Bobby Mackey's for a decade, and in that time I've had many paranormal experiences—it just comes with the territory. Seldom have I felt threatened or afraid. Maybe it's because I'm so used to this kind of stuff, or maybe because I never thought anything would or could actually hurt me. But there have been times when I've been shaken up and have questioned my involvement here.

When the ghosts started following me home and affecting my personal life, I realized you can never be too careful. I can name at least forty resident spirits here, and not all of them are "friendly." I've learned over the years to take precautions, but nothing is foolproof.

Several times I have received strange phone calls and texts from "the other side." Sometimes the call originates from the number 666, which obviously isn't a real phone number, at least not anywhere around here! Other times, I've received strange messages that sounded like screaming or garbled language. And I got a message that sounded like hospital equipment, breathing machines, and a voice screaming.

These messages were so eerie and disturbing, my husband, Wayne, and I decided we needed to find out more. I sent the recordings to some of the sound experts we've worked with over the years. They analyzed the messages, cleaned them up, and deciphered what they were saying.

Most disturbing was, *"Paint her out!"*—an old mob phrase for "Kill her."

"I can't! Her faith is too strong!" said the second voice.

Another message really hit close to home: *"Wayne, get her out!"*

My husband was very concerned about that particular one. Was this a warning or a threat?

These type of otherworldly phone calls kept up for about three months. It's one thing to deal with this at work, and quite another when your work follows you home.

THE GREEN ROOM

Between the gift shop and the gaming area is a small, brightly lit room used as a relaxation and waiting area for Mackey between sets. The "green room" is a private repose for the singer and his wife. They have their own monogrammed chairs with comfy cushions, and a small side table for beverages.

The walls are covered with happy memories from the height of Mackey's performing days, including a giant record that takes up almost a third of the display area, posters and flyers from specific tours, and promotional pictures with famous friends. It's a warm, welcoming, quiet space. But an odd object shocks you back to the club's past.

An enormous safe—a vault, really—sits unmovable against the wall to the right of the doorway. The round gold-hued monstrosity once held the cold hard cash that went in and out of the club daily. Back in the days before checks and credit cards, cash was king—it was nearly untraceable and easy to work with. The mobsters loved it. The safe hasn't moved since the day it was rolled off a truck and moved into the club. The green room, once a counting room and chip exchange, was built around it.

Take the Haunted Tour—The Upstairs Apartment

Relatively few get to see a special area of Bobby Mackey's, the apartment above the bar, though it is included in the private overnight ghost hunt package. The apartment has been variously used as office space, gambling nerve center, living quarters, and storage, and it is now leaky and water damaged.

An enormous numbers board from the gambling days, similar to the *Wheel of Fortune* letter board, sits propped against the west wall, but there's no Vanna White here. Stacks of colorful but faded bingo cards sit ready for action.

A portion of a vintage green felt blackjack table sits tattered and torn in the middle of the room. Thought to be useful as a trigger object for ghost hunters, the table holds memories from a more dangerous era. A baby blanket and a pacifier that seem to have no place in this room add to the uncanny atmosphere.

Bobby Mackey's first wife, Janet, who passed away in 2009, had such a terrifying experience in the upstairs area of the club that she vowed never to return. Janet's account is recorded in a signed affidavit. In 1978, shortly after acquiring the club, the Mackeys were in the process of cleaning up the place and making a few renovations.

Janet, who was five months pregnant at the time, was working upstairs in the apartment. She felt something behind her, something she could feel but not see. Goose bumps covered her body as fear welled inside her.

Suddenly, Janet heard a preternatural voice bellow, "*GET OUT!*"

She froze, and then something grabbed her and pushed her toward the staircase. She struggled fiercely against the unseen force, which to her further horror materialized into a man "dressed from another era," but the entity succeeded in shoving her down the steps, causing her to be hospitalized. Her baby was born prematurely because of complications from the fall, but thankfully survived.

Janet never set foot inside the club again.

Author and historian Douglas Hensley did extensive research on Bobby Mackey's for his book *Hell's Gate*. Hensley was a personal friend of the Mackeys and knew of the reported paranormal doings in the club. He interviewed Janet Mackey about her horrifying encounter. When shown old photographs from a local newspaper account of Pearl Bryan's murder, Janet identified Alonzo Walling as the entity who had pushed her down the stairs. Legend has it that before he swung from the gallows, Walling swore he'd come back and haunt the area, as revenge for his death sentence.

Wanda Kay strongly discourages any pregnant women from investigating the apartment area of the club—several have had complications after ghost hunting or touring the second floor.

In recent years, the apartment was the living quarters of Bobby Mackey's handyman, Carl Lawson. Carl's story is forever intertwined with the history of the building, being one of the most notorious cases of possession/oppression in recent history.

Carl grew up in a house that sat on what is now the far edge of the club's parking lot, and as a teenager he worked for the previous owners of the building until authorities shut the bar down in the 1970s. Carl found himself out of a job until Mackey bought the building and began renovating with the intention of opening a country-and-western club.

Carl offered his services to Mackey, who was happy to have him as an employee. Carl hoped the atmosphere would be more peaceful this time around. Experience had led him to believe that something about the building brought out the worst in people, turning them against each other and stimulating their violent tendencies. He'd been witness to it many times over.

Carl worked and lived at the club, making the apartment space into his home. There was once a working bathroom and kitchen inside the small efficiency. A few reminders of Carl—cigarette butts, empty liquor bottles—are scattered amid the debris, cobwebs, and broken pipes, but since Carl's passing in 2011 the life has been sucked out of the space.

Those close to Carl Lawson describe him as a "sweet, gentle man" but also "a strange old bird" who was plagued with alcoholism, diabetes, and a supernatural attachment, a negative entity from within the club taking over his mind and body, that many believe pushed him over the edge and contributed to his death. Carl's story first came to light on an episode of *The Jerry Springer Show* back in 1991, and again in a 2006 episode of *A Haunting*, a show that put Bobby Mackey's on ghost hunter radar.

Carl Lawson isn't the only one plagued by evil spirits picked up at the club. *Ghost Adventures*'s Zak Bagans, Nick Groff, and Aaron Goodwin all experienced malevolent forces that seemed determined to leave a mark on their bodies and souls. Aaron's life was transformed when a dark entity attached itself to him at Mackey's in the very first episode of the show, leading to the realization that he couldn't have a "normal" life.

In an interview with us on America's Most Haunted Radio, Nick Groff affirmed that he refuses to set foot inside the club to this day, fearing that something might attach and follow him home, putting his family in danger.

Personal Experience—
Wanda Kay

The death of Carl Lawson was devastating to us here at the club. He was part of our family, and things will never be the same without him. After he passed in 2011, the apartment he lived in above the bar fell into disarray. It was once an important part of the history of the building, even before Carl lived here, but now it's a mess.

The paranormal activity has always been up here, one of the darkest areas in Bobby Mackey's. For a while, we chose not to include the apartment on the ghost hunts; it's a dangerous place, especially for women.

A lot of women become very sick to their stomachs as soon as they enter the room. Some have felt something grab their ankles, trying to pull them through the floor. Others have felt something crawling up their backs, grabbing both shoulders and pressing down, shoving them to the floor. But the most common experience is the inability to breathe, their chests feeling like they were going to collapse. One woman told me she felt like a hand was inside her chest, squeezing her heart!

I believe the spirit responsible for these attacks is "Grumpy George." Half a dozen or so people have used the apartment as their living quarters over the years; George Gibhart, Buck Brady's business partner, was the original tenant in the 1930s.

Now his spirit is the dominant one in the entire building.

When the club first started allowing folks in for overnight paranormal investigations, they were often unsupervised. Bobby was a little too trusting, and some took advantage of this. Instead of just collecting evidence, they were collecting souvenirs, taking all sorts of stuff out of the club: bingo cards, poker chips, pictures . . . anything that wasn't tied down!

George was not happy about this and let us know what was happening. Even I wasn't immune to his presence—sometimes I would get that overwhelming heaviness all over when I was upstairs. He didn't like thieves, and he didn't care for females either.

I tried to appease his spirit by making an offering of sorts. I collected a bunch of old stuff that was stored in the basement—blackjack tables, stacks of bingo cards, all sorts of memorabilia—and secured it upstairs in the apartment. I wanted to let him know that we weren't going to let anyone else take anything from the club.

This seemed to work, at least for a while. Over the last couple of years, there have been only a couple of incidents of women being scratched.

Until two weeks ago.

I hosted an investigation with a team of about six people in the apartment. We had a lot of communication through the Ovilus and several EVPs. After a bit, things got quiet. The only response we got was, *"Enough! Enough!"*

George let us know he was done talking to us. One of the team asked that he show himself, just once, in any manner he pleased, and everyone would leave the upstairs. George was happy to accommodate. We witnessed the closet door open and a dark shadow travel across the wall. We watched the shadow move across the floor over to the bathroom door. The bathroom door opened, the shadow entered, and then the door closed. We were stunned!

At this point we were so amazed we wanted to stay, but out of respect for George we kept our promise and headed back downstairs. Now the other half of the group, which had been on the main floor, came up to the apartment. They got the brunt of the activity that we'd stirred up.

It was about fifteen minutes into their session when everything started to happen. One gentleman came down with a huge red welt on his face. He said he had felt something smack him across the face with significant force. The skin was broken and there were traces of blood. Grumpy George was living up to his name!

George Gibhart was one of the rougher characters to grace the halls of this building. Quite a few of these "tough guys" were involved in the nightclubs and casinos that stood on this property. And they were no saints. They were involved in a lot of bad stuff, illegal and immoral acts. I think maybe they've chosen to stay here, guarding the place, so to speak, not out of the goodness of their hearts, but out of fear of what comes after. They don't want to face the music for the things they did while they were alive.

Maybe they'll try to redeem themselves a bit while they're here; maybe they won't. But I can bet they don't plan on leaving anytime soon.

Take the Haunted Tour—The Basement

Below the main floor of Bobby Mackey's is another world, a cavernous hideaway of dusty corners, darkened rooms, and a whole lot of spookery—the basement. Access to the basement is gained through a single door on the south side of the building, from the sunken gravel parking lot that slopes down from the main road.

Inside, high ceilings are covered with wooden crossbeams, pipes, and a web of wiring. Bare bulbs provide harsh light and chase the darkness into the shadows. In the center, a wide open area is flanked on the east and west sides by small storage rooms, utility spaces, and the like. The west side is general storage space filled with excess or seldom used furniture and bar paraphernalia, while the east side is where most of the action is: the old dressing rooms, the Séance or Candle Room, and the notorious well.

Though best known, the well isn't the only portion of the basement where supernatural forces come to play. Each room has its own unique characteristics and tales to tell of paranormal activity, and it's where ghost hunters spend the majority of their time investigating.

Personal Experience—
Matt Coates (Bar Manager)

I have been an employee of Bobby Mackey's Music World for about ten years now, just a little longer than Wanda Kay. I started off as a customer, just coming in and having a good time. One night it got real busy so I asked a bartender if they needed help. I jumped back behind the bar and started washing glasses and I've been here ever since. Now I am the bar manager, overseeing day-to-day club operations. I leave the ghost-related stuff to Wanda Kay.

I'd heard the stories and seen my co-workers get all up in arms about it, but the only spirits I was interested in were the ones in the bottles. I don't scare easy, so I wasn't much worried about any of the so-called demons of the bar. Well, I changed my mind pretty quickly after an incident in the basement that scared the hell out of me.

Back in the winter of 2008, it was real cold out and I was dealing with a few broken pipes in the basement. I was in the central area, right outside the Well Room. I'd been down there working on getting them fixed and everything cleaned up before we opened for the night. Just about finished, I was bent down putting my tools away in my tool bag when I felt this strange uncomfortable sensation on my chest. When I tried to stand up, I almost toppled over.

I figured I was just tired from being downstairs for so long, so I tried to shrug it off. But it got worse. It was this heavy pressure; I felt like I couldn't breathe, like someone was sitting on my chest. I tried to stand up straight to get a deep breath in, open up my lungs.

All of a sudden some type of force picked me up about two feet in the air, right off the ground, and threw me across the room!

I'm 6'1", three hundred pounds. I'm no little twig, so whatever did this had to be very powerful. I didn't trip or fall; I was lifted up and flung backward across the basement like a rag doll. I landed flat against the back wall!

I tore the hell out of the basement, leaving my tools scattered on the ground.

I've never had anything like that happen to me before or since that incident, but it sure did change my ideas about the kind of things haunting this place. This wasn't any shadow person or white silhouette, no creepy noises. I can handle that. This was a violent attack. Something evil was pissed off and tried to hurt me. The only thing I can think of is that I'd been down in the basement working on stuff, changing things around that had been the same for over fifty years. Maybe someone was upset with me, even though I was just doing what I had to do to keep the place running smooth.

I've always been a little sensitive to spirits, but it wasn't some-

Tools of the Trade

Ovilus: a handheld device created by Bill Chappell of Digital Dowsing for direct spirit communication. The Ovilus contains an internal preset library of words heard audibly when "selected" by the spirit during use. The user asks a question of the spirit, which manipulates the device to "answer."

thing I ever really talked about, I didn't really want to believe in ghosts. But after all my years of working here—plus stuff I'd experienced before—I've learned to trust my instincts. Sometimes you just know things. I am a lot more cautious now.

A couple years after this incident, during the filming of one of the *Ghost Adventures* episodes, I had another encounter with something very dark. Before the guys began their investigation, I asked them *not* to provoke any of the spirits here. It's dangerous for them and for the rest of us who are here every day and have to deal with pissed-off ghosts after the cameras are gone. The aftermath is awful.

Well, of course, Zak Bagans didn't listen. He was downstairs doing his usual thing, yelling and taunting the spirits. Provoking, exactly what I asked him not to do. I was pissed off!

When Zak came upstairs, he and I got into it pretty bad. It took a couple guys to keep us apart. We almost got into a physical fight. I was angry, really angry, but it was more than that. I wanted to attack him, really hurt him, *kill him*. I mean, it was crazy!

Bishop James Long—archbishop of the U.S. Old Roman Catholic Church and experienced exorcist—had to take me outside and try to calm me down. I was out of control. He started speaking in tongues or something; I had no idea what the hell he was saying. He laid his hands on me, blessed me, and put some sort of medal on me, some sort of charm.

The bishop said I was borderline possessed, and I believe I was. Something took me over, made me act in a way I wouldn't normally act. Yes, I was pissed, but I usually don't try to kill people I'm upset with. This was something out of my control.

I believe I know who did this. I won't say his name because I don't want to give him the acknowledgment. It gives him power, and he doesn't need any more. He is the supreme deceiver, known by many names. There have been so many ghost hunters and paranormal teams coming in here over the years; some do the stupidest shit. They pour blood down the well and try to summon something dark—it's just ridiculous, dangerous crap. We've tried to put a stop to it. Wanda Kay doesn't let people provoke in the club; it just stirs up trouble. I know what evil force is here. It's attracted to the activity, and now I am extremely careful not to let it take me over again.

This ain't no playground; this is serious stuff. You'd better be prepared if you come looking for ghosts at Bobby Mackey's. You just might find them.

Personal Experience—
Theresa with Eric

On a July 2013 visit, Eric and I got to tour the building with club marketing director R. J. Seifert during the day before the club opened. He gave us the history and filled us in on all the different areas of the building. It was very informative and, though R. J. is agnostic on ghosts, just the right amount of spooky. We had the opportunity to interview some of the employees, including Wanda Kay and Matt Coates, so we had a good sense of what Bobby Mackey's was all about.

I was interested to see if things were different at night.

As evening fell, I was happy to see Mike and Stacey, a couple we had met earlier in the day while we were snooping around outside the building prior to R. J.'s arrival. They were among several people who had come by the club during daylight hours to "feel the place out," or just take pictures.

After a horrific near-death experience several years earlier, Mike had found he was sensitive to ghosts and spirits. During their day visit, Mike had gotten an uneasy vibe from just standing outside the building! Stacey was understanding and supportive but had really wanted to return to the club for a tour. Now they were back, ready to proceed, but poised to bail if things got too heavy.

Eric and I joined Mike and Stacey and the small group on the first tour of the night. We convened in the gift shop area to begin our adventure. Due to the noise level of the now-open club, most of the tour would be of the basement. We went out a door in the vicinity of the mechanical bull, which brought us to the street in front of the building, where our guide, Marky Mark Moore, told us of some of the paranormal history of the club. After a chilling tale or two we moved over to the parking lot and down the hill to the basement door.

The basement was much noisier than before: air-conditioning rattling, refrigeration unit humming, employees coming and going. Noise, people, commotion: It didn't bode well for a "haunting experience," but I resolved to be a good sport and carry on.

We gathered just inside the entrance to the basement while Mark explained briefly what was in store: the dressing rooms, the Séance Room, the wall of faces, and the infamous "portal to hell."

The crowd was fascinated as Mark recounted the tale of Zak Bagans's encounter with a mysterious cowboy apparition at the far north end of the basement, which we could see in the distance. Even with the lights on, the basement was very creepy.

To my immediate left was a tiny storage room. Inside were some boxes and stacked chairs. I positioned myself just in front of the doorway. As Mark talked and pointed off toward the other end of the basement, I felt a strange sensation on my back. Something was touching me!

I dismissed it at first as cobwebs or bugs, but then I felt cold hands firmly press down on my shoulders. I could feel the weight of the hands and shuddered at how unnaturally cold they were. It wasn't a light touch, it was deliberate and unmistakable, so much so that I thought Eric must be behind me, holding on to me for some reason. But Eric was *in front* of me.

As I whipped around to confront whoever was touching me, Mark noticed my fidgeting. "What's the story with this area?" I asked, pointing to the room behind me.

"Ah, well, nothing really, it's just an old storage area with some junk in it. Although lately, women have said they get a weird feeling from it."

The sensation subsided and I just wanted to move on, away from the doorway. The room made me feel weird, "yucky." I thought maybe my imagination was getting the best of me.

On we went, moving in toward the center, approaching the first dressing room. Before Mark could speak, the silence was interrupted by an enormously loud *CRASH!!* The alarming sound of glass shattering filled the air, resounding throughout the basement. The group let out a collective yelp.

Mark chuckled. "It's just the empty bottles from the upstairs bar. Gets 'em every time!"

An ingenious idea: A PVC pipe runs down from a disposal upstairs behind the bar, through the floor, and into a large recycling container in the basement. Every time an empty beer bottle is discarded, it smashes into the waiting receptacle downstairs, making an incredibly loud noise that echoes across the large open area as it lands. The startled group chuckled, and Mark returned to his storytelling.

The dressing rooms are not very big, so I hung back while everyone else tried to pile inside and get a look. Earlier that day I'd spent some time in each of them, so I figured I'd give the others the opportunity to explore. As I watched my companions step up into the room, something drew my attention away.

I turned back toward the area of the creepy storage room. I had the distinct feeling something was about to happen, and I wasn't going to miss it. I readied my camera; instinct told me to do so.

As I strained my eyes in the low light, a large, dark shadow figure poked its head out of the storage room. It was blacker than the surrounding darkness, its outline clearly visible, peeking out from the top portion of the door frame. I estimated it must be at least six feet tall. It was solid, as if it had a definite mass to it. It had a human shape; at least the portion I could see appeared to be that of a man. There were no discernible features, no eyes, no mouth, just cold dead blackness. It was moving, revealing itself slowly as I stared at it, transfixed, terrified.

I couldn't believe what I was seeing. I strained my eyes, focusing intently on the figure. It moved again; I could make out a distinct head and shoulders, but the face was obscured in darkness. I looked through the viewfinder of my camera, and it was there! I snapped a picture quickly, not taking my eyes off it for a second, afraid it would disappear if I did.

"Holy crap!" I said aloud to no one in particular. Everyone else was busy in the dressing room.

I was about to grab Eric and Mark and notify the group what was happening when the shadow man stepped out of the room! Now I could see a complete silhouette of a dark, featureless man. I saw his long, lanky arms. He crossed them over his chest, as if to challenge me, making a firm stand. Although I couldn't see his eyes, I could *feel* them.

This thing was staring right at me. It stepped out and stood tall as if to say, *I see you, and I know you see me.* There was menace to his stance. I felt an icy coldness coming from the black hole where his eyes would be. They bored into my soul, polluting it with gloom. I felt sick to my stomach. I wanted to vomit, to expel the evil creeping up inside me.

"Oh my God, Eric! Eric! Look! Look at that!" I pointed toward the shadow man, who naturally vanished the moment Eric and Mark turned around.

"What's going on?" Mark alerted the group. Now everyone was looking.

"Did something happen? What did you see?" Eric asked as he strained to see what was causing the commotion.

"I swear to God I just saw a shadow man step out of that doorway!"

"In front of that old storage area?" Mark asked.

"Yes, right where I was standing before. It came out of that room, looked right at me, and then disappeared." I was shaking with excitement and terror.

"Did you get a picture?" Eric inquired, thinking first of the book, then of my well-being. Thanks, partner.

"Yes! I saw it through the viewfinder and with my eyes. I got it." I looked at my camera and scrolled back to the picture I had taken. But the shadow man wasn't there. My picture showed nothing but a dimly lit basement and a hazy mist covering everything.

I was stunned. "It's not there! I swear, I saw it through the camera *and* with my eyes!"

Mark wasn't surprised. He said the spirits that dwell in the basement of Bobby Mackey's are sometimes camera shy. I was thoroughly disappointed. I wanted my partner to see this thing. I wanted *everyone* to see this thing, but I guess the encounter was meant for just me.

In all my years of investigating the paranormal, I've had something like this happen only twice before, and never for such an extended period of time or with such an ominous flavor. This was no trick of the light, nor an issue with my eyes. This shadow man was real. He *wanted* me to know he was there. I don't know if this was a human spirit or something more malevolent, but my gut tells me it was the latter.

What did he want? I don't know, but any inkling of doubt vanished at that point. I went from open-minded skeptic to firm believer in the haunting of Bobby Mackey's Music World.

Well done, shadow man, well done.

THE DRESSING ROOMS

Among the most interesting areas of the basement are the old dressing rooms. Latin Quarter performers, including the fabled Johanna, readied themselves for the stage inside these tiny private spaces. Each room has a step up into what is basically nothing more than a large box, with a large mirror and a shelf for makeup and hair accessories covering the back wall. An old clothing bar hangs to the right of each door, a place where elaborate costumes hung, ready for the spotlight.

Two have a single red lightbulb in the ceiling, giving them a "welcome to hell" look. In the third dressing room, the light is blue, which makes it different but just as eerie. The first of the three intact dressing rooms is thought to have belonged to the legendary Johanna. Visitors have heard the sound of singing and have captured EVPs of a crying woman from inside the empty dressing room. People report faces appearing in the mirror, faces that show up on camera occasionally. An apparition of a woman hanging from the ceiling has been reported by terrified visitors.

Another claim often reported is the sensation of being touched. The touch is a pleasant one, more like a caress. Wanda Kay witnessed a man overcome with euphoria while in Johanna's dressing room. Apparently, the dancer took a shine to him and wanted to make him feel welcome. Women report similar feelings in Robert Randall's dressing room. Evidently, Johanna and Robert are still a touchy-feely kind of couple.

THE ROOM OF FACES

One of the larger rooms in the basement is the Room of Faces, aptly named because of the strange facelike markings on the walls. It is also referred to as the Séance Room or Candle Room. Actually, it's just a large utility room with a gated and locked back portion ideal for storing liquor. But other "spirits" linger in the room, and it is a perfect place to communicate with the other side.

A small coffee table sits in the middle of a circular formation of chairs. An oversized candelabra sits on the table, and several small partially burned votives are scattered about. When the light is off in the room, the candles cast an eerie glow on everything and misshapen shadows dance across the walls.

Inconsistencies and pitting in the surface and the paint on the walls combine to form "faces" in the concrete. It is a classic case of matrixing, where the mind finds patterns in random data, like finding an elephant in a cloud or Jesus on a tortilla chip. The "wall of faces" is covered with such shapes: a woman, a cowboy, a child, even a lamb, hidden within the matrix of the wall.

The Room of Faces gained notoriety in 2010 when *Ghost Adventures* front man Zak Bagans was overcome by a "demonic force" that partially possessed him. The episode showed a visibly upset Bagans's demeanor completely change as he collapsed to the ground.

Then, after a chilling experience in the Well Room, Nick was left alone in the Room of Faces to do an EVP session. Sitting on the floor surrounded by candles, Nick tried his luck communicating with the spirits. Upon playback of the audio, Nick heard a sorrowful female voice crying, immediately followed by a whispered male voice saying, "*Precious . . . no,*" as if to comfort her.

Personal Experience—
Mike Hovey (Tour Guest)

I knew of Bobby Mackey's and its haunted reputation from watching shows like *Ghost Adventures*. Between Zak Bagans's account and Carl Lawson's story of possession, I couldn't help but be intrigued. I wasn't sure I bought into all the demonic stuff; it seemed a little overly dramatic and far-fetched. But I was cautious, just in case. I had to be. I have been sensitive to spirits since an accident nearly ended my life, and places with bad energy leave me cold and empty, a feeling I desperately wanted to avoid.

Stacey and I decided to stop by Mackey's in the daytime to kind of "feel the place out" before actually going inside for any kind of tour or ghost hunt that night. We met Theresa Argie and Eric Olsen, who were waiting for someone to open the building. I told Eric the story of my near-death experience, and the four of us compared our thoughts on the paranormal and the bar. As we stood outside in the parking lot, I took it all in. I certainly wasn't getting a pleasant feeling from the place, but I wasn't sure if the negativity was from rehashing my accident with Eric or was coming from the building itself.

In the end, Stacey and I decided we would come back and see what the inside was like. We returned just before the 9 P.M. tour started. I was happy to see that Theresa and Eric would be joining us as well.

The tour started upstairs and moved outside to the front of the building. After a little history and a couple of ghost stories, we moved down into the basement. I was cautious about going down there, remembering the "portal to hell" theory I'd seen on TV. Having a few others around us made me feel a little better, but I couldn't help the feeling that someone or something else was trailing our group, hiding in the shadows. Theresa thought she saw something in the shadows as well, and I kept seeing something out of the corner of my eyes.

By the time our guide, Mark, took us into the Candle Room, I was really on edge. There was a heaviness in the air that I couldn't shake. As Mark gave us the rundown, I looked around at the walls. It wasn't hard to see why people saw faces. The contrast of dark and light was everywhere. I saw all sorts of weird things.

As Mark talked, the crowd listened intently. From my right,

I heard an audible and distinct voice in my ear: "*HEY, over here!*"

I whipped around to see who was trying to get my attention, but no one was there. I was in the back against one of the walls and everyone was in front of me. The voice chilled me to my core. It was a male voice and it was right next to me. I was overwhelmed with different emotions at this point—sadness, anger, fear—all bombarding me at the same time.

I felt shaky and put my hand up against the wall to steady myself. As soon as my palm touched the wall, I heard screaming—not coming from the people around me, but coming from the wall!

I quickly pulled my hand away, shocked by the noise that apparently only I heard. Apprehensively, I touched the wall again, and the screaming returned. It was a thousand voices and one voice all at the same time. It sounded both human and inhuman, almost as if an animal were being slaughtered. I noticed that the area on the Wall of Faces that I was touching just happened to be the part that resembled a lamb and remembered that the building used to be a slaughterhouse.

I kept my hands to myself for the rest of the tour.

THE WELL ROOM

The most interesting and controversial room in Bobby Mackey's Music World, the lure that attracts visitors and ghost hunters from all over the world, is the Well Room. The well is thought by many to be a "portal to hell," a supernatural vortex so dangerous that management cordoned off the area with a wooden fence.

Of course, they also don't want anyone to fall in.

Once used to drain blood and animal waste from the slaughterhouse, "the well" (technically a "drain") was eventually filled in and covered. Rediscovered by Carl Lawson in the 1980s, the well now looks like an oversized gopher hole in the concrete basement floor, about three feet in diameter and about eighteen inches deep. But don't be deceived. The dark energy generated by a river of blood and the alleged conjuring of necromancers lingers thickly to this day, assaulting the sensitive and perhaps still functioning as a portal that has granted God-knows-what manner of malevolence access to our world.

Which brings us to the sensational tale of Pearl Bryan, age twenty-two, and five months pregnant, murdered, decapitated, and dumped unceremoniously in an orchard on John Locke's farm in the Highlands near Ft. Thomas, four miles from where Bobby Mackey's sits today, on February 1, 1896.

Pearl was the youngest of twelve children born to a wealthy farming family in Greencastle, Indiana. Pearl was a lovely and sophisticated music student at Greencastle's DePauw University who fell for a rakish Eastern swell and dental student named Scott Jackson, whom she met through her cousin Will Wood.

Jackson was a charismatic character who had narrowly escaped an embezzlement charge in New Jersey and had come to Greencastle to visit his mother and half sister, and start anew. After a short stay with his mother, he left for Indianapolis to begin dental school but frequently returned to Greencastle and continued his relationship with Pearl, which eventually turned intimate.

In the summer of 1895, Jackson decided to transfer to the Dental College of Ohio in Cincinnati. At the same time he abruptly ended his relationship with Pearl. A couple of months later Pearl discovered she was pregnant, and after a flurry of heated letters, Jackson finally agreed to meet Pearl in Cincinnati, about 150 miles from Greencastle, for the purpose of obtaining an abortion.

After a few days, the abortion had not yet come together and a very loud argument ensued on the street between Bryan and

Jackson, in the company of Jackson's friend and fellow dental student Alonzo Walling.

At dinner, Jackson surreptitiously dumped cocaine into Pearl's drink. Walling left and returned with a livery cab. They guided Pearl, who was now feeling ill, into the cab and headed across the river toward Newport.

Once in Kentucky, they drove in an oddly circuitous route in order to avoid two tollbooths they would have had to pass through on the direct route—clear indication of premeditation. Their path included a jaunt on Licking Pike right past a certain shuttered slaughterhouse and ended up in John Locke's orchard. The two men ushered a groaning Pearl out of the cab. Between two intense and conspiratorial young men, an ill and moaning young woman, an odd yet specific route, and the peculiar destination of a secluded orchard in winter, the driver wanted no further part of the scene and took off on foot, leaving the cab.

After manhandling her into the orchard, Jackson attacked his former lover with a formidable knife. She struggled fiercely, grabbing at the knife, flailing, digging her nails into his arm, causing him to drop the knife. She desperately crawled away, but Jackson caught her from behind by her blond hair, reached around her neck, and slit her throat.

The desperate fiend Jackson finished cutting off her head under the assumption that a headless body would be difficult to identify, which it was, but only for a few days. Poor Pearl was identified by her shoes.

Is it possible Pearl's head ended up in the well of the closed slaughterhouse? Yes, they did drive right past it on the way to the scene of the dastardly deed, and on the way back. But based on the testimony of the killers, the victim's head was almost certainly dumped into the Ohio River.

The conspirators were caught and convicted of the heinous crime. On the morning of their hanging, Jackson made a statement to the sheriff: "I know that Alonzo Walling is not guilty of the crime of murder." The governor agreed to commute Walling's sentence to life if Jackson would confess to the crime and disclose the whereabouts of Pearl's head. But Jackson refused to confess; both men made a final proclamation of innocence and were hanged.

Legend has it that the pair taunted the crowd and proclaimed their devotion to Satan before swinging on the gallows, with Walling cursing everyone involved in his trial and vowing to come back from hell and haunt the place where Pearl Bryan's head was cast. But there is no hint of any of this in newspaper accounts of the very heavily covered public execution.

Head or no head, the well has become a symbol of the darkness that permeates the basement of Bobby Mackey's Music World, and that darkness is very real.

Ghost Adventures—
In da Club

In 2008, *Ghost Adventures* filmed the very first episode of their very first season—an epic and highly controversial episode—at Bobby Mackey's. Zak, Nick, and Aaron came with open minds and left with haunting experiences that have never left them.

While "locked down" in the basement, Zak taunted and full-out provoked the spirits to "come up out of that ground and get us." They obliged.

Zak began to feel sick and dizzy. Cameras rolled as he told Nick and Aaron that his back was burning. Aaron shut off the IR light on his camera while Nick lifted the back of Zak's shirt, revealing three deep red scratches down the center of his spine. Zak walked out of the Well Room as the sick feeling got stronger, then turned around in anger: "Did someone just scratch me?! Who did this?"

The attack continued as more scratch marks formed on his back.

After the guys left the Well Room, they regrouped in the main open portion of the basement. They noticed strange activity over by the north end of the back wall. They focused one of their static cameras in that direction and recorded while they explored the rest of the basement.

A review of the footage yielded the stunning discovery of a silhouette of a man wearing a cowboy hat, who stepped out from behind a pillar and vanished after a few seconds. The cowboy figure had been reported in this area for years, and the Ghost Adventures Crew captured him on camera. The hat on his head left no doubt that this was a legitimate paranormal entity. There were only three men in the building at the time, and none of them wore a cowboy hat!

The Ghost Adventures Crew returned to Bobby Mackey's in 2009 for a public ghost hunt event with a group of fans. The event was not televised but it was well documented, and several disturbing things went down. Nick and Aaron were leading a group investigating the basement when they heard Zak's voice over the radio calling for help.

In a panic, they rushed to see what was wrong, but Zak was fine. He was with a group in another area and had *not* called out to them. When they played back the audio, Zak confirmed that it was his voice . . . but it wasn't him who said it!

Bishop James Long was also present at the event. He had consulted Zak after the first visit to Mackey's, warning him of the danger he faced by messing with the demonic. At this event, the bishop was scratched by an unseen force apparently upset with his presence in the building.

When *Ghost Adventures* filmed the return episode (season four, episode three) in 2010, they invited Bishop Long to come back and rid the basement of the evil spirits. While using the ghost box, the spirits identified Zak and Bishop Long by name. Another voice claimed to be Scott Jackson. When the team switched to a PX device, even more voices chilled the crew as the name Pearl Bryan came over the speaker.

No matter what type of equipment they used, electrifying direct responses and relevant answers resulted. After numerous responses from the spirits, everything went silent.

"Why aren't you talking now?" Zak asked the spirits.

"*Bad . . . memories.*"

"Memories? Of what?" he questioned.

The entity answered clearly, "*I . . . killed . . . Pearl Bryan.*"

They had no doubt they were communicating with the murderer Scott Jackson. But the scariest part of the evening had yet to come.

Bishop Long began a blessing, a minor rite of exorcism used to rid a place of evil spirits or demonic entities. While he prayed and read from his book, a powerful malevolent force appeared to overtake Zak. He was clearly shaken and disturbed as the ritual proceeded.

Even more disturbing was what happened to Aaron. They had to shut off the cameras and leave the building. Later Aaron confessed that he had become so filled with hate and anger toward the bishop that he wanted to hurt him, even kill him.

EVPs saying, "*Hurt . . . Zak*" and "*I'm'a kill your wife*" were only the tip of the iceberg for the team. All three members of the Ghost Adventures Crew were deeply and profoundly affected by what happened to them at Bobby Mackey's. Something followed each of them, crept into their personal lives, attached itself to them in a negative manner that had a lasting effect. Aaron Goodwin told us in a recent interview that his experiences at Bobby Mackey's and their aftermath were at least partially responsible for the breakup of his marriage.

Ghost-hunting is one thing, but battling evil spirits, murderous ghosts, and demonic entities is something completely different. To this day, none of the Ghost Adventures Crew will set foot back in Bobby Mackey's Music World.

Personal Experience—
George Lopez

On our June 2010 trip to Bobby Mackey's, after investigating upstairs, we headed down to the basement. The first thing I noticed about the basement was an immediate sense of something being off-center, askew, not quite right. There was an elusive energy, one that doesn't want to face you directly—cowardice is how I would describe it.

I was interested in the so-called gateway to hell to see if it lived up to its notorious reputation. I was skeptical but needed to find out for myself. Tyler, Jeff, and I were in the Well Room, armed with digital video and audio recorders. I climbed over the wooden fence to get a closer look at the well. I was surprised by how small it actually is.

We did a cursory sweep of the area before starting our investigation. The Trifield meter was giving off some very strange readings, unusual hits with no physical origin. We couldn't figure out where the energy anomaly was emanating from.

I stood in a windowlike opening while Jeff worked the camera. Tyler scanned the area with his flashlight. We were discussing what ghosts are made of and what they are attracted to. Jeff commented that he believed they were made of ultraviolet (UV) light. Our conversation was interrupted by a maniacal, sinister laugh. The disembodied chuckle was loud enough to be picked up on the video camera's audio track. The timing of the laugh was remarkable, as if to mock us, letting us know we really had no clue what spirits are.

At that point, we were certain something was there with us.

Tools of the Trade

PX: an instrumental transcommunication device invented by Bill Chappell of Digital Dowsing. Described as a cross between two of Chappell's other inventions, the Ovilus and the Paranormal Puck, the PX has a larger vocabulary of over a thousand words and an internal speaker that audibly says the words.

It was time to step it up a notch. We decided to divide and conquer. Jeff and I stayed in the basement while Tyler went back upstairs. It was worth a shot.

I wanted to get the full effect, so to speak, so I got into the well—actually stood inside it—to do an EVP session. There was an eerie feeling in the air, an electricity, a disjointed sense of chaos. With this session, I came about as close to provoking the spirits as I dared. I don't believe it's necessary to provoke to get responses, and I'd heard about the horrible repercussions people have faced after pissing off the spirits at Bobby Mackey's.

As I stood inside the well, I said, "We're going to put Tyler in here a little bit later on. You're welcome to scratch him, push him, pull him . . . whatever you need to do."

The EVP response said, "*Fuck him.*"

I knew the spirits got a little physical at Mackey's, but no one was expecting this! I'm glad Tyler didn't hear this EVP until after we had left the building. I think he would have spent the rest of the night hiding upstairs.

The experiences we had at Bobby Mackey's were profound, but I truly believe things could have been worse, much worse. Our visit came not two weeks after *Ghost Adventures* filmed their return episode there. Bishop Long's cleansing and blessing definitely eased the severity of our ghostly encounters.

Nothing harmful or extraordinarily terrifying happened to us. Yes, we got the bejesus scared out of us and I'll never forget the vision of the Woman in White, but we survived intact, without any spiritual attachments or demonic oppressions following us home. And that's a good thing. Unfortunately, I heard that Bishop Long's remedy was only temporary.

The Sad and Mysterious Tale of Carl Lawson

The saddest story to come out of Mackey's in decades is that of long-time employee and possession victim Carl Lawson. Lawson, the club handyman, stumbled upon a boarded-up portion of the floor he'd never noticed before while working on an electrical issue in the basement. When the boards were removed, the old well was revealed. It had been hidden, unused for decades, a remnant of the slaughterhouse days.

Carl believed an evil entity came out of the well and possessed his very soul, ultimately destroying him. Spirits were nothing new inside the club, but Carl released something even more powerful, something dangerous.

Bobby Mackey; his wife, Janet; and everyone close to Carl saw a change in his personality after that. His health declined and he fell into a great depression. An old friend of Mackey's, Doug Hensley, contacted a psychic, who believed that Carl was possessed, or at least oppressed, by one or more evil or demonic spirits.

Doug and Carl believed two of those spirits were Scott Jackson and Alonzo Walling, the murderous dental students who dispatched Pearl Bryan. The spirits were fighting for control of his body, using him to touch, feel, and interact with the physical world.

A Pentecostal priest was called in to perform an exorcism on Carl in 1991, and a legendary battle ensued over his body and soul. Doug Hensley recorded this disturbing and violent ritual,

> ## Tools of the Trade
>
> **Trifield Meter:** a commonly used device that measures the levels of three fields—electric, magnetic, radio—in the environment.

which is available on numerous Internet outlets including You-Tube and recounted in his book *The Exorcism of Carl Lawson*. Although the exorcism seemed to work, Carl was never really the same. He lived out his last years in a sad state, battling other demons, poor health and alcohol, until he passed away in January 2012 at age fifty-three.

The Stairway to Heaven

Within the Well Room, just to the south of the well, is a door that, when opened, reveals a set of stairs that lead . . . nowhere. They climb up steeply and end abruptly at a ceiling that is the underside of the floor of the men's room upstairs. Presumed to have been a secret escape route used during the Prohibition and casino days, it has been inaccessible for many decades.

When the stairs were uncovered, remnants of an old shotgun were found stuffed into the ceiling, likely placed there "just in case." The mysterious "stairway to heaven," as it is playfully called, is appropriately located right next to a "portal to hell."

Personal Experience—
Wanda Kay: Reach Out and Touch Someone . . . Else

In June 2013 I was down in the Well Room with a team that was using the spirit box. The only voices coming across the box were those of children. Over and over again we heard, "*Help me! Help me! Let me out! Let me out!*" Then the doorknob on the door to the "stairway to heaven" rattled.

Those voices were so disturbing, we couldn't wait to get out of the Well Room!

Well, I returned the next night with another paranormal team. I told them all about the activity we'd had the previous evening: door rattling, children's voices, and so on. I said, "Why don't we open that 'door to nowhere' and see what happens tonight."

I was sitting with a K2 meter next to me, and when the door opened the meter maxed out to the red and stayed there. I felt a cold breeze come up around me, and I was covered in goose bumps. The girl next to me didn't feel anything until she stuck her hand by my arm. Then she felt it too, all around me, surrounding me.

Just then I got hit, hard, right square in the chest, knocking the wind right out of me. My head felt dizzy and I became very nauseated. I didn't want to scare the people with me so I tried to stick it out, but within about ten minutes I had to run outside and throw up.

When I finally collected myself, I returned to the people inside who had continued communicating with whatever energy was there. They'd asked what had made me sick and the response was, "*Thing.*"

Besides that horribly cryptic answer, the group told me they'd been communicating with a spirit that identified himself as Alonzo Walling.

We changed tools and started using the dowsing rods, which would cross together for *yes* and move apart for *no*. Using the rods, we asked if Alonzo was the one making me sick. The rods indicated *no*. If Alonzo was around, I figured his partner in crime, Scott Jackson, might be as well. I asked if it was Scott who was making me sick, and the rods said *yes*!

Oh really? Now I was pissed. I said, "Well, you know what, I don't appreciate it much . . ." The rods went to *no*.

I continued, "And you know what else? I'm not going to be on this side forever. When I cross over I'm not going to forget this, and payback is a MOTHER!"

We all watched as those dowsing rods starting spinning like a whirlwind round and round, out of control. The poor folks I was with were scared out of their wits and started panicking: "Oh no, Wanda, you're pissing them off, you're making them angry!"

I said, addressing the spirits, "At this point I really don't care. I'm letting you know I'm going to get even. You can bet on it, mark my words!"

I was so mad. How dare they do that to me; after all these years I've been here and I've always been respectful to *all* the spirits, even those murderous dirtbags! Those dowsing rods just kept spinning until I stopped talking.

CONCLUSION

When we began researching this book, we had a possible list of over fifty places in contention for the top ten spots. Since neither of us had yet visited Mackey's, we had to rely on stories from fellow investigators and the many media reports to gauge how haunted the place was. We weren't convinced. The stories seemed too fantastical to believe.

We were wrong.

When we finally made it down to Wilder in person and spoke with the many folks directly affected by the paranormal activity at the club, we were impressed by their sincerity, loyalty, bravery, knowledge, and intelligence. After having our own experiences—the shadow man in the basement, the cold hands on Theresa's shoulders, the feeling of darkness thick in the building—and witnessing the good vs. evil at work in the bar, we feel Mackey's may be the most dangerous site covered in this book.

Bobby Mackey's is not a place for the faint of heart or the armchair ghost hunter—it can be dangerous for even the most experienced investigator. People have been attacked physically, spiritually, and emotionally and been left with permanent scars.

That's not to say that no one should go there! There is a lighter, happier side to Bobby Mackey's as well. The traditional country music that is the heart of the club brings joy to thousands. Most patrons never have a paranormal encounter, only good times with good friends. Bobby Mackey himself disavows any personal experience with the paranormal at the club. And nothing particularly alarming happened to Eric during our visit.

But Theresa went looking for ghosts, and boy did she find them. She can't help but feel that the building had something to prove to her, wanted to knock her off her skeptical high horse. The spirits she encountered in the club were intelligent and acted with deliberate intent. She can't say for sure that they were "evil" or "demonic" spirits, she only knows that they *knew* her.

There are any number of different entities in Bobby Mackey's. There is residual energy from long ago, some of it good, some of it bad, that is as permanent as the foundation the building rests on, place memory that never goes away. There are intelligent spirits from many different eras interacting at least occasionally with the living, each with their own purposes and ideas of what is happening around them. There are stories that need to be told, wrongs that yearn to be righted, forgotten lives that want to be remembered.

But for all the darkness, there is at least an equal amount of light. Besides the towering focal point of Bobby Mackey himself, longtime employees such as Matt Coates and Wanda Kay haven't been scared away yet. They feel an obligation to Bobby Mackey,

Tools of the Trade

Dowsing Rods: a pair of handheld copper rods bent in an L shape used for detecting spirit energy and as a means of communication. Users ask the spirits to cross the rods in specific directions to indicate *yes* or *no* responses. When used properly, the rods move in distinct and deliberate directions, sometimes vibrating, spinning, or swaying when in the presence of a spirit. Dowsing has been a viable technique used for centuries by those looking to locate underground water wells or mineral deposits. In theory, the rods can be "programmed" by the user's intent to detect whatever is desired.

his bar, and the people who have come before—their strength is enough to keep the evil at bay, under control. The unseen forces have made them stronger, united. They are a family, and they watch out for each other and for those they welcome under their roof.

And there is always the music. But be warned, you enter at your own risk . . .

What You Need to Know Before You Go:

Bobby Mackey's Music World
44 Licking Pike, Wilder, KY 41071

Contact Information:
(859) 431-5588
(859) 291-1689
bobbymackey.com
wandakay.com

Bobby Mackey's Music World is a fully licensed nightclub featuring live music and a variety of entertainment, including pool, a game room, and Turbo the mechanical bull.

Bobby Mackey graces the stage every weekend along with a multitude of other local and national traditional country music acts. Wanda Kay leads the crowds with karaoke between sets.

Besides the traditional honky-tonk festivities, Bobby Mackey's offers several choices for the paranormal enthusiast.

Additional Reading:
Wicked They Walked by Wanda Kay Stephenson
The Exorcism of Carl Lawson by Doug Hensley

Tours:
Basement Tour: 30-minute guided tour of the basement and "the well." Every Friday and Saturday night. First tour starts at 9 P.M.
Two-Hour Paranormal Tour: Tours are given Monday through Thursday during the day when the bar is closed for business. All ages. Call for reservations and to choose a time.
Five-Hour Paranormal Investigation: By appointment only. Call Wanda Kay for available times and dates. Limit 20 people. Extra time may be purchased.

Lodging:
Country Inn Wilder, (859) 441-3707
10 Country Dr., Wilder, KY 41076
countryinns.com/wilder

Embassy Suites Cincinnati—River Center, (859) 261-8400
10 E. Rivercenter Blvd., Covington, KY 41011
hilton.com

Commonwealth Hotels, (859) 261-5522
50 E. Rivercenter Blvd. #600, Covington, KY 41011
commonwealth-hotels.com

Cincinnati Marriott at River Center, (859) 261-2900
10 W. Rivercenter Blvd., Covington, KY 41011
marriott.com

Travelodge Newport/Cincinnati Riverfront, (800) 578-7878
222 York St., Newport, KY 41071
travelodge.com

The Stanley Hotel

Estes Park, Colorado

INTRODUCTION

The Rocky Mountains are home to some of the most spectacular scenery on earth—a place of magnificent natural wonders, and supernatural wonders as well. Just outside the north entrance to Rocky Mountain National Park, the majestic neo-Georgian Stanley Hotel sits "7,500 feet above the ordinary" with stunning views in every direction, including inward.

Freelan Oscar (F. O.) Stanley was a man of wealth who had everything money could buy except good health. He made his fortune through a series of successful business ventures and inventions, including the legendary "Stanley Steamer" line of steam-powered automobiles and the Stanley Violin. Like thousands of other Americans at the turn of the century, Stanley had tuberculosis.

In 1903 his doctor suggested a visit to the Colorado mountains, where the dry fresh air would be beneficial to his delicate lungs. After staying in Denver for a month, Stanley saw no particular improvement. A friend offered the use of his cabin in Estes Park, northwest of Denver, and F. O. and his wife, Flora, immediately fell in love with the area, resolving to build a luxury resort as soon as the property could be purchased. Construction began in 1908 and the Stanley Hotel opened on July 4, 1909.

Stanley conjured up a place for his wealthy friends to relax and enjoy the therapeutic climate and stunning scenery. Among the first-class amenities Stanley offered guests were running water, indoor toilets, electricity, and telephone service—a new concept to travelers at the time. The only thing missing was heat, but that wasn't an issue as the hotel was designed to be a summer resort.

The long, arduous trip up the mountain in Stanley Steamer buses was well worth the effort to those who could afford it, and notable guests included *Titanic* survivor "Unsinkable" Molly Brown, Teddy Roosevelt, the emperor of Japan, J. C. Penney, John Phillip Sousa, Harvey Firestone, and a number of Hollywood notables.

The Stanleys spent much of their time at the resort, as it did prove to be beneficial to F. O.'s condition. He survived to be an old man of ninety-one, outliving his original bleak prognosis by decades. He took great pride in every detail and was by all accounts a genuinely warm and welcoming host. Music and merriment filled the hotel daily, making the Stanley attractive to musicians and entertainers from every corner of the country. Stanley also built an enormous state-of-the-art hydroelectric power plant nearby, which not only supplied power to his hotel but helped the surrounding area blossom as well.

Although reports of eerie happenings stretch back to its early days, the hotel's reputation for spookiness gained momentum when horror author Stephen King was inspired to write his novel *The Shining* while staying in room 217 of the near-empty Stanley, just before it closed for the winter in 1974. Today that room is said to be one of the most active on the property. The fictional setting of the book, the Overlook Hotel, bears an uncanny resemblance to the Stanley, upon which it was likely based.

Employees have reported hearing what sounds like a party, only to find the ballroom or concert hall empty upon inspection. Guests sometimes spot F. O. smiling and tipping his hat to them in the lobby as they check in for the night, and many report hearing small children run through the halls when no children are present. A dutiful housekeeper haunts the halls, still busy with her work, making guests feel welcome or unwelcome, depending on their marital status.

Violin maker F. O. loved music of all kinds, and his wife, Flora, an accomplished pianist, is known to now and then tickle the ivories of her piano, which sits in the ballroom. It's no wonder the Stanley has captured the attention of paranormal enthusiasts.

Ghost Hunters's Jason Hawes brought his team to the hotel twice, once for a live televised event, and encountered some astounding paranormal activity. While Hawes was sleeping, a glass sitting on the nightstand shattered for no apparent reason. Grant Wilson witnessed a chair "jumping" almost two feet. The two of them also recorded some noteworthy disembodied voices while investigating the employee tunnels under the hotel.

Bill Murphy of Syfy's *Fact or Faked* worked with scientists, researchers, and paranormal investigators to create a thought-provoking documentary titled *The Stanley Effect: A Piezoelectric Nightmare*. Murphy claims that a combination of the minerals found naturally in the mountains and the power plant built nearby contribute to the hauntings and unusual activity at the hotel.

The *piezoelectric effect* revolves around the notion that properties in the environment can act as a sort of amplifier of paranormal activity. Crystals are thought to direct, absorb, and multiply energy, and the mountain is full of crystals. Murphy states that "unusual properties of the ground's ability to hold and release energy" are at the core of this effect.

Whatever the causes, natural or unnatural, the "hauntingly beautiful" Stanley Hotel is as famous for its spirits as for its spectacular view. The paranormal reports keep pouring in from ghost hunters and guests alike. Several guest rooms are deemed "haunted," but no single area is immune to the supernatural. From the tunnels hidden below the main building to the bustling hotel lobby, the basement under the concert hall, and the spirited fourth floor, ghostly phenomena lurk in every neat and tidy corner.

Between the scenery, the setting, and the spirits, the Stanley Hotel is one of the most inviting places in America to hunt ghosts.

Take the Haunted Tour—The Tunnels

Among the most unusual features of the Stanley Hotel are the tunnels underneath the main building, built as protected passageways for employees' use during harsh weather. Carved right out of the mountain, the low-ceilinged tunnels are rough-hewn rock lined with pipes and electrical wires. A basic lighting system guides those who travel the eerie catacombs. Like most basements, the Stanley tunnels are the perfect setting for a spine-tingling ghost story.

Personal Experience—
LeeAnna Jonas (Paranormal Investigator,
Spirit Realm Investigative Project)

It was a cool Colorado fall in October 2010 and I was one of many attending a Darkness Radio event at the Stanley. The gathering was led by Darkness Radio host Dave Schrader, an experienced ghost hunter and *Ghost Adventures* researcher. The event featured several well-known paranormal personalities such as journalist Aaron Sagers, EVP experts Mark and Debby Constantino, and Zak Bagans from the Ghost Adventures Crew. I was surrounded by some great new friends and some familiar spirits!

After a day of informative lectures and photo ops, the guests broke off into small groups to investigate the hotel. As the evening wore on, I found myself in the dark, mysterious tunnels under the lobby. The tunnels have low ceilings, bare pipes, and loose rocks. They are creepy but not unbearable. The cavelike system has been used by staff since the early days of the hotel. I remember watching an episode of *Ghost Hunters* where Jason and Grant had an amazing encounter in the tunnels.

Aaron Sagers led a few others and me in a series of experiments using various pieces of equipment, such as digital recorders and the Ovilus. We had had no luck capturing EVPs, but the Ovilus was another story.

Aaron asked the spirits for a message, a name. "*Derrick*" was the name that popped up. Aaron asked for clarification, and again "*Derrick*" was the name on the Ovilus. Getting a name on a random word generator such as the Ovilus is nothing new, but to get one particular name over and over can be meaningful. No one recalled hearing any stories about a spirit with that name at the hotel. Sagers asked if there was a Derrick in the group, but there wasn't anyone by that name among us.

"Does anyone know anybody named Derrick?" he asked again. I bit my lip, waiting to see what would happen next.

I asked for more information, "What is your message? What are you trying to tell us?"

"*Derrick*" came up once again.

"Derrick? Is that your name?" I asked apprehensively.

"*Derrick . . . rope*," answered the Ovilus.

Aaron was puzzled, "Did it just say 'rope'?"

I felt my heart drop. I was shaking uncontrollably. "Yes, it said 'Derrick' and 'rope.'"

After that, things went hazy. I was shocked by the session, although my fellow investigators had no idea what I was going through. Finally, after much soul searching, I explained to Aaron why I was so affected by the words from the Ovilus.

In 1997, I suffered a severe tragedy, something that changed my world forever. My twelve-year-old stepson took his own life. By hanging. My stepson's name was Derrick.

This Ovilus session was the first of many attempts Derrick made to contact me. For some reason, he chose this particular day at this place to do so. Maybe he knew his message would have meaning only for me. Maybe he wanted me to be around people who would believe or appreciate what he was doing. Maybe he loved this area as much as I did and it brought back happy memories from his short life. Whatever the reason, it became a special place for the spirit of Derrick and me to connect.

I've used a variety of tools during my years of investigation, including the Ovilus and similar equipment, but never has the name of my stepson come up. Except at the Stanley Hotel. This wasn't Derrick's only attempt to communicate—another coincidence came to light a year later.

In September 2011, my team and I were on the reality competition show *Paranormal Challenge*. Our episode was filmed on the USS *Hornet*, docked in San Francisco. This was quite a way from our home in Colorado, but we were happy to have the chance to be showcased on national television. The producers had offered us a location a little closer to home, but circumstances had made that impossible, so we packed up and headed to California.

The experience was wonderful and I couldn't wait to share it with the world! The night our episode premiered, we had a big celebration, a viewing party at one of our favorite gathering spots.

A ton of guests showed up, some I knew, some I didn't. One young lady named Crystal came up and introduced herself. She was a local paranormal investigator who had participated in *Paranormal Challenge* on the Jerome, Arizona, episode.

We chatted a bit and she expressed her condolences for the loss of my son. Derrick's tragedy had come to light during filming at the *Hornet*, so now the whole world knew of my heartache. Crystal told me she had suffered through the death of her best friend, Derrick Perez, when he was only twelve. He had hanged himself. She had seen his apparition shortly after he had passed, and it was that incident that had led her to the paranormal. Needless to say, I was shocked. This was my Derrick.

It turned out that Crystal had grown up only a few miles from me, in the same area as my ex-husband, who had Derrick on the weekends when I didn't.

My head was spinning at this point. I believe Derrick had a hand in this. If things had fallen into place, my team would have filmed our episode in Jerome, where I certainly would have met my son's best childhood friend. When that didn't work out, he made sure we met at the viewing party a few months later. Even stranger, after a long conversation I discovered that Crystal had been at the same Stanley event as I in 2010! Although we hadn't met that evening, Derrick hadn't given up.

Derrick went to great lengths to connect his best friend and his stepmother, two people dear to him in life who welcomed his message of love from beyond—a message that came through loud and clear at the Stanley Hotel.

Personal Experience—
George Lopez

Like any good son, I got my parents what every couple wants for their wedding anniversary: a trip to the Stanley Hotel. My interest was, of course, in the paranormal activity at the hotel, but I knew my folks would enjoy the beauty of the place as well. It was a win-win for everyone.

It was November 2009, a spectacular time to be in the heart of the Rocky Mountains. Although it's not the most picturesque area of the Stanley, I talked my parents into exploring the tunnels under the Stanley with me.

I had just watched the live Halloween episode of *Ghost Hunters*, where Jason and Grant had captured the disembodied voice of what sounded like a little girl or young woman in the tunnels. It was creepy and astounding, and I hoped for something similar.

The tunnels are cramped, with low ceilings and sometimes narrow passageways, but not as bad as Mom and Dad had imagined. We spent some time trying to re-create the *Ghost Hunters* experience, but things were quiet. With plenty more cave to explore, we moved on, and that was when the excitement started!

The three of us were on the opposite side of the caves, behind a small shacklike structure. We wondered aloud what it might have been used for. As we talked, we were interrupted by the unmistakable sound of a little girl's laugh. I couldn't believe my ears! The ghostly giggle was identical to what Jason and Grant had heard during the *Ghost Hunters* episode.

And then another shocker. From the darkness came a disembodied "*Hello.*"

It was the same voice I'd heard on TV, the voice of a little girl. She was trying to communicate with us. My body erupted with goose bumps and an icy chill traveled down my spine. My mother froze, eyes as wide as saucers. Dad was speechless.

"*Hello?*"

"Who's there?" I asked the darkness. The response was an eerie, echoey giggle. I tore around to the other side of the tunnel, frantically trying to catch someone messing with us. We were alone.

Who is the girl with the happy laugh who hides in the shadows, amused by those who explore the caves under the Stanley? I don't know, but I hope we get the chance to meet again.

Take the Haunted Tour—The Concert Hall

The Concert Hall is a large open gathering area, set with tables and chairs ready to accommodate all but the largest groups. Sound echoes off the walls and high ceilings. A state-of-the-art sound booth sits high above the hall floor. Large open windows allow a full view of the scenery. The stage awaits musicians and performers with its high platform and thick draped curtains.

When the room is empty, its elegance and detailed craftsmanship are clearly visible. It is warm and welcoming, bright and well lit during the day. But the Concert Hall takes on a more ominous feel at night. A ghostly party carries on at all hours of the evening, dissipating when the living open the wide double doors. There is always an event happening in the Concert Hall, even when nothing is scheduled.

The connection between music and the Stanley harks back to days long before the first guests arrived at the hotel. Before successful business ventures with photographic dry plates, x-rays, steam-driven vehicles, and the hospitality industry, music was the family business. Freelan Oscar's father was a world renowned maker of fine concert violins, passing the craft down to his sons. The boys, F. O. and his twin brother, Francis Edgar, created their first miniature instruments at age ten, and their first full-sized at sixteen. The Stanley Violin was one of the most sought-after instruments of its time. Today, fewer than seventy original Stanley Violins remain in existence, making them almost as rare, if not as expensive, as Stradivarii.

F. O. and Flora Stanley retained a deep appreciation and love for music and hosted musical events of all kinds. The Concert

Hall (then called "Stanley Hall") and the more intimate Music Room were often filled with the sweet soothing sounds of orchestras, bands, and soloists. For the grand opening of the hotel in 1909, the Stanleys invited marching band superstar John Phillip Sousa to perform. Flora, a gifted pianist, bought a 1904 Steinway piano, which sat proudly in the Concert Hall and remains on display in the Music Room of the hotel today.

Guests and staff report music coming from the concert hall on a daily basis. A spectral Flora Stanley often plays her piano happily, entertaining guests and staff from the afterlife. Paranormal enthusiasts incorporate music into their investigations, often with great results.

Personal Experience—
Bill Murphy (Paranormal Investigator, Filmmaker, TV Personality)

During the filming of the documentary *The Stanley Effect: A Piezoelectric Nightmare*, my team and I had number of unexplainable experiences. During a vigil in the Concert Hall with sensitive Erika Frost, investigator Patrick Burns, investigator Jeannette Baker-Shaw, and a few other participants, we made contact with an entity that wasn't happy about us being there. Erika led the group, having us hold hands while forming a circle. We placed several devices, including a K2 meter, in the center while two cameras recorded the event.

Erika asked the spirits to communicate by lighting up the meters to indicate *yes*. We received a steady stream of responses as the K2 lit up like a Christmas tree. As we delved deeper into specifics of the vigil, strange noises echoed all around us. We heard a rush of water from no apparent source. Patrick heard an odd voice from the back, but couldn't make out what it said. We all heard a ghostly conversation and a strange moan but were unable to pinpoint the source. We were being bombarded with disembodied voices, all coming from *inside* the Concert Hall.

Erika said, "We have a few people here with us who don't want us to be here."

It was obvious we were not alone. Jeannette sensed a change in energy, and the K2 blinked wildly.

"They don't want us here; they're tired of all this. They want everybody to go!"

Erika was obviously distressed.

The atmosphere in the room changed drastically. A palpable negativity enveloped the group. Erika tried in vain to assure the spirits that they were safe within the circle and it was okay to speak with us.

"I keep hearing, '*It's not okay*,'" Erika told us.

Could she explain what wasn't okay?

"There's something about the basement of this place that's not okay. Something came from the basement up this way . . . and I feel that it's a man."

We'd all heard the stories of something in the basement, something that seemed more aggressive than other Stanley Hotel spirits. Something that liked to throw objects—sometimes large ones like tables and chairs—at visitors and staff.

With the unease intensifying, we felt it was time to end the vigil. We left the Concert Hall and followed whatever force was leading us to the basement below.

Personal Experience—
George Lopez

I attended a Darkness Radio event held at the Stanley Hotel in March 2008. The weekend was chock-full of celebrity lectures, paranormal demonstrations, ghost hunts, and charity auctions. Up for bid was an after-hours private ghost hunt with Jason

Hawes and Grant Wilson. As luck would have it, I won the opportunity! I invited five friends to join me in the haunted excursion.

We were a group of six, along with Jason and Grant, investigating the Concert Hall. On display was an old black-and-white picture of Flora Stanley, who spent many joyful hours playing piano in this room. For some strange reason, I was immediately drawn to the photograph. I felt a connection to her that I couldn't explain. It was if she *wanted* me to talk to her.

I knew this was a good place to start. I asked Flora if she'd like to communicate with me. I had my recorder and my EMF meter out and I got a few positive responses, but I needed something a bit more concrete.

"Mrs. Stanley, could you give us a sign that you're here?"

The moment I finished my question, I heard an enormous crash to the right of the stage! It sounded like someone had thrown a cafeteria chair down the stairs. Before I could turn to my companions to ask if they had heard the noise, Grant Wilson flew by me, running toward the stairs to investigate the sound, the rest of us right behind him.

We expected to find a broken chair mangled at the foot of the stairway, pieces of hardware scattered everywhere, but we found *nothing*. We were absolutely shocked. This incident got our blood pumping and chased away any sleepiness we had at this point in the evening!

Within minutes, we confirmed with Stanley management that no one had been in the area at the time. A more thorough investigation of that part of the hotel left us scratching our heads. Nothing was out of place. Nothing could account for the crash.

The timing and intensity of the mysterious crash convinced me that we were dealing with something paranormal. My intuition led me to the Concert Hall and to Flora Stanley. Although I would have preferred the soothing sounds of the ivory keys, the deafening crash was an unmistakable way to let us know we were not alone.

Personal Experience—
Frank Polievka (Paranormal Investigator, Filmmaker, AdventureMyths)

In April 2012, I made the long trek from Maryland out to the Stanley Hotel to film a documentary for AdventureMyths, a paranormal team and production company that I founded in 2006. We spent five days investigating, interviewing, and filming for our project, which we called *Shining Secrets of the Stanley Hotel*. Highlights from our amazing adventure are documented on the DVD.

During our second night at the hotel, I met a young woman named Cailey Noone who was celebrating her eighteenth birthday at the Stanley with her family. I invited them to join us for part of our investigation. Having non–team members on the hunt helps validate paranormal activity from a different perspective, plus it was a really cool gift to give Cailey for her birthday!

There were ten of us sitting at a large table in the Concert Hall: my team; Cailey and her family; and two Stanley representatives, Clay Johnson and Lisa Nyhart. I had a camera filming us as we tried to communicate using the Ovilus. We asked questions for fifteen minutes with no response. All was quiet and we were about to give up and move to another area of the hotel. Jonathan Ness stood up slowly, sort of stretching as he rose. Immediately after he got up from the table, the Ovilus spoke!

"Sit down!"

This was the only response we got from the device the entire session, and it firmly barked this order at Jonathan as if it could see what he was doing! I was ecstatic to get the response, although our novice guests were a little freaked out.

We gathered our equipment and moved downstairs to the basement of the Concert Hall, an area known as Lucy's Room.

Take the Haunted Tour—Lucy's Room

Underneath the large elegant Concert Hall of the Stanley is a small storage area with a notorious reputation known as Lucy's Room. Legend states that back in the early days of the hotel, long before central heating, a homeless woman named Lucy sneaked into this hidden area of the Stanley, seeking shelter from the harsh Colorado winter. Unfortunately, one night the cold was too much and poor Lucy froze to death inside this unheated storage room underneath the main floor.

Ghostly activity attributed to Lucy has been reported in this area for years, so much so that it has become one of the paranormal hot spots at the Stanley.

Our research and that of several others, including Adventure-Myths and Stanley management, has been unable to confirm the story of Lucy's death. But countless people have encountered her emaciated apparition and heard her sorrowful cries in the basement and the Concert Hall. Lucy appears to still be hanging around, sometimes in the Concert Hall, sometimes in the room named for her. It looks like she has found a home and she is not alone anymore.

Personal Experience—
Bill Murphy: Battle of the Psychics

After leaving the Concert Hall, we made our way down to the basement storage area known as Lucy's Room. Erika led us in another vigil, but this time the energy was different, unpleasant. Erika attempted to make contact with the entity, assuring it we meant no harm and only wanted to communicate.

Erika opened her eyes and looked up at me, glaring intently in my direction. She asked me if I was feeling okay. At the time I was, but not for long. Within seconds, I became extremely ill.

"I'm feeling sick," I told the group. I had the feeling of being smothered, like my chest was being crushed.

Jeannette became very dizzy and felt overwhelmed with sadness.

Erika received a strong message from the spirit. "We need to go; I'm getting '*GET OUT!*' I'm getting '*GET OUT!*' Let's please just acknowledge it."

Erika sensed something behind me, which is why she had asked if I was okay. She felt very strongly that the entity was something negative, that we should leave the area and leave it alone. I was having difficulty breathing and needed air, so we all quickly vacated the area.

Later, we returned to the basement with an additional sensitive, psychic Chris Fleming. Chris and Erika have similar abilities but divergent views on certain aspects of the spirit world. They also had different ideas on how to proceed. Erika wanted to stop the session and vacate the area, but Chris wanted to carry on, using the K2 to get answers. He tried to decipher the spirit's identity.

Chris, with a positive response from the blinking K2, established that the spirit was that of a child. Or at least it seemed to be.

Chris asked the entity, "Are you telling me the truth?"

Yes, was the response.

"How do you know you can trust he's telling you the truth?" Erika was very perturbed.

Chris continued. "Is there another spirit down here, a nonhuman spirit?"

Again, *yes* was the response.

As Chris continued to communicate with what he thought to

be a child and a nonhuman spirit of some sort, Erika interjected and explained her position on the entire session. She strongly believed that there were imprinted emotions from children present in the space, but not spirit children. She does not believe children can be earthbound, or "stuck," and haunt our world in spirit form.

Erika was confused and upset because Chris continued to communicate with something that claimed to be nonhuman *and* trusted it to be truthful. If it truly was a nonhuman entity, it could pretend to be the spirit of a child, or anyone else for that matter, essentially using that persona as a disguise.

Tensions rose, as did the feeling of foreboding in the room. The session continued under protest from Erika, who felt it was completely inappropriate.

"Make a believer out of me," Chris said to the entity.

"Don't say that, dude. Trust me." A concerned voice rose from the crowd.

"Show yourself! Can you manifest?" Chris pushed on.

Erika said aloud to Chris, "There is not a child here, there are imprints of children here; the emotions of the children are here. There is a man wandering this area. I swear to you."

Erika was very upset and insisted Chris stop all communications.

As the session wore on, Chris's attitude changed. He explained to the group that whatever he was communicating with was not going to tell the truth. It was a deceiver. He stopped the session.

Erika Frost and Chris Fleming discussed their different impressions of what exactly they were communicating with, comparing notes from this and the sessions each had had in the basement. Chris believed there was a female energy, child spirits, a male presence, and something else, something not human.

Erika clearly saw a male entity standing behind me and thought it was the only spirit down there. This was the same entity we had encountered upstairs, the one that had lured us into the basement.

The conversation began as a discussion on who or what was lingering in the basement and turned into a heated debate on basic concepts of the afterlife: Who or what is a spirit? Why does it chose to remain earthbound? How do you know if it's telling the truth?

Erika obviously had very different ideas about who and what haunts our world, including the idea that there are no such things as demons.

A puzzled Chris asked, "Have you ever been with a demon and—"

"They *don't* exist!" Erika quickly cut him off.

"Yes, they do."

This event illustrates the very different ideas that people, especially psychics, have on the spirit world. Is there good? Is there evil? Can children become ghosts? What are nonhuman entities? Do demons exist? And who or what, exactly, is haunting the Stanley Hotel?

Personal Experience—
Frank Polievka

The Concert Hall had lived up to its reputation and we were anxious to explore the rest of the hotel. We continued investigating downstairs in Lucy's Room. We invited Cailey—our non-team member/birthday girl—to spend some time inside the room alone, with no equipment, using only her senses as tools.

Reluctantly, she agreed.

She reported feeling very uncomfortable inside the room, as if someone were watching her from the shadows. She felt eyes boring into her soul from somewhere in the dark. Her body broke out in goose bumps, anticipating that something "bad" was going to jump out at her.

Cailey twice saw a strange mist manifest in front of her, moving out of the corner and across her path. She was terrified by this misshapen, cloudlike apparition moving erratically right in front of her eyes! Something, possibly Lucy, tried to manifest and take form inside the darkened room. This was the closest thing to a ghost the young woman had ever encountered.

Happy eighteenth birthday, Cailey!

Cailey's experience got the team charged up and ready to continue investigating. Joining us were Stanley employees Karl Pfeiffer (winner of season one, *Ghost Hunters Academy*) and Clay Johnson. We set up flashlights to play the on/off game. I was also eager to try a new tool, something I picked up just for this investigation: a singing bowl from Nepal.

The metal bowl came with a wand called a striker. The user gently encircles the rim of the bowl with the striker, creating a soothing musical sound that vibrates softly in the air. Music is often a trigger for spirits, especially at the Stanley. Spirit Lucy seems to be particularly fond of music and is known to enjoy interacting with people who incorporate it into their investigations.

I held the bowl in my outstretched hand, circling slowly and rhythmically with the striker. Karl asked Lucy to turn on the flashlight. She did. Karl asked her to turn off the flashlight. She did. Whenever the bowl was "singing," we got responses from a spirit. When we stopped, the spirit stopped as well.

We were all amazed at the consistent responses, but we didn't want to overstay our welcome. It was time to wrap up for the night, but I wanted to try one more thing. I set up a static video camera in front of the door to Lucy's room. Everyone vacated the area, but I left the camera focused on the open door. Security guards, Stanley staff, and other investigators have reported Lucy's door slamming shut on its own. If Lucy wanted us to end our investigation, she would let us know by closing the door to her room.

The next morning, I returned to Lucy's room to retrieve the camera. I noticed that the door we had left open was now completely closed. I didn't jump to conclusions just yet—anyone could have shut the door. Maybe a living person had come along and closed it.

But when I reviewed the tape some time later, I was shocked! The video showed the door slowly but firmly closing. The tape also showed that no one had come by the room while the tape was rolling. No one tampered with the tape, no one manipulated the door. Lucy shut it, in a sense closing the door on our investigation.

Take the Haunted Tour—The Second Floor

The elegance and grandeur of the Stanley Hotel begins at the front door and ascends skyward toward each of its upper floors. The cocktail lounge invites visitors to sit back, relax, mingle with old friends and make new ones along the way. If you're in the mood for a bite to eat, the Stanley has several dining options to titillate the most discriminating taste.

As you travel toward the grand stairway, magnificence beckons onward and upward toward enchanting guest suites. The wide stairway bends with gentle curved angles, wrapped in polished wood and covered in rich burgundy carpeting. The smooth white handrails stretch like open arms welcoming guests to their place of respite on the second floor. Portraits of past Stanley dignitaries adorn the walls; proud faces look off into a the distance while others keep a watchful eye on all who walk by.

ROOM 217

Room 217 is one of the most requested rooms in the hotel, and for good reason if you're into ghosts. It is often referred to as "the Stephen King room," the room in which the famous author stayed while at the resort in 1974, and where he was inspired to write *The Shining*.

Much like in the novel and film, the hotel was vacant of guests when King and his wife arrived at the end of October, just as it was shutting down for the winter. It wasn't until 1982 that heat was installed and the remodeled Stanley became a year-round resort.

King stayed in the Presidential Suite, the original 217 (which was much larger at the time), and experienced horrific nightmares there. He also reported some sort of vision while eating dinner at the hotel, and a barrage of terrifying images as he gazed into a mirror. Were these the writer's imaginative process, a trick of the mind, or spirit activity?

Regardless, the incidents inspired him to write his most successful novel, *The Shining*. Inside the room that bears his name, a collection of King novels lines a shelf, ready to set the mood for fans of the paranormal.

Today room 217 is plush with a hand-carved four-poster bed in a caramel brown wood finish, matching dressers and side tables, and a modern flat-screen television hanging on the wall. A ceramic clawfoot bathtub, an amenity not often found in modern hotels, screams elegance and luxury. Soft drapes and sheers hang gracefully from the windows, framing a spectacular view of the Rocky Mountains. It is a welcoming, comfortable room with a chilling history.

In June 1911, hotel housekeeper Elizabeth Wilson was given the task of lighting the acetylene lanterns throughout the hotel after a thunderstorm knocked out the electricity. The gas lanterns had been installed by F. O. Stanley as a backup lighting system.

The dutiful Miss Wilson carried her candle into each room, lighting each lamp along the way. When she opened the door to room 217, an explosion rocketed through the hotel, blasting

Wilson through the floor to the MacGregor Ballroom (then the dining room) below. A gas leak had filled the room with colorless, odorless acetylene, and Wilson's lit candle sparked the mighty eruption. A significant portion of the hotel was blown to bits, shrapnel from the blast scattering over a half mile of valley landscape.

Wilson was badly bruised and both of her ankles were broken, but remarkably she survived the explosion. F. O. Stanley felt responsible for his loyal employee and oversaw her care until she fully recovered and returned to work. Wilson remained an employee of the Stanley until her retirement many years later. She passed away peacefully at home in the 1950s, but many believe she returned to the hotel after death.

Her apparition appears in the room where she was almost blown to bits. Miss Wilson likes to helpfully pack or unpack suitcases, arrange shoes and toiletries neatly, and tuck visitors into bed when sleeping. She does *not* approve of bachelors staying in this or any room in the hotel. In her day, unmarried men stayed only in the Manor House, segregated from the women in the hotel proper.

Personal Experience—
Jesse Freitas (Guest Services Manager, Stanley Hotel)

As a guest services manager, I've worn many hats at the Stanley. Before my current position, I often worked the front desk. I've heard countless reports from visitors about ghostly encounters they have had during their stays. One of my favorite accounts illustrates and reinforces room 217's haunted reputation.

Early one morning I was approached by a couple who had spent the night in 217. They seemed tired, as if they hadn't slept well the night before. I asked them how their evening had been, and they responded with a question: "Is that room really haunted?"

"Yes, we believe it to be. Many of our former guests have had paranormal experiences there. Why? Did something happen to you?" I was intrigued.

The woman continued, "Well, I've heard something likes to move your belongings around and stuff like that."

"Yes, that seems to be a frequent claim."

"Well, nothing was touched. Our bags are where we left them, but we both felt something in our bed last night." She was visibly shaken as she spoke.

The gentleman added, "I swear it felt like something was between us, physically pushing us apart."

"I felt it too, like an invisible but solid barrier." Her voice cracked slightly as she spoke.

I'm not sure my response was much comfort. "Are the two of you married?"

Slightly embarrassed, they replied, "Uh . . . no, we're not."

"That explains it! It was most likely Miss Wilson, who was very proper, as was expected back in her day. She probably didn't approve of the two of you spending the night in the same building, let alone the same bed! She wanted to physically keep you apart."

I sent the tired couple on their way, hoping the sleepiness would fade but the memory of their Stanley Hotel experience would remain forever.

ROOM 230

Another room on the second floor also deserves mention, 230. During the filming of Bill Murphy's documentary *The Stanley Effect*, a guest, Chloe Engle, participating in the Darkness Radio event being held at the hotel that weekend, encountered a terrifying entity that left its mark on her for good.

During the first evening, Chloe, along with two of her companions, was investigating in the hallway outside their room. The trio noticed a strange temperature drop while conducting an EVP session. Chloe, who was crouched down on the floor with her back against the wall, suddenly felt a forceful push that knocked her off her feet sideways. Before she could fully rise and steady herself, she was pushed down again.

Word of this terrifying encounter got back to Bill Murphy, who along with psychic Chris Fleming met with Chloe on the second night. After getting details of Chloe's attack, Fleming attempted to make contact with the nasty spirit. He implored the ghost to leave Chloe alone and do no harm, and then Chloe began to feel a strange sensation on her back, as if mosquitoes were biting her.

Concerned for her safety, Fleming moved her away from the hallway and back into room 230. Things escalated quickly, and within minutes Chloe felt a sharp pain on her back. She lifted her shirt, revealing her back, which was now covered with five deep red scratches that began to bleed. Fleming pulled out a Bible and had Chloe read from Psalms 90 and 91. While she read the powerful verses out loud, she was attacked again, on a different part of her back.

Something unseen was trying to stop her from reciting the holy words. She continued reading until she no longer felt anything touching her. The powerful prayers quelled the angry spirit, at least temporarily, but Fleming warned Chloe to make sure she reread the verses before she went to sleep.

As with any haunted location, the spirits are unpredictable— a word of warning for anyone who lifts the veil on the shadowy world of the paranormal.

ROOM 237—THE ROOM THAT ISN'T THERE

The most requested rooms at the Stanley Hotel are the "haunted" ones: 401, 408, 428, 217, 418, and 1302. But there is one missing from this list, the most notorious room of all: room 237. Any fan of *The Shining* will immediately know why: room 237 is the fictional Overlook Hotel's most horrifying guest room.

Jack Torrance's shape-shifting demon lover rises from the bathtub, welcoming poor Jack in her deadly embrace. Little Danny's roaring Big Wheel zips past 237 with much trepidation as he instinctively knows something about it isn't right. The references to 237 and its supernatural fright fest abound. Some hit you right in the face, but some are subtle and almost go unnoticed. Almost.

Rodney Ascher has noticed, as have a number of conspiracy theorists. Ascher directed the 2012 documentary *Room 237*, which presents various theories as to what the director of *The Shining*, Stanley Kubrick, was trying to say in the film. According to one of the theories presented in the film, Kubrick was involved with NASA in faking the Apollo 11 moon landing, directing the "hoax footage" broadcast around the world in 1969. Kubrick's guilt over this fraud perpetrated on the American people compelled him to "confess" through a series of symbols and hidden messages throughout *The Shining*. Every time the script deviated from author Stephen King's original story, some sort of visual clue arose onscreen, as the theory goes.

Wild theories and repetitive patterns (such as parallel lines thought to represent the number 11 as in Apollo 11) are everywhere in the film, according to the true believers presented in *Room 237*. Kubrick's guilt is expressed through his characters Jack and Danny, who each represent a different side of him, split in two by his conflicted psyche. Sometimes Kubrick is Jack, sometimes he is Danny. Sometimes he is the Apollo mission, the rocket that never made it to the moon. Once you accept the idea that Kubrick could have hoaxed the moon landing, the pieces of the puzzle fall into place.

And it doesn't stop there—several other juicy conspiracies are revealed throughout the film. *Room 237* also references the

Holocaust, the slaughter of Native Americans, and, less disturbing but just as weird, the fairy tale *Hansel and Gretel*. It's a dizzying array of theories dumped in a big bucket of crazy.

Room 237 isn't the first or the only film to point out such "obvious" messages: the documentary *The Shining Code* does much the same thing, zeroing in on many of the same symbols. The theories are outrageous—interesting, fascinating even—but outrageous. What drives the theories is nothing but matrixing, also known as *pareidolia*: the mind finds patterns that aren't there. It's the brain's way of making sense out of chaos. But it's a parlor trick, a head game. Try it. Next time you watch the film, look for your own personal codes. You'll find them too, just like you'll find "structures" on the moon or Mars if you look at enough photographs and squint your eyes, or the face of the Virgin Mary in shower mold or piecrust.

The Shining took moviegoers on a psychological thrill ride through madness, pulling them deeper and deeper into the dark abyss of the human mind gone awry. Kubrick's other masterpieces include *Dr. Strangelove*, *2001: A Space Odyssey*, *A Clockwork Orange*, and *Full Metal Jacket*. His cinematic genius is unquestionable, and Kubrick, who passed away in 1999, should remain personally unsullied by such conspiratorial lunacy.

Maybe room 237 *should* be on the Stanley Hotel's room list. Would the ghost of Stanley Kubrick come back to address these allegations? Now *that* would be a room worth renting.

Take the Haunted Tour—The Third Floor:
Age Can Be a Delicate Topic

No place is safe from the ghosts that roam this exquisite Estes Park retreat, not even the "quieter" third floor. Guests who prefer not to pay a premium for one of the "most haunted" rooms may be quite pleased with the activity elsewhere. Guest services manager Jesse Freitas is familiar with every guest suite and believes they are all "paranormally charged."

As recorded in Bill Murphy's *The Stanley Effect*, hotel guests Char Quinn and her two daughters, Matty and Abby, recorded some remarkable EVPs while staying in room 336.

The clarity and personal connection within the recordings is alarming. During the conversation Matty said, "We really like talking to you." A childlike voice answered with a clear but breathy whisper, "*I . . . like . . . Abby.*"

This EVP was the first ever captured by the trio, and it chilled them to the bone. As excited as they were to capture the remarkable evidence, the reality of speaking with the dead terrified them. Further communication with the spirit revealed more disturbing information. The ghost was a five-year-old boy born in 1954. He believed the year was 2005.

Murphy joined the girls in a subsequent EVP session in room 336. Along with the audio recorders, he placed a series of EMF meters on the bed. He asked the girls to reestablish contact with the spirit of the little boy. They asked a few more questions, and then Murphy joined in.

"If you could tell us your age . . ."

He was cut off immediately by the frightened girls. "No, no, we know, seriously we refuse to ask him that!" Abby and Matty said in unison.

Puzzled, Murphy asked, "Why 'no' on the age?"

The girls answered, "He gets mad. We've asked him that too many times already!"

They were adamant about this. And rightly so. On playback, the recorder picked up several more EVPs. After Murphy asked the spirit's age, an angry and forceful voice said, "*NO!*"

Some other responses picked up included a plea for "*Help,*" and a statement that the spirit was "*Right here, right now.*"

The camera went out of focus on one occasion and the K2 meter continually blinked in response to their questioning. Char, Abby, and Matty experienced activity that most paranormal researchers only dream about, and it happened on their first time out.

Take the Haunted Tour—The Fourth Floor

The top floor of the Stanley originally was an attic, but early on it was converted to living quarters for female employees of the hotel and the nannies of wealthy guests. The rooms were small but comfortable. The hallways were an indoor playground during bad weather for rambunctious children. While their parents socialized downstairs, the kids played happily on the fourth floor.

Today the fourth floor is bustling with activity. Guests often request one of the haunted rooms, paying a premium for the privilege, and seldom are they disappointed. The sounds of giggling ghostly children running up and down the corridors is a common report. Guests sometimes leave offerings of candy for the spirit children, enticing them to interact.

Tour guide and four-year Stanley veteran "Scary Mary" demonstrates this phenomenon by placing small lollipops, Dum Dums, in someone's hand and asking the spirit children to take the candy. They oblige by manipulating the candy, turning the sucker over as if attempting to open it. Guest services manager Jesse Freitas has witnessed this several times, adding that it is such an amazing sight, it sometimes freaks guests out a little too much. Scary Mary's bond with the spirit children on the fourth floor is incredibly strong, and they obviously feel comfortable enough that they don't mind "performing" for her. Or maybe they just really want some candy.

Personal Experience—
Scott Felger (Paranormal Enthusiast)

I'm an avid paranormal enthusiast from Youngstown, Ohio, and the Stanley Hotel has been on my radar for many years. Unfortunately, my wife, Allison, does *not* share my passion! She's a believer, but likes to believe from a safe distance. Somehow, I talked her into taking a trip to Estes Park and the haunted Stanley.

It was late September 2012 and the snowcaps were just beginning to form on top of the mountains. The view was breathtaking, more beautiful than I'd imagined. The summer heat was giving way to an autumn coolness. It put me in the mood to find out if the legends of the ghostly happenings were true.

The inside of the hotel was equally impressive, with its grand staircase and elegant décor. We were offered room 1302 in the Manor House, the one where Grant Wilson had such an amazing experience on *Ghost Hunters*, but I couldn't put Allison through that. It meant the world to me that she had agreed to stay the night at the Stanley. True love wins again!

We ended up in room 409, which is situated on the very haunted fourth floor of the main building. Some of the claims coming from this floor include the sounds of children laughing and running in the hallways. I couldn't help but hope we would experience something similar during our two-night stay.

The hotel's guided ghost tours were all sold out, which left me disappointed and my wife relieved. Fortunately, the spirits of the Stanley are not confined to stops on the tour. After settling in to our room, we decided to head downstairs to the restaurant for a nice romantic dinner. There are two sets of stairs that lead down from the fourth floor. I wanted to use the smaller one, which I believed to be the servants' stairwell, at the other end of the hall from our room.

Allison and I walked leisurely in that direction, passing several guest rooms along the way. As we passed one particular room we heard an odd sound. I stopped and looked at my wife, who seemed puzzled as well. We heard it again, the unmistakable sound of a door handle jiggling. I assumed someone was about to exit the room, but the door never opened.

Once again, we heard the jiggling of the metal handle. I couldn't take my eyes off it as it rapidly *click-click*ed up and down.

I put my ear up to the door but heard nothing from the other side. What was making the lever-type handle move? I looked through the tiny sliver of an opening under the door, trying to catch lights or shadows from inside. Nothing. I tried to re-create the handle movement by walking back and forth in front of the room, but that had no effect at all.

My poor wife was a little freaked at this point, her eyes like saucers. Such a small movement, but it gave her quite a scare! She pulled me away from the room before some ghoulish phantasm could jump out at us. Later, we asked the front desk if anyone was staying in that room. They assured us it was unoccupied, at least by any living guests.

ROOM 401—LORD DUNRAVEN'S ROOM

Lord Dunraven, Windham Thomas Wyndham-Quin, the fourth Earl of Dunraven, an Irish journalist, landowner, entrepreneur, sportsman, politician, and aristocrat, was once the largest landowner in the Estes Park area, after claiming fifteen thousand acres via the Homestead Act.

When F. O. Stanley bought 106.4 acres of the land from Dunraven, Stanley intended to name his new hotel after him. But the locals were very resentful of Dunraven, who was not an American citizen, which prevented him from legally homesteading. A cunning man, Dunraven had found ways around those pesky laws, persuading others to homestead for him, paying them only a tiny percentage of what the land was worth. Increasingly unpopular and besieged with litigation, Dunraven was run out of town, and Stanley was compelled to name the hotel after himself instead.

Although Dunraven engaged in shady practices, his story is an important part of Stanley history. A very special room bears his name. The room is similar to others on the floor: large comfortable bed, soft upholstered chair, cream-colored walls, tasteful bathroom fixtures, and the spacious closet has plenty of room for belongings. Just be careful of the door: It tends to open and shut on its own.

Of all the rooms on the fourth floor of the Stanley Hotel, room 401 seems to be the most haunted. After the first TAPS investigation, the team decided to stay the night, each member taking a different room. Jason took room 401. It was clean and roomy and had a great reputation for paranormal happenings.

Jason settled in, IR camera rolling so he wouldn't miss anything while asleep. During the night while he slept, the camera caught the closet door moving. It opened just slightly before closing *and* latching on its return!

The sound of the closet door closing woke Jason, and he was even more startled to find that the drinking glass sitting on the nightstand next to his bed had cracked apart. Upon closer examination, Jason noted that it looked as if it had broken from the inside.

What could have caused such a violent outburst from the other side? Was there an angry spirit in the room with him, or was something trying to prevent him from getting a good night's sleep? Luckily, both incidents were caught on tape and aired on the season two episode of *Ghost Hunters*.

Maybe Lord Dunraven's spirit has returned to Estes Park to reclaim what was once his, starting with the room that bears his name.

Personal Experience—
LeeAnna Jonas

In October 2011, I was with one of my girlfriends, Wanda, who is a metaphysical Wiccan, for a weekend at the Stanley Hotel. We met a couple of other gals, Michelle and Stacey, and planned to investigate together later on that night. Toward the end of the evening, our new friends approached us asking for help with a paranormal problem they'd run into. After spending time in room 401, Lord Dunraven's room, Michelle felt as if she were under some sort of spiritual attack.

While doing an EVP session she felt a flood of anger overtake her. It was as if she'd been bombarded with negative energy. She'd almost started a fight for no reason, and she wanted the key so she could go back to her room. Michelle was not a high-tempered or violent person, so this feeling really scared her.

The women left room 401, but something followed them back to their own room. Michelle was not herself. She felt an oppressive presence overtake her physically and mentally. They said the room was unusually cold, and no matter what they did they couldn't get it warm. It was an unpleasant and disturbing night. The situation had become unbearable—they needed it to stop.

They hoped Wanda and I could help. As a Wiccan healer, Wanda was experienced with that sort of thing. I was well versed in cleansings as well. The four of us returned to room 401 to confront whatever malevolent force was messing with Michelle.

I could tell something was different. The air was stagnant, stale, as if we were in a vacuum or something. Room 401, like all the rooms at the hotel, is beautiful—there is nothing inherently scary or creepy about it at all. But at this moment it felt dead. We sat in a circle on the floor and tried to make contact with this thing, to implore it to release our friend from the negative bond. Was Lord Dunraven's spirit responsible for this, or was it one of the female entities that he's associated with? What-ever it was, it was *not* happy.

We held hands and did a basic cleansing ritual, during which I almost leaped out of my skin as the negative force jumped from Michelle to me! A wave of emotion washed over me, starting from the top of my head then shooting down through my ex-tremities like an electric shock. My hair stood up on end and my heart was beating so hard it felt like it would burst out of my chest. My face felt flushed, my body on fire.

Suddenly I was very angry, filled with hate. I tried to fight it, but it was powerful and extremely frightening. I yelled out loud, "Don't you dare! You're *not* gonna do this! Leave me alone!"

Wanda immediately approached, trying to get this thing off me. Just as I started to feel like myself again, the entity jumped *again*. As Wanda cleansed me, Stacey started crying, just bawling uncontrollably like a baby. Before Wanda could deal with her fully, this thing jumped back to me! I started sobbing and weep-ing just as Stacey stopped!

The four of us witnessed this bizarre phenomenon as the entity jumped from Michelle, to me, to Stacey, back to me, and around again! All of us felt the same extreme personality change and flood of emotion.

Wanda finally seemed to get everyone more or less back to normal, and we decided we'd had enough of Lord Dunraven's room. The four of us went downstairs to the lobby and took a seat in the restaurant. We gathered ourselves, still shaken by what had happened.

All of a sudden, Stacey stood up and slowly walked away. The look on her face was blank, as if she were in a trance. She didn't say anything. We called to her, but she didn't seem to hear us. We got her to sit back down and asked her what she was doing. She didn't answer; instead she got back up and rambled off again! She walked into the courtyard; Wanda went after her. Wanda got her to snap back to reality, finally, and asked her what the heck was going on. Stacey started crying; she was visibly upset, trembling and weeping.

"I don't know what's wrong with me! I don't feel like myself!"

"You picked it back up, Stacey; it transferred from LeeAnna back to you again."

Wanda sat down with her, trying to calm her down and cleanse her the best she could. Stacey seemed a little better, although not fully herself for the rest of the weekend. And poor Stacey's ordeal didn't end after she left the Stanley. Months afterward, she called me in a terrible state. Since that night she had been constantly ill, back and forth to the doctors, but they couldn't figure out what was making her so sick. She was miserable.

"LeeAnna, something followed me home and I can't get rid of it." The anguish in her voice was undeniable.

She continued, "I think it's the spirit of a woman or maybe a little girl. It's been with me since the Stanley. It stopped being mean to me, but I know that's what's making me so sick."

"I'll get you in contact with Wanda. She can help you get rid of this attachment for good . . . hopefully." I felt so sorry for her. She was at the end of her rope.

After that, I didn't hear back from Stacey, and unfortunately I don't think she ever sought the help she needed. Last I heard she was still dealing with this. It's very sad, and very rare for something like this to happen. I'm not sure why the spirit chose Stacey and why it wouldn't let go. I know that I never felt anything take hold of me like that spirit did that night. I hope I never do again. I felt powerless, not in control of myself. I felt someone else's emotions, and it was awful.

That was the only truly negative experience I've had at the Stanley. I don't believe the ghosts there are evil, but I do think they might be aggravated. The constant ghost hunts and paranormal teams that come, asking for the spirits to come out and talk, must be annoying to them. I think they want to find peace, a peace they had in their living days at the gorgeous Stanley.

Personal Experience—
George Lopez

Over the last four or five years I've made many trips to the Stanley Hotel. I have never been disappointed—the paranormal literally radiates from that place.

On this particular trip in 2010, my girlfriend and I were lucky enough to have access to many of the reported hot spots of the hotel. I had built up a good rapport with management because of my work with Jason Hawes, Grant Wilson, and the crew of Darkness Radio. I had a set of keys that unlocked the most active areas of the hotel, including room 401.

The fourth floor has a spooky vibe to it. Phantom children creep me out. I wasn't sure I was ready to run into any ghostly rug rats. We took room 401 by storm, stepping out from the hallway into the darkened room. We were standing by the bed, perfectly still, letting our eyes adjust to the cumbersome darkness. Something was "off" in this room—the hair on the back of my neck stood at attention.

Suddenly, out of the corner of my eye I saw a shadow dart across the floor. It was fast, a blur. I couldn't make out any detail. And then it happened again, this time moving in another direction. At first I thought my eyes must be playing tricks on me. This *couldn't* be happening. But my girlfriend saw it as well; I looked at her and saw she was looking in the same place my attention had previously been drawn.

This activity continued and seemed to pick up strength with each pass. Even more unsettling, the shadows would at times slow down and appear to be crawling around the perimeter of the bed. Back and forth, under the bed, and then out the other side. I would have been terrified if I hadn't been so mesmerized!

In a matter of about ten minutes, we witnessed many more of these strange shadow anomalies. Crawling masses of concentrated darkness moving all around us as if we were being herded! My girlfriend suddenly jumped, letting out a little noise. Before I could ask her what was wrong, something brushed by my legs, something with structure and intent. Not only could we see these phantom shadows, now we could feel them too!

That was enough for us—we made a hasty exit out the door.

Personal Experience—
Jonathan Ness (Paranormal Investigator, Filmmaker, AdventureMyths)

While shooting the AdventureMyths documentary *Shining Secrets of the Stanley Hotel*, my partner, Frank Polievka, and I had some amazing experiences, some of them caught on camera. Although I consider myself fortunate to have been able to document this evidence, the camera can't quite capture how truly intense and profound these experiences were.

The AdventureMyths team was able to spend a good deal of time in the "most haunted" rooms, including room 401. While we slept, we kept static cameras rolling, just in case. Our cameras picked up all sorts of strange noises, including the sounds of children laughing and running down the hall. Of course, I cannot be sure those sounds were paranormal—there were other people (although very few) staying in the hotel that weekend. As a responsible paranormal investigator, I have to disregard those sounds because they could have been made by real living people.

The team and I set up in room 401, Lord Dunraven's room. We were told that whenever someone was inside the closet, the door would mysteriously close. This happened more frequently with women than with men. I wanted to test this theory for myself. After a close examination of the closet door, I was convinced that it would not close without physical force manipulating it. There was no swing to it and the latch mechanism worked perfectly—no defect in the door would make this phenomenon occur.

I asked Victoria "Vikki" Rickett, the only female present at the time, to sit inside the closet while we tried an EVP session. She apprehensively took a position inside the dark, cramped closet. The entire room was pitch black; the only light was the eerie greenish glow from my camera. I had a good shot set up in the viewfinder. I could see Vikki inside the closet and a nice portion of the area around her.

All of a sudden, I saw a small white mistlike form come in from the right side of the frame. It was oddly shaped, almost like a large outstretched hand. It appeared to manifest instantly out of nowhere and shoot across the room toward the door of the closet.

Then, to my amazement, it slowed down, changed directions, and moved downward out of frame. I had never seen anything like this before; it was like a phantom arm reaching out, trying unsuccessfully to grab something and then pulling away.

I tried several times to debunk this; maybe it was a feather from one of the down pillows, or dust, or some other weird light source that created the effect. Nothing I did to re-create the anomaly even came close.

Tragically, the original footage was lost when an unfortunate mishap destroyed the camera. Luckily, Frank had rerecorded it with another video camera almost immediately in order to show our friends on staff at the hotel. We would have lost not only an expensive piece of equipment but some of the best visual evidence ever captured at the Stanley as well. The camera could be replaced, but the experience could not.

Taking another one for the team, Vikki spent the night in room 401 that evening. She focused a static camera on the closet door. Although no other anomaly was captured on the camera, the audio confirmed that she was not alone.

In the middle of the night, the disembodied voice of a small child called out mournfully, "*Vikki?*"

ROOM 428

Next on the list of haunted rooms is room 428, larger than the other rooms on the fourth floor and in a different configuration. It has a big comfortable bed and matching furnishings, including a small table for two that sits by the window. A corner cabinet holds a flat-screen television, and ceiling fan blades turn gently, offering a soft breeze instead of air-conditioning.

The terrifying sounds of boots striking the roof outside have kept overnight visitors wide awake, especially those who know that the roof above them is slanted and no living soul could walk there without climbing equipment.

Scarier still is the apparition of a cowboy, out of place and unwelcome, keeping guests cowering under the bedsheets until daylight mercifully streams through the window. No one is quite sure who this cowboy is or why he favors room 428, but numerous guests have encountered him there. They describe him the same way: a tall, dark silhouette with broad shoulders, wearing a wide-brimmed cowboy hat, which he tips as if to say hello.

His face is unclear, his features hidden in the darkness. He appears at the foot of the bed, occasionally walking around toward the headboard before vanishing into thin air. Several guests have also seen him pacing methodically back and forth at the foot of the bed before dematerializing, vanishing as he walks through the closed door.

ROOMS 407 AND 418

Two other rooms on the fourth floor are considered highly active: rooms 407 and 418. The layouts of each room are almost identical: huge beds, rich wood furnishings, clean lines and simple elegance. Besides the ghost children parading up and down the hallways at all hours, there is plenty of action inside the rooms, including subtle but unsettling things such as the alarm clock going off at random hours. The time on the clocks often changes as well. So often do guests report this that management recommends using their wake-up service instead of relying on the clock.

Another common occurrence in rooms 407 and 418: The televisions tend to turn off and on by themselves. Skeptics argue that the timer must be responsible, or the remote is somehow triggered, but even replacing the television didn't seem to fix the issue.

Manager Jesse Freitas has stayed in each room on several occasions and experienced this phenomenon himself. He has studied the timers and examined the TVs carefully, searching for a logical explanation to the problem, but has found nothing that could account for them turning on and off by themselves. Notably, on each occasion the television has turned on at exactly 3:07 A.M., "the Devil's hour." The 3 A.M. timeslot is thought to mock the Holy Trinity, taken to be the exact opposite time of the death of Jesus on the cross (3 P.M.). That midpoint, the darkest hour of the night, is thought to be the most active for ghosts and spirits.

Jesse has experienced this same phenomenon in room 311, which is not even on the hotel's haunted room list. *Any* room at the Stanley can be a haunted room.

Jesse believes it is the spirit children who like to play with the clocks and the televisions throughout the hotel. They are fascinated with our modern technology and, like most children, like to push buttons and play tricks. One particular spirit, named Matthew, is often blamed for the mischief. Matthew likes to follow Scary Mary around during her tours, probably because she brings candy.

Matthew seems to be the dominant spirit on the fourth floor, but he is not alone. Another spirit, possibly of one of the nannies, make her rounds in room 407, room 418, and all the guest rooms on the fourth floor. Guests, especially children, often report the sensation of being "tucked in" at night by unseen hands. Freshly made beds suddenly appear to have a handprint on the comforter. Unmade beds are suddenly made, long before housekeeping makes it to the room. Helpful, yes, but unsettling. At least the extra help isn't on the payroll.

During the filming of *The Stanley Effect*, Bill Murphy and his crew investigated room 418. Hypnotist Russ Clarke joined them. Investigator Syd Schultz and Murphy noticed a very strange and extremely high electromagnetic field emanating from Clarke. The cell sensor and other devices registered readings well over the 5 milligauss the human body normally produces.

Lights blinked in rapid succession and the meter buzzed steadily as Murphy traced the magnetic field around Clarke's body. As the readings climbed, Clarke became dizzy and fell to the floor as if he'd been hit by a stun gun! Schultz and Murphy had to lay him against the wall, unconscious.

The crew could find no explanation for this event. Readings in the area surrounding the fallen man were well within the normal range. Somehow, Clarke had become a conduit of energy, which knocked him for a loop, rendering him helpless. Skeptics claimed that the walls or light fixtures caused this massive surge in the magnetic field, but those who witnessed the event disagree. Something powerful was at work, something paranormal.

Take the Haunted Tour—The Lodge

Next to the main building of the hotel is a smaller, yet nearly identical one, the forty-room Lodge. The Lodge was completed shortly after the main hotel, in 1910. Once referred to as the

Manor House, the Lodge was used for housing unmarried bachelors during the Stanley's early years. The idea was to segregate the women, married or unmarried, from the single men, "proper etiquette" for the time.

F. O. wanted the Manor House to be as comfortable and luxurious as the main building, and he spared no expense in making it so. Besides all the trimmings the main hotel offered, it also featured a game room, smoking lounge, and bar. The Manor House was a clubhouse for privileged young men who enjoyed all the luxuries the hotel had to offer.

As the years went by, the Manor House was used less frequently, eventually falling away from its former magnificence. Recently, an extensive renovation restored the building to its original charm and glory. And the Lodge has its own paranormal tales to tell.

ROOM 1302

Room 1302 is nicknamed the "Bachelor Pad" because of the many reports of partylike sounds coming from the room, even when it is vacant. Male voices conversing happily echo out into the hallway, sometimes deep into the night. Women who stay in this room often report the sensation of being watched through the darkness. Interestingly, if there are ghostly gentlemen residing in room 1302, they respectfully keep their hands to themselves.

Room 1302 garnered its reputation and secured its place on the hotel's most-haunted-room list after a televised incident on *Ghost Hunters* (season two, episode twenty-two). Grant Wilson, investigating with Dave Tango and Lisa Dowaliby, entered room 1302 and immediately sensed something different about the room. They decided to stay and investigate further. Lisa and Dave were situated across the room from Grant, who was sitting at a small round table next to the tripod in order to change the tape on the mini-DV camera.

As usual, Grant was accompanied by cameraman Kendall Whelpton. Grant asked Kendall to use the light from his LCD screen to illuminate the camera, as it was completely dark inside the room. Tango started an EVP session, asking any spirits present to give them a sign.

As if on cue, the table and chair "jumped" under their own power.

Kendall yelped and jumped back.

Grant sat frozen at the table, bewildered. His hands shook visibly.

Tango, who could hear but not see what was happening, asked what was up.

Grant, almost at a loss for words, tried to verbalize what had just happened. Kendall, usually behind the camera, was now part of the story, having reacted so strongly to the bizarre event.

Luckily, the incident was captured by both the crew's camera and the TAPS camera. Before-and-after camera shots clearly showed that the table moved as well as the chair, making it impossible for Grant's leg to have caused the jump.

Kendall explained that out of nowhere, the table and chair had lifted up forcefully. He had never seen anything like it and couldn't explain it.

Grant and the team tried to find a natural answer for the moving furniture but were left with no concrete answers. They

---

Tools of the Trade

Cell Sensor: an EMF meter designed specifically for ghost hunting that can also detect electromagnetism given off by cell phones and other similar devices and thereby eliminate them as energy sources.

felt very strongly that it was indeed paranormal. The episode was one of the most intently scrutinized of season two, and enticed many curious visitors to come to the Stanley and discover for themselves the secrets of room 1302.

CONCLUSION

There are haunted hotels, and there are *really* haunted hotels. The Stanley is among the latter. It is really, really haunted. Really. There has always been something special about this place. It seems to have a magical effect on people, including F. O. Stanley, who built the hotel. Diagnosed with tuberculosis, he thought the fresh mountain air would do him good, and he was right. Stanley lived to the ripe old age of ninety-one.

Stephen King reintroduced the world to this beautiful mountain resort with his novel *The Shining* in 1977, and Kubrick's subsequent movie version in 1980, though not filmed at the Stanley, brought even more attention. (King supervised a television adaptation of his novel in 1997, which *was* filmed at the Stanley.) The public was horrified and mesmerized at the same time. Behind the psychotic madness and terrifying phantoms of the story's fictional Overlook Hotel was a majestic and beautiful setting: the Stanley.

As people flocked to the Estes Park getaway, reports of ghostly activity escalated and have continued unabated. What exactly is happening at the Stanley and why?

The Piezoelectric Effect
When some materials, like crystals, vibrate or are put under pressure, an electric charge is generated; in some cases the reaction also creates visible light, such as when you bite into a Wint-O-Green Life Saver. Known as the piezoelectric effect, this phenomenon has a fascinating application to paranormal theory.

The energy created can draw, amplify, and perhaps even generate paranormal activity. The flip side of the effect is that steady electrical energy causes uniform vibration within the materials, and that vibration may store energy, such as emotional energy, leaving an imprint of the past that can be released and replayed like a motion picture.

When Stanley broke ground to build his hotel, he literally had to carve it out of the mountain. Considered a "free-floating building," the Stanley shifts and moves with the mountain. The Stanley Hotel sits on this superconductive, supercharged natural battery.

Bill Murphy has studied this phenomenon in depth and concluded that the Stanley is, in fact, *A Piezoelectric Nightmare.*

Bill is not alone in his beliefs. Dr. Simeon Hein studies "subtle energy sciences," including remote viewing and instrumental transcommunication (ITC). He explains the piezoelectric effect in reference to crystal theory. Unique properties of crystals—orderly latticelike structures in a repeating pattern that grow outward—make them "superconductive" when energy moves through them. It is this superconductivity that contributes to their connection in paranormal phenomenon, in Hein's view.

Nobel Prize–winning physicist Dr. Brian Josephson, who discovered superconductivity, also believes this phenomenon is responsible for paranormal activity and psychic functioning. Josephson was chastised by his peers for this statement, but he believes it can explain much of what we consider paranormal. Kudos to Dr. Josephson for not being afraid to straddle the great divide between science and the paranormal.

The Stanley unabashedly capitalizes on its paranormal appeal. Historic tours run several times a day, every day, and the hotel has its very own in-house paranormal team that takes the public on guided paranormal investigations several times a week, fifty-two weeks a year. Major public paranormal gatherings, such as the popular Darkness Radio events, are held regularly.

The Stanley Hotel is the perfect mix of majesty and mystery. Whether you're into history or hauntings, the wildlife or the afterlife, the Stanley has something for everybody. It welcomes visitors from all over the world, inviting them to discover for themselves the beauty of the Rocky Mountains and the shining secrets of America's most haunted hotel.

What You Need to Know Before You Go:

The Stanley Hotel
333 Wonderview Ave., Estes Park, CO 80517

Contact Information:
(800) 976-1377, (970) 586-3371
stanleyhotel.com
info@stanleyhotel.com

The Stanley Hotel is a historic travel destination near Rocky Mountain National Park in Estes Park, Colorado, about an hour from Denver. The Stanley operates as a lodging and event facility, but non–hotel guests are welcome to come and enjoy any of the daily tours, nightly ghost hunts, and seasonal activities. The hotel has a museum, a gift shop, and its very own in-house psychic! The Cascades restaurant, the Lodge Table, and the Whiskey Bar are open to the public, and the Sunday brunch is a five-star dining experience. The Riverspointe Spa provides the ultimate in relaxation and luxury.

Tours:
Please contact the tour office for more details on times, dates, and availability. Ask for veteran Stanley tour guide "Scary Mary" for the ultimate haunted experience. Lisa Nyhart and Karl Pfeiffer

are the Stanley ghost hunters-in-residence and can usually be found at the hotel for weekend paranormal investigations.

The Stanley History Experience: A 45-minute tour of the Archive room with time at the end to browse.

The Stanley Tour (Ghost and History Tour): A 90-minute walking tour.

Night Ghost Tour: A 2-hour tour. No children under 10 are permitted on the ghost tour.

Ghost Stories: Family friendly. All ages welcome.

Paranormal Investigations: A 5-hour ghost hunt. Ages 18 and over only.

Private Tours: Sunday through Thursday for the Stanley Tour only. Call the tour office for details at (970) 577-4111.

Fire Engine Tours: A break from the ordinary!

There are several tour opportunities at the Stanley Hotel; some run several times daily, others on nights and/or weekends. These tours sell out quickly, so please call ahead for details, times, and reservations.

Other seasonal events offered include the **Murder Mystery Dinner** and **The Shining "Masquerade" Ball**. Activities of interest in and around the Stanley include **The Butterfly Encounter at the Cascade Garden, The Stanley Sculpture Garden,** and **Rocky Mountain National Park** recreation such as hiking, fishing, biking, golfing, snowshoeing, and cross-country skiing. Please check the website for all the upcoming events.

Lodging:

The **Stanley Hotel** features a range of historic and spacious guest rooms and suites to suit every taste and need. The main hotel offers four floors of guest rooms, including many of the popular historic and "haunted" rooms. Besides the main building, guests can stay at **the Lodge, the Presidential Cottage,** and any of the one-, two-, or three-bedroom **Overlook Condos.**

Please contact the reservation desk for options, rates, and availability. Haunted rooms are offered at a premium rate and sell out quickly.

The Stanley Hotel is located in the beautiful Rocky Mountain National Park area, which offers a full range of outdoor activities and lodging options, including cabins, camping, and traditional hotels and inns. Check out the Visitors Bureau website at visitestespark.com for more information.

Comfort Inn, (970) 586-2358
1450 Big Thompson Ave., Estes Park, CO 80517
estescomfortinn.com

Hotel Estes, (970) 586-3382, (800) 798-2130
1240 Big Thompson Ave., Estes Park, CO 80517
hotelestes.com

Best Western Plus Silver Saddle, (970) 586-4476, (800) 528-1234
1260 Big Thompson Ave., Estes Park, CO 80517
bestwestern.com

Pine Haven Resort, (970) 586-3184, (800) 586-3184
1580 Fall River Rd., Estes Park, CO 80517
estesparkcabins.com

Lemp Mansion

St. Louis, Missouri

INTRODUCTION

The saga of the German immigrant Lemp family is an all-American tale of hard work and innovation, fabulous success, lavish opulence, and recurring, often self-inflicted tragedy, making it one of the most haunting in American history.

Johann "Adam" Lemp emigrated from Eschwege, Germany, in 1836. He settled in the American heartland of St. Louis among a burgeoning German population on the south side of town, and in 1838 he opened a small grocery store that sold a variety of goods, including homemade vinegar and beer. Utilizing brewing skills learned as a young man in the old country, he crafted German lager, a light and effervescent departure from the heavier English ales and porters popular in the United States at the time.

Lemp's discovery of a nearby limestone cave helped propel him from corner grocer to brewing mogul in a few short years. When stocked with ice chopped from the nearby Mississippi

River, the cave provided a refrigerated environment ideally suited for fermenting and storing his product.

Upon his death in 1862, Adam Lemp passed down the thriving Western Brewery to his son William Lemp Sr. To improve efficiency, William, an acute and innovative businessman, built a modern new brewery and bottling plant, which ultimately grew to five city blocks, directly above the caves.

In 1876, William and his wife, Julia, inherited an impressive Italianate-style home from her father, Jacob Feickert, conveniently located a block from the brewery, which the Lemps lavishly remodeled into a thirty-three-room Victorian showpiece, complete with a subterranean tunnel between the brewery and the mansion. Among other mansion attributes were three room-sized, walk-in vaults where the family locked up their paintings, jewelry, and other valuables when they traveled.

After installing the first artificial refrigeration system in a U.S. brewery in 1878, Lemp began converting the caves to other uses, including a private auditorium and theater, which could be reached from the basement of the mansion.

The Lemp family fortune grew along with the popularity of their beers. By 1895 the brewery employed seven hundred people, making it the eighth largest in the country. Their beer was shipped from coast to coast via its own Western Cable Railway Company.

William Sr. and Julia raised eight children (a ninth died at birth) in a majestic lifestyle befitting local royalty. William's fourth and "favorite" son, Frederick, was groomed to lead the business into the next century in conjunction with three older brothers, all trained in the art and business of brewing. But the hardworking Frederick's health took a turn for the worse, and in 1901, after what seemed to be an encouraging upswing in his condition, the twenty-eight-year-old died suddenly of heart failure.

William was devastated. His demeanor changed drastically;

he withdrew from public life and lost interest in the business. William's grief was compounded when his best friend, Frederick Pabst, father-in-law of his daughter, Hilda, and fellow beer mogul, also died suddenly. On February 13, 1904, just before the family was about to launch its Falstaff brand at the St. Louis World's Fair, William took his own life with a .38 shot to the head in an upstairs bedroom of the mansion. He was sixty-eight.

William's $10 million fortune was left in the hands of his widow, Julia, who was stricken with cancer in 1905 and died in the family home in March 1906. William Lemp Jr. (Billy), who was short of stature and temper but big on bravado and business savvy, now took his turn as captain of the Lemp ship.

Billy had married beautiful, eccentric heiress Lillian Handlan, famous for her enchanting smile and purple wardrobe, in 1899. The "Lavender Lady" employed a staff of seamstresses who steadily fashioned appropriately purple apparel for her. She also had a carriage accessorized and upholstered in her signature hue. But beneath the vibrant violet surface, all was not well in the Lemp household. The main bright spot in the couple's union appears to have been their mutual devotion to their only son, William III, born in 1900.

In 1908, Lillian filed for divorce, charging that her husband drank to excess, threw mad parties with prostitutes, beat her, threatened her with a revolver, and mocked her Catholic religion. Billy shot back, accusing his wife of "excessive wearing of the color lavender to attract public attention," using profane language, smoking, and being unfaithful.

In sensational and salacious divorce and custody proceedings that eventually went all the way to the Missouri Supreme Court, the couple's private lives were laid bare, and the inner sanctum of the privileged Lemp domain became fodder for a giddy press. Lillian was eventually awarded a lump-sum alimony payment of $100,000, the largest ever awarded in Missouri at that time.

Among highlights of the postdivorce custody battle for William III: Lillian cited Billy's habit of shooting neighborhood cats among the reasons for denying her ex-husband access to their son. William retorted that he did not kill cats for pleasure, only to depopulate the area of those felines that disturbed his sleep.

Following the very public divorce, Lillian retreated from the spotlight, never remarried, and lived—lavender still—to age eighty-three. Billy remodeled the mansion into offices for the company in 1911, moved to the country, and in 1915 married Ellie Limberg, the daughter of Columbia brewery kingpin Casper Koehler. But whatever happiness he attained was short lived as a new nemesis loomed on the horizon—the temperance movement and Prohibition.

The Eighteenth Amendment to the Constitution of the United States—which made production, transport, and sale of alcohol illegal—was ratified January 16, 1919, and set to take effect on January 17, 1920.

Prohibition, obviously, took a devastating toll on the brewing economy. The Lemps had a number of factors—including aging equipment, costly overhead, and outdated brewing methods—against them, and, unable or unwilling to compete in a vastly reduced market, Billy, without warning, closed the brewery doors for good in 1919.

The next blow came in March 1920, when Billy's youngest sister, Elsa Lemp Wright, thirty-seven, was found dead of an apparent self-inflicted gunshot wound to the heart in her bed at her 13 Hortense Place home. Oddly, her husband did not call the police when he found her, but called a doctor, a family friend, an attorney, and his wife's brothers. When he arrived, Billy said only, "This is the Lemp family for you." The Wrights had been remarried for just twelve days after a previous nine-year marriage and a year of divorce.

The dissolution of the family business was heartbreaking.

Records show that the floundering Lemp brewery sold at auction for a paltry $585,000, a fraction of its pre-Prohibition value of $7 million. The third family suicide came in February 1922, when a distraught Billy, presiding over the liquidation of the brewery's assets, shot himself in the heart—twice—in his Lemp Mansion office. He was fifty-five.

Like father, like son.

In 1929, William and Julia's third-oldest son, Charles, a life-long bachelor, moved back into the family mansion, where he lived a secluded life, attended by only two servants and a pet dog named Cerva. A germophobe who had obsessive-compulsive disorder (OCD), Charles became increasingly bitter and arthritic with age. In 1949, Charles shot himself—and allegedly his dog—with a .38-caliber Army Colt revolver. He was the only Lemp to leave a suicide note; his read, "In case I am found dead, blame it on no one but me." Okay then.

Charles was the last Lemp to live—and die—in the family mansion. In 1950, the mansion was converted into a boarding-house. Odd reports began to surface from the residents. Paranormal activity was commonplace until the boardinghouse closed two decades later. The once palatial estate sat empty, collecting dust and ghost stories.

After years of neglect, Richard (Dick) Pointer Sr. purchased the property in 1974, with hopes of restoring this important piece of St. Louis history.

Paul Pointer remembers the circumstances that led his family to become the new caretakers of the famous St. Louis landmark: "My older brother and my father were interested in history and knew of the significance of the property when they bought it. We didn't plan on buying a haunted house. It was a combination of the historic setting and the restaurant space. The hauntings just came along with it."

With renovation came renewed paranormal activity. Workers

were so frightened by strange noises and unusual sights that they walked out before finishing their daily tasks. Richard Pointer realized that sometimes the spirits were being helpful. Original antiques and artifacts would "turn up" just as they were needed, as if the spirits were assisting the Pointers in their quest to restore the Lemp home.

After the mansion finally opened as a restaurant, many reported ghostly figures roaming the dark hallways. Some said they resembled Billy Lemp, while others claimed to see Lillian.

Other reports included objects moving by themselves, puzzling and sometimes pungent smells, shadow figures, unexplainable cold spots, and baffling disembodied voices. Visitors have also spotted a phantom dog along with an ominous male spirit. Psychics say the man is Charles Lemp, accompanied by Cerva, his ill-fated canine companion.

Over the years, staff and guests have reported sightings of the so-called Monkey-Faced Boy. His small figure has been seen staring out the attic window or playing a ghostly game of hide-and-seek. He is alleged to be Zeke, youngest child of William Sr. and Julia, kept hidden away in the mansion attic because of his physical deformities. Others speculate he may have been the illegitimate child of Billy Lemp, product of an extramarital affair and born with Down syndrome. However, there are no records to support either claim.

Paranormal investigators have been drawn to the Lemp Mansion for years, hoping to unlock its many mysteries. Some investigations have yielded incredible results, most notably those of TAPS in a 2010 episode of *Ghost Hunters*. Other programs that featured the Lemp include *Ghost Lab*, *My Ghost Story*, and *Children of the Grave II*.

Theories as to why the mansion is so haunted come in all varieties. Some believe the Lemp family was cursed. For the superstitious, it is interesting to note that the number 13 comes up quite a bit in relation to the family. Billy was born on August 13, his father died on February 13, and the home where three family members committed suicide was located on South 13th Street. Elsa Lemp Wright lived at 13 Hortense Place.

The Lemp Mansion lures like a siren with its bizarre history of fortune and calamity, and now with a new family breathing life back into the building, it has been born again.

Take the Haunted Tour—The First Floor

Jacob Feickert built the historic home located in the quaint Benton Park district of south St. Louis in 1868. Jacob's daughter Julia married William Lemp Sr., and in 1876 the opulent three-story, stone-and-brick structure became the Lemp family residence. Situated in a beautiful hilltop setting, the Millionaire's Row home was a symbol of wealth and power for one of the city's leading families.

Today, the Lemp Mansion Restaurant and Inn stands proud with castlelike turrets, winding wrought-iron stairs, and a majestic fountain. The side of the building is emblazoned with the trademark Lemp logo. The Missouri Highway, a necessary evil with its constant hum of traffic, runs along the back of the mansion.

A curbstone carved with the Lemp name sits front and center, next to a replica hitching post shaped like a giant bottle of Lemp lager (in humorous contrast to the modern parking meter and street cleaning sign next to it).

A set of double doors at the top of the stone steps opens to the wondrous world of an American legend.

THE OFFICE

Personal Experience—
Theresa

In February 2013, I spent a weekend in St. Louis with fellow Haunted Housewife Cathi Weber. We were eager to check out the Lemp Mansion from both a paranormal and historical point of view—the Lemp family saga is an American *Downton Abbey*.

We rented a suite for the night, and as soon as the restaurant closed we were free to explore the mansion at our leisure. All staff went home and the place became eerily quiet. The ten other mansion guests, mostly couples, had retired to their rooms. It was Valentine's Day weekend, and perhaps they had things on their minds other than dead Lemps. But not me. The weekend auspiciously took in the anniversaries of William Sr. and Billy Lemp's deaths (February 13 and 15, respectively), and my mind was on affairs of the grave.

Immediately to the left of the entrance is a small dining area, once the brewery's office, where Billy Lemp committed suicide. Cathi and I were drawn to this area, a perfect spot to start our investigation. We sat down at a small table in front of the huge fireplace and silently took in our surroundings.

It was dark, very dark, which made the room feel smaller than it actually was. It took a while for my eyes to adjust, but my body could sense a strange electricity in the air. My spidey-senses were tingling.

I thought about Billy Lemp, wondering if I was sitting in the spot where he committed suicide. A life-size portrait of Lillian hangs prominently on the west wall, as if to mock her ex-husband's memory. The purple hues of her outfit, highlighted by a small spotlight from the frame, add the only color visible in the room.

As I studied the painting, a cold chill slowly slid its fingers up my spine. Maybe it was a draft from the uninsulated windows. I angled myself closer to the old steam radiator.

We decided to start with an EVP session. I set up a small digital video camera alongside my voice recorder, while Cathi sat across from me at another dining table.

The silence was unsettling.

"William, William Lemp Jr., are you here right now, here at the Lemp Mansion?" I asked.

My recorder picked up a faint response: "*I am.*"

I asked a few more questions, but the spirit was silent. Cathi tried her luck.

"Who or what caused you to become so despondent that you took your own life?"

"*I failed!*" The response was clear. And loud! Was this the spirit of Billy? We needed more information.

I asked, "What was the name of the beer you brewed at the brewery?"

"*Falstaff.*" That was unmistakable.

Goose bumps instantly covered me. My partner was equally affected, as was evident by her body language. Incredible!

At the time, neither Cathi nor I knew the particular names of the beers the Lemps brewed. What can I say? We're *wine* drinkers. The following day we discovered Falstaff was one of their most popular brands. The name came from the comedic Shakespearean character, Sir John (Happy Jack) Falstaff, who embodied the idea of "the good life" where one should "eat, drink, and be merry."

When the brewery closed, Billy sold the name and the trademark label to another brewery but retained the family recipe. The Falstaff name continued to be a successful brand for subsequent breweries for decades after the Lemp era and was produced until 2005.

THE PARLOR

Directly across the hall from the office is the parlor, a large dining area with tables and chairs neatly positioned in a staggered formation on each side of the room. Against the wall sits one of two twin fireplaces, both with exquisitely hand-carved African mahogany mantels. Dick Pointer said the discovery of these fireplaces, their beauty marred by years of neglect, was one of the reasons he decided to buy the property. After the layers of thick paint were removed, the wood was found perfectly preserved beneath.

On the ceiling is an incredible hand-painted, fully restored fresco. In the daylight, it is easy to appreciate the intricate artwork. As the ornate light fixtures add little illumination to the room, night obscures the royal blues and golden yellows edifying the ceiling high above.

THE MUSEUM AND GIFT SHOP

Tucked away in the back of the main floor is a museum and gift shop, originally one of the three Lemp family vaults. Life-size cutouts of Billy and William Lemp peer out from the wall behind the display case. The room is deeper than it is wide and utilizes every inch of space. Once filled with priceless artwork, the former vault now offers a variety of knickknacks, books, T-shirts, novelty items, and the ever-popular *I Got Nailed at the Lemp Mansion* underwear.

Opposite the modern, even gauche, souvenirs are locked glass cases taking up the entire wall, which hold Lemp memorabilia including newspaper articles recounting great historical events, personal items, handwritten notes, and brewery artifacts such as label artwork, bottle caps, and promotional items.

One of the few pieces of original furniture left in the mansion, a beautiful hand-carved chair, is displayed proudly and prominently. Over the years, the Pointers have made great efforts to obtain Lemp treasures, hoping to preserve as much of the family history as possible.

Personal Experience—
Betsy Belanger (Lemp Tour Guide, Psychic)

The rooms on the first floor of the mansion are connected by a common hallway, which leads from the front entrance, past the stairs and the bar, back to the family dining room. My most frightening paranormal encounter happened in that hallway.

Many years ago, when I first became involved with researching the Lemp family, I hosted a Supernatural Slumber Party and invited several guests to join me in an overnight stay at the mansion. After a fun night of history and exploration, it was time to go to sleep. My partner, Jason, took the settee in the hallway, and I had a roll-away bed set up next to it.

This was the first time I'd stayed the entire night in the mansion. I had spent plenty of time in the building but had never actually tried to sleep there. It seemed like a good idea at the time, but as it got later and later, I started to feel differently.

I was struck by my surroundings, which took on a different vibe at night, and thought to myself, *I don't know if I can do this; it's so scary!* The darkness was broken only by some dim light leaking through the stained-glass windows in the bar. So I lay down on the bed, pulled the covers over my head, and cowered in the fetal position.

It wasn't long before I heard a long, drawn-out screeching sound. It was a distinct sound, a familiar sound. I knew exactly where it was coming from: the door to the men's room. I called out to Jason, but he was sound asleep.

So I lay back down, trying not to think about it, when *screeetchhhh!* I heard it again! I called, "Jason, Jason!" and this time he woke up, saying he had heard it too. We got up to investigate the noise. We looked down the hallway to see if anyone was wandering around. There was no one on the first floor, no one in any of the other rooms.

Eventually, we gave up, lay back down, and tried to go back to sleep. I pulled the covers over my head and shut my eyes as tight as I could, hoping nothing else would happen.

After a few minutes I could *feel* someone walking around. It wasn't just the sound; this time I could actually feel the vibrations through the floor! The footsteps were getting closer and closer to my bed. Then, all of a sudden, they stopped. Right where my head lay on the pillow! Even with my eyes closed I could feel this energy. I took a quick peek, opening one eye at a time, but saw nothing.

My heart was pumping so loud I could hear it. But then I heard another sound, even more terrifying. It was a horrible moaning, just like a spooky ghost on TV. *"Ohhhhhh ohhhhhh."* I was petrified!

The sound just kept going and going. *"Ohhhhh ohhhhh."*

Jason was sound asleep. Everyone upstairs was sound asleep. I was shaking, just scared to death at this point.

I didn't know what else to do, so I just said aloud, "I'm just too scared, you *have* to go away. Please, I'm too scared!"

I was thinking, *They're dead, I'm the living one here. I should have the power.* But I was so frightened. I closed my eyes and repeated over and over, "Please, just go away!"

And then it stopped. There was stone silence. I was so afraid it would come back, I didn't move a muscle until daylight. When morning came, I had to get out of there. It was too much.

But then I thought, "Wait a minute, I had an encounter. I had communication. An undeniable personal experience with a spirit. It *worked*!"

That was my breakthrough. Maybe it was some sort of test. Maybe since I wasn't scared off that first time, they didn't have any problems with me being here. After that initial incident, I've had numerous encounters with the ghosts and spirits at the mansion. I feel I have a duty to be a caretaker of sorts for the Lemp. Just as the Pointers preserve the building, I preserve the memories of the great family who lived and died here.

THE ATRIUM

On the east side of the building, just behind the parlor, is the aviary or atrium. This circular room was designed to allow sunlight to stream in through the windows, creating a greenhouse effect perfect for tropical plants and exotic birds. A glass ceiling once sat atop the atrium but was removed when more living space was added on the second floor.

Today the atrium is a dining room. A decorative planter, once a beautiful stone fountain, sits in the middle of the room. The mosaic tile floor is original to the mansion, and green-hued jungle murals on the walls have been restored as well. Heavy wrought-iron tables set against the curved walls make the most of this small space.

The room's bright features are best appreciated during the day when the sunlight bounces off the walls, illuminating everything it touches. In the evening, decorative candles flicker dangerously close to the airy curtains adorning each window, but the atmosphere seems "right"—everything is as it should be.

Though it's the least creepy room in the house, strange things have been reported in the atrium. A heavy wrought-iron chair slid away from its table and several feet across the room. It's always disconcerting when furniture takes on a life of its own.

Personal Experience—
Grant Nevala (Lemp Restaurant Employee)

As a seven-year veteran of the Lemp, I've seen and heard a lot of strange things. You get used to the weird noises and strange shadows after a while. You learn to push your fear aside in order to do your job properly. I love working here, so I'm not going to let a few ghosts scare me away! That's not always true for our customers.

An incident that sticks out in my mind happened to one of my regulars a few years ago. This couple came in about once a month for the great food and service, not particularly interested in the ghost stories. One night, after dinner in the atrium, they decided to finish the evening with a nightcap. It was a little past closing time and they were the last patrons to leave the bar, the last to leave the whole restaurant, actually.

I bid them good night and showed them out, locking the door behind them. All other staff had gone home, and there were no guests staying in any of the suites that night.

I completed my nightly duties and locked up, never leaving the first floor. A short while later, I was in my car and on my way home.

The next day, I was surprised to see these "regulars" back so soon. Their demeanor was very different from the previous night's visit. After an awkward dinner, the couple asked, "How many guests stayed at the mansion last night?"

I told them, "None; no one was in any of the suites last night."

"How many workers were still in the building after we left?"

"Just me," I assured them. "I left a few minutes after you did. Why do you ask?"

"We saw a bright light on upstairs, and a strange figure staring out at us from a second-floor window."

This "someone" was looking right at them and continued watching them intently as they drove away. There was something familiar, intrusive, and deeply unsettling about this figure, which they believed to be a woman. The woman looked at them as if to say GO AWAY with her eyes. The whole experience creeped them out.

I tried to calm their fears as best I could, stating in a very matter-of-fact voice, "That kind of stuff happens here all the time; consider yourself initiated into the Lemp Mansion experience!"

I'm not sure my words were any comfort to them.

Another time, about a year ago, there was a young couple, first-timers to the Lemp, who eagerly sat down for dinner in the Atrium. It was early and they were the only table seated in the room at the time. They had come to dine and "check out the ghosts," well aware of our haunted reputation.

I welcomed them and gave a brief rundown of the dinner options and Lemp history. They were all smiles and almost giddy with excitement, claiming to be big fans of the paranormal. After bringing their drinks and an appetizer, I excused myself and went to put in their dinner order.

A few minutes later, I returned to find the formerly carefree young couple obviously upset, the man trembling and the women on the verge of tears, both scrambling to leave the table. Their drinks were barely touched, as was the appetizer.

Puzzled, I asked if everything was okay. The wide-eyed young man replied, "No, it's not okay. We can't stay here. This place is too haunted!"

They threw some money on the table and made a mad dash for the door. I don't know what happened to them, but it was apparently so terrifying they felt the need to rush out of the building without touching their food. It's a shame, really. The food is to die for.

Personal Experience—
Theresa: Billy Lemp Approves

Cathi Weber and I investigated the atrium, following up on claims of activity reported by staff. I situated myself at one of the small iron tables, which gave the feeling of being outdoors or at a garden party (not that I've ever been to a garden party). It had a "livelier" feeling than most other areas of the house.

I grabbed my equipment, changed the tape in my camcorder, and made sure a fresh battery was attached.

Cathi was sweeping the room with a K2 meter when out of the corner of her eye she spotted some movement in the bar area. A dark form blocked out the light for a brief moment. Almost immediately, I also saw a shadow, just over five feet tall, with a distinctly human shape to it, move quickly left to right across the doorway leading to the next dining room. I quickly turned the camcorder toward it, frustrated that I had missed it the first time.

We sat silently in the dark, hoping our other senses would aid us in our investigation. Odd sounds were happening all around us, eerily echoing off the tile floors and stone walls.

I heard a soft tapping coming from the hallway. At first I thought it was something mechanical, but the rhythm was irregular. *Tap tap tap*—pause—*tap*. Then it stopped abruptly, only to start a few seconds later with a different pattern. I tried not to think about the sound, more interested in seeing the shadow figure again. After a while, with no further movement, we decided to start an EVP session.

Cathi began, remarking on the beauty of the atrium.

"Was this your favorite room in the house? Did you invite guests in here when they came to visit?

I joined in. "What sort of birds were kept in here?"

Unfortunately, the recorder didn't pick up anything and the room itself was still. Maybe we were alone. Or maybe no one wanted to talk. Not ones to give up easily, we continued with our line of questioning.

"Who are we speaking to?" I asked.

Three distinct syllables: "*Bil-ly-Lemp.*"

"Are you a member of the Lemp family?" I asked.

"*OF COURSE!*" the voice yelled back at us.

Cathi followed with, "Do you think the Pointers are doing a good job with the Lemp Mansion?"

"Beautiful job."

It was a clear, assertive male voice. Apparently, the Lemps are very pleased with the new owners of their former family estate.

I couldn't wait to tell Paul Pointer that his efforts have not gone unnoticed.

THE FAMILY DINING ROOM

The formal Lemp family dining room sits in the back of the building on the first floor—its large wooden doors open, welcoming visitors. This room is special: a meticulously restored, hand-painted fresco on the ceiling; stunning light fixtures; an ornate decorative fireplace. You can almost hear their chattering voices as you imagine dining with American "royalty."

Several smaller tables have replaced the original large one, making for more flexible dining arrangements. The Pointers are to be commended for making this area usable for the restaurant while still retaining as much of its original character as possible.

THE BAR

The restaurant has a cozy, full-service bar, where guests can enjoy some spirits with their spirits, or, more appropriately, a beer with their fear. Stained-glass windows in the likenesses of Lillian and Billy Lemp add a shock of color to the dimly lit room. Billy's image is slightly distorted, but Lillian's, in her signature lavender dress, is unmistakable. It's ironic in light of their sensational divorce that their images linger side by side, bound together in glass.

THE WOMEN'S RESTROOM

The private bathroom designed by William J. Lemp is one of the odder features of the mansion. After William's death, the room was locked and sat untouched for decades, even during the building's stint as a boardinghouse, and it remains much as it was during the Lemp era.

Now it is a public ladies' room, and guests get a glimpse into the esoteric world of the weird and wealthy. Two modern toilet stalls seem out of place next to the opulent fixtures, including a rare glass-legged sink and a ceramic foot bath. But the most notable and bizarre feature is a massive glass-enclosed marble shower stall that sits in the middle of the room, which historians agree was the first free-standing shower in St. Louis.

William discovered these eccentric furnishings while traveling in Italy and brought them back for his personal enjoyment. It's undoubtedly a shock when women walk into the restroom and the first thing they see is an enormous see-through shower. We assume no one has actually tried to use it, at least not during business hours.

Personal Experience—
Cathi Weber

Eager to check out the famous shower, I excused myself after dinner and headed to the ladies' room to wash up. The layout of the room is peculiar and confusing; I had to walk around the enormous shower stall to reach the sink, which sits on one side, with the toilet stalls against the opposite wall.

As I was making my way around the shower, I heard the door to one of the stalls open and shut. Thinking someone would need to use the sink, I waited. No one appeared. Maybe they went *into* the stall? Oh well. I brushed the incident off and turned the water on to wash my hands.

Over the running water I heard the sound again, but this time louder, more distinct. I turned off the faucet and listened quietly. I kept glancing in the mirror, sure that I would turn to find someone standing behind me. It was suddenly very chilly, as if the air-conditioning had kicked on.

I heard the same creak again, like a sound effect from a haunted house or kid's cartoon. I half expected to see Scooby and the gang jump out from behind the door. I quickly dried my hands and quietly crept over to the stalls. Hands trembling slightly, I opened each door and ducked my head inside, but found them empty.

I got the feeling I wasn't alone. I couldn't see anyone, but I could *feel* them. What's worse is I kept thinking that this was William's private bathroom; maybe *he* was watching me. I quickly washed up and returned to the table, anxious to fill Theresa in on what had happened. For the remainder of our stay at the Lemp Mansion, I only used the private bathroom in our suite!

Take the Haunted Tour—The Basement

Access to the underground wonderland of the Lemp empire starts in the mansion's basement. Descending the narrow stairs to the low-ceilinged rooms, one might expect to feel confined and claustrophobic, but it's actually quite inviting. The mansion's basement is the perfect environment for seasonal and weekend activities such as the popular Lemp Comedy-Mystery Dinner Theater.

The space provides an additional dining area and a service bar. The old rathskeller, used to store beer and wine, is still visible. An old stained-glass window hangs horizontally off the ceiling in the hallway, adding an unexpected blast of color to the room. Memorabilia of all kinds adorns the walls, including personal photographs of the Lemp family and brewery.

In 1904, the grand staircase was replaced by an elevator, remnants of which can still be seen. Modern renovations began in the basement, the first area to be opened to the public as a restaurant. The former family kitchen has been converted for commercial use. Storage areas that once held Lemp treasures are now used for restaurant supplies.

The most fascinating feature of the basement is the bricked-up entrance to the cave system that once ran from the mansion to the brewery. The caves, with their consistent cool temperatures, were a huge part of the Lemp success story. They were large enough to accommodate a horse-drawn carriage and served as an underground transportation system for people and goods.

When electric refrigeration became available, the caves were converted to other uses. The family added a theater and entertainment rooms, among other things. The three levels of tunnels expanded for miles, and were as deep as two hundred feet belowground in some places. Only those close to the Lemps ever used the labyrinth of caverns and hidden rooms.

Some caves were closed and sealed after Prohibition, leaving an unseen and nearly forgotten world under the city.

In the 1950s the caves were "rediscovered." The new owner brought in diggers, who unearthed some unusual bones. Paleontologists from the Museum of Natural History in New York determined them to be of a peccary, a type of Pleistocene-era wild boar. Most of the remaining caves were sealed or destroyed when Interstate 55 came through in the 1960s.

Take the Haunted Tour—The Second Floor

THE LAVENDER SUITE

The Lavender Suite is the largest and most impressive Lemp Mansion bedroom. Two lavish high-ceilinged rooms are connected by an enormous set of pocket doors. An oversize mirror hangs above the mantel of the exquisite marble fireplace, complete a with jolly Flagstaff effigy inlaid in cast iron.

Two huge brass and copper chandeliers hang above a dining table and a king-size bed. The windows are covered by nonadjustable shades that remain half closed at all times. Once it gets dark in the Lavender Suite, it stays dark. A comfortable couch and an oversized armoire complete the decor. Some say this was the children's room, although its size indicates it was more likely the master suite.

The grand private bathroom is an impressive, bright, open space. Every appointment in the room is white, from the porcelain toilet to the ceramic bathtub. What it lacks in color it makes up for in grandeur. The rare marble shower's unusual twisted system of brass pipes spurts water out of dozens of strategically placed holes, offering the user a sensual, tickly experience.

In the center of the white mosaic tile floor is a short-legged round table, suitable for reading materials, fresh flowers, or what-not. Angled in the corner is a locked leaded-glass cabinet containing artifacts and heirlooms from the Lemp era, including antique medicine bottles, vintage soap dishes, and other washroom necessities. It's like having a mini-museum inside the bathroom.

Personal Experience—
Cathi Weber

It was past midnight. The mansion was dead quiet except for the muffled sound of traffic from the interstate. Theresa was asleep, exhausted from a long day of traveling. I couldn't sleep. Maybe it was the excitement of actually being at the Lemp Mansion, or maybe it was the strange setting; either way, I was wide awake. I tried watching television but quickly gave up on that idea.

Armed with my brand-new purple amethyst pendulum, I decided to try a little solo spirit communication. I could feel the crystal vibrating before I even began the session—was something trying to get my attention? I didn't want to wake Theresa, so reluctantly I put the pendulum away and decided to try something different.

Our suite had three exits, one from each room, all leading out into the hallway. Quietly, I unlocked the bedroom door and glanced out, curious to see if any other guests were up exploring. All was still. Disappointed, I shut the door, locking it behind me. Trying to make the bedroom more "cozy," I closed the heavy pocket doors from the dining room. I lay back down, trying to force myself to sleep.

Less than a minute later I heard an unsettling noise: the sound of the knob on the bedroom door jiggling, as if someone were frantically trying to open it! I sat up abruptly, staring at the door for a second, before hearing the sound again. In the darkness, I could just barely make out the knob jiggling around.

I jumped out of bed and sprang toward the door, about six feet in front of me. I threw the door open to find nothing. There was no one behind the door—the entire hallway was deserted. I made a quick check of the area, venturing as far as the bottom of the first-floor stairs and the top of the servants' stairwell, but found no one.

That was it for me. After that, I didn't sleep a wink; I sat there wide-eyed and freaked out, waiting for the sun to come up. I was stunned by this experience and pissed that Theresa had slept right through it!

In the morning I asked the other guests if they had been out of their rooms during the night. All said no. Later we discovered that one of the most common occurrences reported by guests is the sound of someone or *something* jiggling doorknobs in the middle of the night.

THE WILLIAM LEMP SUITE

Across the hall from the Lavender Suite is the William Lemp Suite. It is elegant in its own right, although smaller than the former. It consists of two spacious rooms connected by floor-to-ceiling pocket doors, with ample living and sleeping space for overnight guests.

One of the most remarkable paranormal events to occur at the Lemp involved both of these suites.

Ghost Hunters—
TAPS Investigation

In 2010 TAPS filmed an episode (season six, episode sixteen) of their hit Syfy show *Ghost Hunters* at the historic mansion. The team uncovered a plethora of paranormal phenomena—the house was alive with spirits.

At one point, Grant Wilson, seated on the couch in the Lavender Suite, became visibly unnerved, got up, and walked across the hall to Jason Hawes, who was lying on the bed in the William Lemp Suite.

Grant told Jason he had just heard a loud whisper in his left ear and might have caught it on his recorder.

Jason smiled oddly.

Grant said that someone had whispered "*Atlantis*" in his ear.

Just moments before, Jason had tried an unusual experiment, asking any entities in the room to carry a message to Grant across the hall. To his amazement, it had worked!

Once more, without informing Grant, he tried the experiment again, this time with the word *comet*.

After about ten uneventful seconds, Grant again looked startled. Dumbfounded, he returned to Jason saying he had heard another word, something that sounded like "comic" or "karmic."

Jason shook his head in bewilderment and wondered out loud how this was possible.

Grant was obviously puzzled by Jason's reaction. Until the secret was revealed. Jason played his recorder for Grant.

Jason's voice on playback said the new word was *comet*.

Surprise and excitement flashed across Grant's face at this revelation, and he indicated he had chills all over his body.

Both men, although thoroughly excited, were frustrated that the entity wouldn't make itself known in a more definitive manner. Grant speculated that it might be a child spirit, just playing a game. It's impossible to know for sure.

THE CHARLES LEMP SUITE

The Charles Lemp Suite sits at the top of the stairs, off the servants' hallway, across from a shared public restroom. It is as beautiful as the other two, although significantly smaller. It has a nice view of the city and comfortable period furnishings, and it currently holds one of the few original pieces of Lemp family furniture: a table once used by the housemaids to fold laundry, which doubles nicely as a small dining table for overnight guests. An old piano sits against the wall; though usually silent, it's been known to play on its own.

One famous Lemp legend involves Charles, younger brother to Billy and the fourth Lemp to commit suicide. He was a loner, control freak, and eccentric, and his many phobias kept him out of the public eye. On the night Charles shot himself with a .38, he (supposedly) killed his dog, Cerva, first. Charles went to great lengths to put all his business and personal affairs in order before he pulled the trigger. According to the suicide note found by his servant, he wanted to make sure no one took the fall for his death. Neat and tidy, and completely neurotic.

In researching this book, the authors found no evidence that Charles Lemp shot or even owned a pet dog. There was nothing in the suicide note, nor in any official reports of his death, and no mention of it in any public or private records. The story came from Betsy Belanger, who has worked the ghost tours at the mansion for sixteen years. It is from her communication with the spirits of the Lemps that many of the family legends arise.

She claims the obsessive Charles thought his beloved pet would be better off dead with him than sad and neglected without him. Betsy also claims the name Cerva (named after the Lemp nonalcoholic beer) came directly from the spirit of Charles. Although it is known that the Lemps kept many animals, nothing about this dog can be verified.

That being said, this doesn't disprove the account either. In fact, there have been numerous claims of a phantom dog at the mansion. The spirit of Cerva is said to be the constant companion of the ghost of Charles, faithfully by his side even in death.

In February 2013, a couple sleeping in the Charles Lemp Suite claimed they were awakened during the night by "the cold, wet nuzzle of a dog's nose" and the distinct sound of a "whimpering animal." They flipped the light on but saw nothing. No dog, no animal of any kind. The confused couple were too frightened to leave the bed until morning.

That same night, women staying in the William Lemp Suite, just down the hall, claimed they heard the disturbing howls of a large dog; curiously, the sound was coming from *inside* the building, not outside.

Personal Experience—
Theresa

I was touring the second floor with Cathi Weber and Betsy Belanger when something strange caught my eye: the shadow of a stocky man, about five feet tall, in the glass door of the room next to the Charles Lemp Suite. It was just a quick glimpse, but the silhouette was unmistakable. It was very similar to what Cathi and I had seen in the atrium the night before.

Before I could alert the girls, the shadow reappeared, stopping momentarily in the framed window of the doorway. As soon as I said something to my companions, it dashed off to the left. I tried to peer inside, but the opaque glass was difficult to see through. I kept my eye on the area for a while longer, but the odd figure didn't reappear and no one was inside. Betsy told us the locked room was used for storage and no one but the manager had the keys. Other than the three of us, only the cleaning lady was in the building at the time, and we could hear her vacuuming upstairs.

Take the Haunted Tour—The Third Floor

THE LOUIS AND FREDRICK LEMP SUITES

The top floor of the mansion is accessible through the servants' stairway that reaches from the cellar to the attic. An outdoor, open-air deck overlooks the carriage house and offers an unobstructed view of the city and the highway.

Major renovations over the last century and a half have transformed the former attic into comfortable living space. The former servants' quarters have been turned into three gorgeous guest rooms.

The nearly identical Louis and Frederick Lemp Suites are located directly above the Lavender and William Lemp Suites on the second floor. These updated rooms each have their own modern bathroom, which makes up for their substantially smaller size. There is one notable difference in the two bedrooms: the Louis Lemp Suite has a door, locked and nailed shut, that opens to a set of stairs leading to the mansion's Widow's Walk, a railed rooftop platform that was a traditional feature in large Victorian homes.

That locked door hides a secret and birthed a paranormal legend.

Tools of the Trade

Crystals: crystals (such as quartz, amethyst, tourmaline, and aventurine) can be used for their metaphysical healing and energy-giving powers, with each stone delivering specific qualities. Pendulums made with crystals are useful for scrying. Spirits communicate using the movement of the pendulum to indicate *yes* or *no* answers. Crystals are also known to vibrate when held during scrying sessions. They can be paired with special boards or mats to obtain more specific information as well. Scrying can also be performed by looking deeply into a mirror or other reflective surface in a dark room and concentrating on seeing past your own reflection.

The legend in question involves the ghost of a little boy named Zeke, also known as the Monkey-Faced Boy, an unflattering and cruel name for this unfortunate child afflicted with a physical disfiguration. The Booth Brothers, paranormal documentary filmmakers, believe that Zeke had neurofibromatosis, more commonly known as "Elephant Man's disease," which causes tumors to grow wildly throughout the body, leading to massive deformities and eventually death.

Zeke has been reported at the Lemp mansion since the early 1950s. A St. Louis police officer remembered a little boy who had "something wrong" with his face watching him from a small window on the third floor. He saw the sad boy looking out at him from the attic almost daily for about a year, until the last of the Lemp family left the mansion.

Apart from the police officer's story, all information about Zeke comes from psychic medium Betsy Belanger. She says Zeke's spirit contacted her during mansion renovations. She received more information from the spirit of Billy Lemp, who claimed to be Zeke's brother.

Betsy developed a special relationship with Zeke and shared her discovery with the world several years ago. Zeke has become one of the Lemp Mansion's most touching tales, drawing dozens of professional and amateur investigators, who come to seek their own encounter with the shy and playful ghost.

Children of the Grave II—
Filming and Investigation: The Booth Brothers, Keith Age, Betsy Belanger, and Spiritchaser Anita

In 2011 the Booth Brothers, enticed by the story of Zeke, came to the Lemp to film *Children of the Grave II*. The tragic tale of the deformed boy hidden away like a dirty secret was a perfect fit for their heart-wrenching paradocumentary.

At one point, Betsy, along with investigator Keith Age, opened the locked doors in the Louis Lemp Suite, giving them access to the Widow's Walk. Once the doors were opened, Betsy spotted Zeke hiding in the shadows.

Sitting on the stairs leading up to the Widow's Walk, Spirit-chaser Anita—a Native American ghost hunter who claimed to have no previous knowledge of Lemp legend—felt the presence of a shy but curious child spirit. She thought he had something over his face, as if to hide his appearance. At the same time the Booth Brothers, who were filming Anita with a thermal camera, captured the startling image of a face, just behind her left shoulder.

Keith Age noticed an anomaly on the thermal: a face, a deformed face!

Christopher Saint Booth peered into the thermal camera and also saw the face.

Anita carried on a conversation with Zeke as the crew watched the features of the image become clearer and more distinct.

Anita indicated Zeke was right beside her.

Christopher saw him in the viewfinder.

A screen shot from the thermal camera showed what looked like a face with misshapen eyes and a deformed nose and mouth. The image appeared to morph into a head with a covering or mask on it.

Betsy became upset, the face of the spirit child bringing her to tears. Her compassion for Zeke was obvious. His story, if true, is a hard one *not* to get choked up over. However, there is no documented evidence that this child ever existed: no birth records, no death records (although Betsy claims he died from a fall at age sixteen), no medical reports, nothing.

Official records of the Lemp lineage show that Julia and William Sr. had nine children, one of whom died in infancy. There is no mention of a tenth child, who would have been the youngest. Julia would have been sixty-three in 1904, the year of Zeke's supposed birth, which seems exceedingly unlikely.

A variation of the story claims Zeke was the bastard child of Billy Lemp, the product of an affair with a family servant. There is no record of Billy Lemp fathering another child, illegitimate or otherwise.

The word of a psychic is proof enough for many, and the sightings of Zeke over the years seem to support the claims. There is the possibility, however slight, that a child did exist without any official birth or death records—most babies were born at home in those days. It wasn't uncommon for children with special needs to be kept hidden and sequestered from society during the Lemp era. Was this done to protect the child from prying eyes, or the family from shame?

Besides a small unmarked grave in the Lemp family plot, the

only morsel of "tangible" proof of Zeke's existence is in the dusty eaves that run horizontal to the connected suites. There, Betsy claims, is a faded and worn spot created by the boy's constant pacing in front of the windows for so many years.

Another possible explanation for sightings of the Monkey-Faced Boy is derived from the legend that the Lemps, who were large supporters of the St. Louis Zoo, were allowed to bring exotic animals to their mansion. Eyewitness accounts of zebras, giraffes, and other such creatures roaming the grounds of the Lemp estate have surfaced over the years. Included in the menagerie were various species of chimps and monkeys. It is possible that "Zeke" may be nothing more than a misidentification of one of these animals. These reports could not be verified, but it is well documented that Edwin Lemp, the youngest son of William Sr., kept such animals at his personal estate, Cragworld. Edwin's 140-acre property housed one of the largest private collection of birds and animals in the United States at the time.

It is possible people may have confused and combined these stories over the years, leading to the tale of "Zeke." It does not, however, explain the numerous ghostly sightings decades after the fact.

Personal Experience—
Betsy Belanger

When I started at the mansion, there was much to be done—the top floors of the mansion hadn't been touched in years! The Pointers were renovating the place from the bottom up, starting with the basement.

As they worked on the top floors, many things were uncovered, both physically and spiritually. I began to make contact with Lemp family spirits. I've been blessed with this ability, and it's allowed me to have a special relationship with certain members of the Lemp family, especially Billy. I get a lot of my information from my spirit communications with him.

But my most treasured relationship is with Zeke. He is a beautiful child spirit who was very much loved but born with some difficulties. Zeke has the mind of a four-year-old but the body of a sixteen-year-old. People have called him very hurtful names because of his deformities. He's like any child—he just wants to be loved.

The Booth Brothers were filming *Children of the Grave II* on the third floor, using all sorts of fancy equipment—expensive cameras, meters, recorders, and so on. Bill Chappell (Digital Dowsing) hooked up an Ovilus—a random word generator—to the computer.

We'd been asking all sorts of questions, trying to contact *someone*, with no luck. Just nothing was happening. When we got to the area where Zeke hides, the computer started to blurt out messages. What came through that machine was one word—a child's voice saying "*Mommy, Mommy, Mommy!*" It was completely heartbreaking. This was at the same time the thermal camera picked up the image of Zeke.

THE ELSA LEMP SUITE

The final guest room on the third floor of the mansion sits at the top of the servants' stairs and boasts a magnificent view of the St. Louis skyline. The Elsa Lemp Suite is decorated with a functioning fireplace and antique furnishings, including a king-size bed with a lighted headboard. Some claim that the Elsa Lemp Suite is *the* most haunted room in the building, although we think it's impossible to bestow that title on any one room of the spirit-saturated Lemp.

Elsa was once the wealthiest single woman in St. Louis, the youngest child of William and Julia, born in 1883. Her fortune grew in 1910 when she married Thomas Wright, president of the Moore-Jones Brass and Metal Company. The marriage was far from a happy one and after nine years of misery, Elsa was done. Claiming emotional and physical detachment by Thomas, she was quietly granted a speedy divorce in 1919.

In an unexpected turn of events, Elsa and Thomas reconciled a year later. Friends and family were stunned by their reunion, even more so when, on March 8, 1920, Elsa remarried the man who had caused her so much grief. Eleven days later, Elsa was dead, victim of a self-inflicted gunshot wound to the heart. She was the second Lemp family member to commit suicide. Or was she?

There was much controversy surrounding Elsa's sudden rec-onciliation with her husband and her death just days later. Elsa reported high spirits and reasonably good health, other than a chronic case of indigestion. More questions arose when Thomas Wright didn't immediately report the incident to the police.

Now perhaps Elsa Lemp's spirit has returned to her former family estate, a place of great joy and comfort, unlike the marital home she shared with Wright. Maybe she wants the truth behind her alleged suicide to come out, whatever that truth may be.

CONCLUSION

One paranormal theory holds that a haunting occurs when a person dies suddenly or tragically, such as by freak accident or suicide. That alone could account for many of the ghosts at the Lemp Mansion. Another theory is that the spirit of someone with a strong attachment to earthly things (or people) can remain after bodily death. It is evident that the Lemps were "attached" to their family, their money, and—with beer running through their veins—their business.

With so many of the Lemp family wanting to "exit" this world by their own hands, it seems ironic they would choose to remain earthbound. Maybe they had second thoughts, or maybe it wasn't a choice. Maybe they feared what was waiting for them if they crossed over, or maybe they are still here because they have a story to tell. It could be they want to be remembered, or they just want people to know the truth.

A bit more esoteric is the idea that a haunting can be "created," that the power of belief or assumption can actually manufacture a spirit. Some of the most well-known ghosts of the Lemp Mansion have no documented basis in fact. They may have never "been." This invites the question, "Which came first, the haunting or the ghost?" If enough people hear a story, believe a story, repeat a story in a spiritually charged place, can that story become "fact"? This phenomenon may have a bearing on the "Zeke" spirit.

Theresa was fortunate to meet several members of the Pointer family, owners and proprietors of the Lemp Mansion Restaurant and Inn. The Pointers purchased the historic property with plans of turning it into a restaurant. Richard Pointer Sr. had known the building was rumored to be haunted dating to his days as a street cleaner in the late 1950s. He and his sons, Richard (Dick Jr.) and Paul, knew they had an important task. The more they learned about the Lemps, the more they couldn't deny the paranormal aspects of their new business venture.

"Once we knew the significance of the tragedy and the hauntings, there was no putting that genie back in the bottle," Paul Pointer said in a recent interview.

Several correlations exist between the Lemps and the Pointers. Both combined family and business. Both had nine children. Both had a deep love and respect for the mansion. The strong blood ties that kept the Lemp empire together are reflected in the

Pointers' desire to keep the Lemp Restaurant a family venture. The spirits of the Lemps feel a kinship with the new family. Maybe this is why they feel comfortable staying on in their former home.

What You Need to Know Before You Go:

Lemp Mansion
3322 DeMenil Pl., St. Louis, MO

Contact Information:
(314) 644-8024
lempmansion.com

The Lemp Mansion is open year-round. The six suites are available for overnight accommodation. Prices differ per suite, day, and time of year. Please call for details and availability.

The restaurant is open for both lunch and dinner. Lunch hours are 11 A.M. to 2:30 P.M. Monday through Friday, and dinner is served Tuesday through Saturday from 5:30 P.M. to 11 P.M. (September–December) and Tuesday through Saturday from 5:30 P.M. to 10 P.M. (January–August). An all-you-can-eat chicken dinner is served on Sundays from 11:30 A.M. to 8 P.M. year-round.

The popular **Comedy-Mystery Dinner Theater** runs every Friday and Saturday night at 7 P.M. It is a lively period-piece whodunit featuring a delicious dinner and audience participation. The show sells out quickly and reservations are highly recommended. Show changes seasonally.

The Lemp Experience: This is a guided public ghost hunt through all three floors of the mansion.

Haunted Tour with Betsy Belanger: Take an informative tour through the mansion with Lemp family historian and sensitive Betsy Belanger, the foremost authority on all things Lemp. Tours

run on Mondays. Call Betsy for prices and details at
(314) 644-1814.

Other events at the Lemp include an evening with Edgar Allan
Poe, the Lemp Mansion Halloween Bash, and the Annual
Pumpkin Carving Contest. Please check the website or call for
exact dates and details.

Lodging:

There are plenty of places to stay in St. Louis, but I highly
recommend you stay at the Lemp Mansion if at all possible.

Holiday Inn Express, (314) 773-6500
2625 Lafayette Ave., St. Louis, MO
hiexpress.com

Sheraton St. Louis City Center, (314) 231-5007, (886) 627-8096
400 S. 14th St., St. Louis, MO 63103
sheratonstlouiscitycenter.com

Residence Inn by Marriott, (314) 289-7500
525 S. Jefferson Ave., St. Louis, MO 63103
marriott.com

Westin St. Louis, (866) 716-8137
811 Spruce St., St. Louis, MO 63102
stlouis.com/westin/

Waverly Hills Sanatorium

Louisville, Kentucky

INTRODUCTION

Tuberculosis (TB), the "white plague," has been stalking human-kind since ancient times, but the rise of cities and their poor sanitary conditions allowed the highly contagious and usually fatal lung disease to sweep across Europe in the seventeenth century and the United States in the nineteenth. Though the pathogen was identified in the late nineteenth century, it took another fifty years until an effective treatment was devised, but the understanding that the disease was contagious gave rise to the sanatorium movement in an effort to isolate, comfort, and perhaps cure the stricken. Edward L. Trudeau founded Adirondack Cottage Sanatorium, the first tuberculosis sanatorium in the United States, at Saranac Lake, New York, in 1885.

Waverly Hills Sanatorium was originally a modest two-story frame building that opened for business on July 26, 1910, and could accommodate forty tuberculosis patients. The location was specifically chosen for its isolation from populated areas and its elevation high on a hill above Louisville, Kentucky. As TB raged through the area over the next decade, the little clinic filled with more than 140 patients, making it obvious that a much larger facility was required to keep up with demand.

The massive, Gothic-style sanatorium you see today opened in 1926, could accommodate over four hundred patients, and was considered one of the most modern and well-equipped facilities of the time, with two beds to a room and each bed equipped with phone, radio, bell signal, and electric light.

At the time, fresh air and sunshine were the primary weapons in the war against tuberculosis. Arthur Loomis and the firm of D. X. Murphy of Louisville teamed up to design Waverly Hills so that the back of the batwing-shaped, redbrick building faced southwest to catch the prevailing breeze and afford maximum exposure to the sun, allowing fresh air and sunshine to consistently flow through the corridors and into the solarium and patient rooms.

The building served as a tuberculosis hospital until 1961, by which time antibiotic treatment had virtually wiped out the disease. It was closed down and quarantined, then renovated. In 1962, the building reopened as Woodhaven Medical Services, a geriatric facility. Woodhaven was closed by the state in 1980 because of overcrowding and allegations of abuse.

The patient rooms that line the vacant halls of the building are now in various states of decay, although current owners Charlie and Tina Mattingly have made great strides in cleaning up after years of neglect. Pipes dangle haphazardly from the ceilings of some rooms, while ivy invades through broken windows in others; peeling paint flakes off in sheets, and bits of plaster and glass linger in corners.

The number of people who died at Waverly Hills is a topic of dispute. Some accounts claim that at the height of the epidemic, patients died at the rate of one an hour, putting the total death toll as high as 63,000. But over the last several years, historians and researchers have concluded that a facility with 400 to 500 beds operating for thirty-five years (plus the sixteen years the smaller facility operated) could not have generated a death toll higher than 8,000 or so, and a figure in the 5,500 to 6,500 range is most likely.

Some of the spirits reported at Waverly are what one might expect at such a facility: tortured souls who lived out their last attenuated days isolated from the world until disease squeezed the life out of them. Visitors hear their labored coughs echoing through the long corridors and glimpse their pale, sunken faces lurking in the shadows. But these spirits are not alone. Visitors often report glimpses of ghostly doctors and nurses in the building as well, and phantom children still play with balls left for them by the living.

The spirit of a suicidal nurse, a vagrant and his dog, and a little lad named Timmy make their presences known on a regular basis.

Most disturbing is the Creeper: an inhuman, dark entity, spiderlike and faceless, that crawls along the graffiti-covered walls and deteriorating ceilings with movements almost too quick for the human eye. Emerging suddenly from the darkness, this sinister figure frightens even the most seasoned investigators.

Waverly Hills is a veritable paranormal playground; spirit activity seems to happen here *every day*, as if the ghosts *need* to be noticed. A trip to Waverly Hills should be near the top of every ghost hunter's bucket list. Some claim that it is one of the scariest places on earth, and we know from experience that it is one of America's most haunted.

Take the Haunted Tour—The Grounds and the
First Floor: A City on the Hill

The contagious nature of tuberculosis required patients and staff to be sequestered from the local community and their loved ones. The hospital became a self-sufficient city with its own zip code, providing those who lived there all the necessities of day-to-day life.

The first floor of the main hospital building featured a lobby, various medical offices and labs, a nurses' station, therapy rooms, x-ray, maintenance, storage areas, and a morgue.

Among on-site services and facilities were a salon, barbershop, dining room, dentist's office, library, post office, school, various workshops and training rooms, a power house that supplied electricity to the entire facility, and a separate-but-not-equal hospital for African American patients.

A working farm provided fresh meat and produce prepared by an extensive kitchen staff, and a bakery turned out fresh bread and other baked goodies. A nutritious, well-balanced diet was part of the treatment of tuberculosis. Although not a cure, it certainly didn't hurt.

Doctors, nurses, and other staff had dormitory-style living quarters on the grounds. Children of Waverly patients who had no other family to care for them were housed in a dormitory on the property; those who were infected stayed in the main building.

THE MORGUE

The dead made one final stop before exiting the hospital: the morgue. Postmortem exams were routinely carried out on the dead in the hope that doctors would learn something useful about the dreaded disease that claimed so many of their patients, and Kentucky required autopsies be performed on a certain percentage of those who died inside state-funded hospitals.

The morgue is located on the main floor not far from the entrance to the body chute. The room is surprisingly small and separated into two areas: one for the living, where doctors busied themselves with work, and one for the dead, where the bodies were prepared and stored.

Personal Experience—
Theresa

After being contacted by a casting director, Cathi Weber, Darla Spector, and I—the Haunted Housewives—were chosen to participate in a new reality television show for the Travel Channel, *Paranormal Challenge*, created and hosted by *Ghost Adventures* star Zak Bagans. Each episode featured two three-person teams of paranormal investigators in a head-to-head competition at some of the most haunted locations in the United States. We were delighted when producers sent us to Waverly Hills, which was at the top of our paranormal wish list!

During our three-day shoot in May 2011, we engaged in a battle of nerves, technical skills, teamwork, and historical knowledge against our worthy competition, Dark Alley Paranormal. Each team simultaneously investigated the building, armed with the same equipment, in an extremely limited time frame.

A cameraman and sound technician followed us throughout the night investigation. Special areas were designated as "solo" spots, where a team member investigated alone rigged with a POV camera. A panel of expert judges monitored the teams remotely via stationary and robotic cameras placed throughout the building.

The sanatorium was electric with paranormal activity, and both teams captured amazing evidence. But, alas, there could be only one winner. The Haunted Housewives reigned victorious and were awarded the grand prize: bragging rights.

When we returned to Waverly Hills in August 2012, my teammates and I had the opportunity to explore the building at a much less televised, much more leisurely pace. Without the pressures of judgment and a ticking clock, we were able to spend more time investigating properly.

We entered the morgue with much trepidation. The space felt tight and confined, even though it was nearly empty, with most of its original equipment long gone. What remained sent shivers up my spine.

The most disturbing aspects of the room were the body trays. The drawerlike structures were built into the wall in a group of three, one on top of another like a double oven, containing sliding slats that allowed access to the bodies. They were still in working order, although the doors were missing.

My mind quickly painted a picture of an emaciated corpse, pale and bloodless, lying faceup on a cold slab, waiting for its turn on the autopsy table. The trays made a horrible screeching sound as they were pulled out, strenuously objecting to being disturbed.

On my previous visit to the sanatorium, while filming *Paranormal Challenge*, I had bravely (or stupidly) lain down on one of these slats and had my teammates slide me in, thinking this would be a good way to stir up some spirit activity. After a two-minute eternity, my fear and claustrophobia had chased me out.

This time I passed on the nap in the death drawer—once was more than enough for me. Instead I made my way over to the autopsy table, which looked like an ordinary table except for the strange grooves along the edges leading to an unplugged hole. The grooves were channels for blood to flow through as it drained from lifeless bodies, outlining them in parallel rivers of red. All evidence of the table's past had long been scrubbed away, but in the dark it was easy to imagine what a macabre scene it must have been.

The three of us gathered around the autopsy table. Cathi and I placed two digital voice recorders, a video camera, and a spirit box neatly on the table. Darla, our videographer, set up to film the session. We were hoping to catch an EVP or get some real-time responses through the spirit box. The room took on a sepulchral vibe and we felt the temperature drop. Unnatural sounds emanated from the shadows. Suddenly, a rusty metal chair in the corner rustled as if someone were getting up or sitting down on it. Of course, the chair appeared to be empty.

I tried not to think about the noises—there was work to be done.

Hoping to entice the spirits to talk to us through our equipment, we began the session with a few basic questions.

"What should we call you?"

The radio spewed out a series of names: "*Rick . . . Garth . . . George . . . Dave . . . Sonny . . . Dan . . . Mike . . .*"

"How many of you are in here?"

"*Seven,*" the box said.

"Are you patients here?" I asked.

"*Yes . . . seven.*"

"Seven? Is that correct?" Cathi reiterated.

"*Yes.*"

Someone was clearly talking to us through the box. Voices cut through the static and white noise, every word a distinct, intelligent response to our questions.

"Do you know what room we're in right now?" I asked.

"*Morgue,*" came the response, loud and clear.

Mind blown—chills gripping body.

"Can you see us? How many women are in this room?"

"*Some.*"

"Do you know our names? Do you know what my name is?"

"*Theresa.*"

Uncomfortably personal.

At that exact moment, my camera shut off. The battery was fully charged; it was as if someone had physically pushed the power button and turned it off.

"Did you just shut my camera off?" I demanded of the spirit.

"*YES*," came the forceful response.

Many find it easy to dismiss the disjointed "answers" that come from the spirit box, chalking them up to coincidental radio chatter. But unequivocal responses to direct questions can help corroborate paranormal activity.

After the most successful spirit box session *ever*, we continued our investigation.

While conducting an EVP session, I thought I heard footsteps from within the room. Cathi heard a noise as well but believed it was coming from the autopsy table, which, upon approach, we noticed was vibrating, shaking our equipment against its metal surface.

"Oh my gosh, Theresa, feel this!" Cathi exclaimed.

The cold surface was indeed vibrating. Like a washing machine on spin cycle, it shook lightly but rapidly.

Between the temperature drop, moving-chair sound, camera malfunction, autopsy table vibrations, and remarkable responses from the spirit box, we undoubtedly communicated with the dead of Waverly Hills Sanatorium in the morgue that night.

Personal Experience—
Aaron Sulser

Aaron Sulser regularly brings his team Dark Alley Paranormal to investigate Waverly Hills. On a spring night in 2011, Dark Alley took a short break from pursuing spooks in the main-floor common room. Refreshed and ready to resume the hunt, Aaron bantered briefly with Waverly owner Tina Mattingly, then told her he was heading off to the morgue with new team member Alex Meiring.

As he said this, Tina's tiny female terrier, who had been quietly at her side the entire night, began barking insistently at Aaron. Then she growled nervously and bit onto his pant leg, pulling with as much force as her five-pound frame could muster.

"What is she doing?" Aaron asked Tina.

When you own a haunted location, such as Waverly Hills, you become familiar with subtle and not-so-subtle signs from the spirit world. It was apparent to Tina Mattingly that this was a sign.

"She doesn't want you to go back in!"

Many researchers think animals possess a higher degree of psychic ability than most humans. Could this dog, so accustomed to the paranormal activity of the sanatorium, be "tuned in" to the spirits and energies all around her?

Despite the warning, Aaron and Alex headed off to the morgue.

The two men were alone on the first floor while other team members investigated the top section of the building. Once in the morgue, Aaron headed straight for a body tray with the intention of connecting empathically with any present spirits.

"I was lying on the body tray and we could hear a lot of banging down the hallway, so we knew something was kind of weird."

While Aaron lay in the death drawer, Alex saw a looming, human-shaped shadow quickly approach him, blocking out the light as it came. Shadow figures are nothing new at Waverly, but this was a first for Alex, who was shaken but remained vigilant at his post, watching uneasily over Aaron, now completely enclosed inside the drawer.

Aaron settled himself as best he could inside the tray, his arms folded across his chest. He closed his eyes, imagining the sensations of those who had lain there before him.

"I was lying there and I decided to do the one thing you're not supposed to do as a paranormal investigator, which *nobody* should do. I said, 'You can get into my head and let me feel what you felt.'"

An "invitation" to allow a spirit to enter your mind or body is very problematic: You are opening yourself with no way of controlling who or *what* may take you up on the invitation. In an attempt to experience total empathy, you may actually experience oppression, or worse, possession, by the spirit or spirits with whom you commune. It is a dangerous game best left to psychics and mediums, who may spend years honing their ability to channel the dead.

"It got cold around my face. It was chilly to begin with, but this was noticeably different. My legs grew very heavy, as if something were pushing on them or weighing them down. It was hard to move."

As Aaron struggled against the pressure growing on his lower body, his arms, folded against his chest "like a mummy," began "seizing and curling up, like muscle spasms."

Aaron was trapped inside the body tray, and becoming trapped inside his own body. He felt lightheaded, nauseated, distant from himself as he summoned the will to struggle against the unseen force overtaking him.

In the room outside the tray, Alex sensed something was wrong.

"Are you okay in there?" he called to Aaron. "Do you want out?"

Once the drawer is closed, you cannot open it from the inside. Dead bodies are typically content to stay put.

Aaron tried to calmly assure his teammate (and himself) that everything was okay, but it was not. He could feel the invading force growing stronger as the last vestiges of his self-control slipped away.

After thirty more seconds, Aaron knew he had to get out before it was too late and called to Alex to release him.

Alex pulled him out and again asked Aaron if he was okay. The look on Aaron's face gave him the answer. Aaron sat up slowly and tried to collect himself. He was dizzy and disoriented.

"I finally stood up and started to walk down the hallway," still recovering from the encounter. "I thought, 'I can't go on, I've got to get out of here!'"

Aaron made a hasty exit from the building, trying to get far away from the morgue and the negative force he had encountered. He was so shaken by the experience that it was more than thirty minutes before he could go back inside the building.

After Aaron finally pulled himself together, he realized he had left Alex inside, alone, with no walkie-talkie and no way of communicating with the rest of the team. Alex had been freaked out and more than a little scared after witnessing Aaron's alarming episode. Now he was alone in the dark, inside a cavernous abandoned tuberculosis hospital, trying to navigate through the maze of corridors while spooky shadows danced and chilling noises echoed around him.

Alex's initiation into the haunting world of Waverly Hills was now complete.

As for Aaron, an entity had invaded his mind and body to the extent that he had nearly lost control. This was a lesson learned and a shining example of what *not* to do.

Paranormal investigation involves attempting to communicate with entities or energies that cannot be positively identified. Unless you are a psychic, how do you *really* know who you're communicating with? The location's history may offer clues, and EVPs can sometimes help, but how do you know for sure? How can you trust the information coming through from the spiritual realm?

People lie, frequently. It would stand to reason that ghosts, who were once people, lie too. You can take it a step further and say that demons lie; that is their very nature. So how can anyone be certain of who or what they're communicating with? What Aaron Sulser encountered may have been a spirit simply answering an invitation, or it may have been something more dangerous and malevolent. Whatever Aaron crossed paths with that night made an indelible mark on his psyche and taught him a frightening but valuable lesson.

Ghost Adventures—
Waverly Hills Sanatorium

Ghost Adventures Crew front man Zak Bagans said that if death has a home address, it's Waverly Hills Sanatorium, to open the season four episode of their hit Travel Channel show filmed at the shuttered tuberculosis hospital.

In the episode, which aired in October 2010, viewers were treated to a softer side of Bagans, a man known for his in-your-face, aggressive style of investigating.

Tina Mattingly insists that *everyone* follow a basic rule of respect. To her, the ghosts of Waverly Hills are no different from the living and deserve to be treated properly by visitors to *their* home.

The kinder, gentler Bagans even flourished a bouquet of flowers to honor a patient, Lois Higgs, who died of tuberculosis at age twenty-eight at the sanatorium. Her tattered picture is displayed in the museum area to remind visitors that those who lived, suffered, and died here were very real.

While investigating in the morgue, Zak lay down inside one of the body trays while teammates Nick and Aaron explored the laboratory down the hall. He became very lethargic, feeling an intense pressure on his body.

Zak said he felt like bodies were lying stacked on top of him and he couldn't move.

As Zak described what he was feeling to the camera, his audio recorder picked up a disturbing EVP.

"Yer not gonna make it."

(Between Aaron Sulser's, Zak's, and Theresa's experiences, we feel confident in advising against The Body Tray Experience.)

During the lockdown, GAC member Aaron Goodwin was, as usual, sent off by himself, this time to explore the fourth floor, where he saw unexplained movement and heard strange sounds, including labored breathing reminiscent of a tuberculosis patient. Zak and fellow investigator Nick Groff caught up with Aaron and ordered him back to the area of activity. His protestations were in vain as he reluctantly wandered back into the darkness as "bait."

Meanwhile, the guys reviewed the full-spectrum static camera that had been left running on the third floor. To their amazement it had captured a large black mass manifesting on camera in one of the long corridors. It was human-shaped and appeared to be walking toward the camera before changing directions and disappearing into a wall.

Zak took this piece of evidence to an outside expert who concluded there wasn't just one shadow figure on the tape, but another, smaller figure right behind it.

The paranormal activity at Waverly Hills made such an indelible impression on Zak that he would later make it an investigation site for *Paranormal Challenge*.

Take the Haunted Tour—The Body Chute

As if the 180,000 square feet of Waverly Hills weren't scary enough, there's another 500 feet or so attached to it that are truly terrifying. The aptly named "body chute" is a concrete tunnel that descends at an angle from the main floor of the hospital to the outside world below. The tunnel was originally used to bring goods and supplies into the facility during inclement weather and as a secondary entrance/exit for employees.

At the height of the epidemic, doctors and administrators realized that the sight of so many expired fellow patients being removed from the facility was unsettling to those still clinging to life inside, and the tunnel took on the function of surreptitiously transporting bodies out of the sanatorium. The deceased were lowered by a series of pulleys and rails down the 485-foot tunnel into a waiting hearse below. This was done under the cover of night and out of view of patients.

Personal Experience—
Theresa

During our *Paranormal Challenge* visit to Waverly, producers wanted an "alone in the dark" feel to the body chute segment, so I was sent to investigate the tunnel solo armed only with handheld equipment and a POV "banana cam" strapped to my back. This camera's purpose was not to record what I was seeing, but to record *me* as I was seeing it.

The area was rigged with stationary cameras that were monitored from a central command center. I wore a microphone for sound.

I had my recorder and my courage but little else as I inched down the tunnel in the pitch black. No flashlights were allowed, which made it difficult to navigate the grated steps and protruding rebar that stuck up like metal stalagmites through the cement floor. On the right side of the tunnel is a ramp with remnants of the pulley system still evident, on the left a series of platforms and steps in a repeating pattern all the way down to the bottom.

I had to look through the tiny viewfinder of my infrared camera to see anything in the pitch black. It took my focused concentration to not fall and become the latest casualty of Waverly Hills.

Knowing that my every move was being watched and judged, *and* would be watched again by millions of viewers, was unnerving enough, but the realization that I was literally in a *death* tunnel and my claustrophobia was kicking in nearly paralyzed me.

With every step, I felt the tunnel getting narrower and narrower, swallowing me in its concrete throat. But I took a deep breath and again resolved to investigate to the best of my ability.

I could *feel* something watching me—and I'm not talking about Zak Bagans and the other judges, but something unseen and very *present*.

My sense of hearing kicked into overdrive, every sound amplified by the curved tunnel walls.

As I gingerly navigated each step, I heard the echoes of another set of boots. One, two, three, four, platform, stop. One, two, three, four, platform, stop—my echo. The pattern repeated over and over as I made my way down.

But then the footfalls continued at a different pace, more slowly. This was not my echo, nor the rhythmic sound of water dripping from the ceiling.

I stopped completely, remained perfectly still, silent.

Clomp clomp clomp. The sound of boots on pavement.

"Hello?" I asked the air. "Who's down here?"

I expected to see one of the producers or judges coming out of the darkness to save me from this exercise in terror. But there was no answer. I continued my way down: same pattern, ears wide open, eyes fully dilated. Each time I stopped I could hear the phantom footsteps coming from what I perceived to be *right behind me*.

Muffled voices murmured. I couldn't make out what they were saying, but they were uncomfortably close. I started doing short-burst EVP sessions each time I stopped.

Finally, after an eternity, I made it to the bottom of the body chute. I touched the locked metal gate through which so many had passed over the decades, collected myself, and turned around for the return journey. Again, I heard the echo of boots whenever I stopped. Icy chills racked my body.

The trip up the tunnel took far less time than the trip down. If I could have run the entire distance I would have. I was done.

Later, when I reviewed the audio from my digital recorder, I found several EVPs, including the sound of footsteps and strange voices speaking a language I couldn't understand.

In another EVP I asked, "Is this how you left Waverly Hills, through this tunnel? I'm not leaving the way you did. I'm going up and out."

In response, I heard, "*It's upside down, man.*"

Was this a comment on the bizarre commuter traffic of the tunnel, with the living going up and the dead coming down?

The body chute was one of the most harrowing experiences of my paranormal career. Investigating while being filmed for a reality television show was just another layer of the experience. More layers would reveal themselves as the night wore on.

Take the Haunted Tour—The Second Floor

Though each floor appears identical and all are active, the paranormal activity reported on each is quite different.

In season two, episode fourteen of *Ghost Hunters*, TAPS team leaders Jason Hawes and Grant Wilson captured one of the most striking pieces of visual evidence ever recorded.

While investigating the second-floor corridor between the solarium and the terminal rooms with a thermal imaging camera, Jason and Grant captured a humanoid figure, three to three and a half feet tall, darting from the right side of the hall to the left and disappearing into the wall or open doorway. A quick head count of team members and production crew by Jason and Grant revealed they were alone in this part of the building at the time.

When they reviewed the footage more closely, the pair saw a child-sized figure with distinct legs and an opaque upper half, ruling out the possibility of it being a living person! Tina and Charlie Mattingly verified that they too had seen a similar figure on the second floor, as well as in other parts of the building.

The hunters concluded that the figure was the ghost of a boy named Timmy, a friendly spirit who likes to play games with visitors. So often is Timmy seen at Waverly that the staff has taken to leaving out toys and balls of various sizes with which he might play. Paranormal investigators often use the balls as trigger objects in an effort to interact with little Timmy.

TAPS has made several trips to Waverly Hills and captured interesting evidence on each visit, but this piece of thermal footage sticks out as most compelling. It made such an impression that thousands of ghost hunters from all over the world have flocked to Waverly hoping to have their own playdate with death.

Take the Haunted Tour—The Third Floor

Patients were housed in some capacity on all floors of the sanatorium. The sunporch, or solarium, offered mountain views, sunshine, and fresh air for the infected. There were no windows, just mesh-covered screens that allowed for exposure to the elements year-round. Patients were propped up and their beds wheeled out on the promenade side by side, taking full advantage of the location even in winter—snow was simply brushed aside.

On the opposite side of the hallway, directly behind the solarium, were the small, dark, bare terminal rooms where the doomed were moved to make room for those who might yet be saved.

This area of the hospital is the lair of the Creeper. Its dark spidery limbs move swiftly and unnaturally throughout the patient rooms. It is thought to be a bad omen, an inhuman, negative elemental born from tragedy and pain. Visitors who have had run-ins with it report feeling physically ill or uneasy, even after leaving the building. Some believe it will seek vengeance on anyone who provokes or disrespects the spirits of Waverly Hills.

The Creeper has been variously spotted crawling the walls and ceilings of the second, fourth, and in particular, third floors, hiding in the corners of the angled hallways. This freakish entity is often spotted in the terminal rooms, perhaps drawn to the echoes of death still embedded in the peeling paint.

THE ELEVATOR SHAFT

Not every ghost at Waverly Hills is a former patient or worker from the sanatorium. After the facility closed as a TB hospital, it reopened as Woodhaven Geriatric Hospital in 1962. This was a home for the aged, the infirm, and the forgotten. Labeled a "retirement facility," it was as much an overcrowded dumping ground for the unwanted. Until it was closed by the state because of "inhuman conditions" in 1980, the building was further soaked in misery, decay, and death.

After this, the building remained dormant for over a decade. During this time it became the domain of vagrants, youth gangs, drug addicts, and the homeless. In the 1980s, one poor soul was "allowed" to stay inside the building with his dog in exchange for watching over the place on behalf of the owners. This arrangement worked reasonably well for a time, but then the man disappeared and after a few days a strong odor began to seep through the elevator doors on the third floor. The man and his dog were found dead at the bottom of the elevator shaft.

Authorities deemed the deaths "suspicious," surmising that someone had either pushed the pair to their deaths or tossed their lifeless bodies down the hole after killing them, but the case was never solved.

The story doesn't end there. On the third floor Tina Mattingly saw the full-bodied apparition of a man with long, disheveled hair wearing what appeared to be a trench coat, with a large white dog lying by his side. They both evaporated as she approached. Tina's description of the man and his dog—and similar reports by visitors—match the unfortunate pair found at the bottom of the elevator shaft decades earlier.

Personal Experience—
Theresa

During our *Paranormal Challenge* visit to Waverly Hills, I spent some time on each floor in pursuit of ball-playing ghostly children and the fallen man/dog pair.

After an uneventful search of the second floor, we came upon the infamous third-floor elevator death shaft. The metal doors were covered in spray paint and pockmarked with dents and gouges. The story of the man's ignominious end struck a chord with me, perhaps particularly because of the dog.

My teammates and I decided to do an EVP session, hoping to contact the spirit of the homeless man or perhaps the dog. Gently, respectfully, we began to ask questions.

"What is your dog's name?" my teammate Cathi asked. I wasn't the only one interested in the dog, it turned out.

"Do you know who hurt you?" We walked gingerly around the subject of his death.

We took turns questioning and commenting, trying to get some interaction.

"It must have been terrible. What a horrible way to die, down the shaft." I thought of the terrifying three-story fall.

We didn't know it at the time, but one of our recorders picked up a male voice.

"Down the shaft."

I was astonished by this EVP. I scoured each tape and reviewed the camera footage confirming that none of us had said it. This was a "Class A" EVP. The voice was either mocking me or commenting on the precipitous manner of his own end—either way, darkly humorous and chilling.

Take the Haunted Tour—The Fourth Floor

Waverly Hills doctors were desperate to find a cure for tuberculosis. Before the age of antibiotics, fresh air, nutritious foods, and plenty of rest were the established treatments. When rest and fresh air failed to heal the sores left by active pulmonary tuberculosis in the lungs, physicians had the option of several surgical procedures to collapse the diseased lung, as it was thought that closing up the lung would give it a better chance to rest and heal. Such procedures came to be known as "compression" or "lung collapse therapies."

Surgeries used in the treatment of tuberculosis had such daunting names as phrenicotomy, pneumothorax, lobectomy, and pneumoectomy.

Thoracoplasty was a particularly grim, last-ditch effort in which the chest cavity was opened and several ribs were removed in order to mechanically collapse the lung. This operation left patients disfigured and sometimes killed them outright.

Waverly Hills doctors performed these procedures in a state-of-the-art surgical suite, tucked in a corner of the fourth floor of the sanatorium. The room feels surprisingly small for a facility of this size and is barren but for a large operating light, dangling from the ceiling like the Eye of God waiting to pass judgment on those close to death, and the sanitation station, resembling a built-in oven, where surgical tools were readied for use.

It's hard to imagine that any spirit would chose to stay in this area after death, but it seems clear that some have.

THE SURGICAL SUITE

Personal Experience—
Cathi Weber

During the filming of *Paranormal Challenge*, I had a chance to investigate the surgical area of the hospital. Windows freshly replaced with glass took up two of the four walls, and the moonlight shining in cast an eerie glow on everything around me.

I decided to use the Mel Meter. We had had no luck using the Mel the entire first half of the night except for a few random beeps out on the solarium, which we had attributed to a jet passing overhead.

I placed the Mel in the middle of the floor, stepped back, and began.

After establishing who I was and what I was doing there, I explained what the device could do, assuring any unseen entities

Tools of the Trade

Trigger Objects: objects used in paranormal investigation to essentially "trigger" spirit communication. In the case of Timmy, investigators used a child's toy ball as a trigger object, hoping to entice him to "play" or move the ball. Trigger objects can be personal items such as jewelry or photographs, or something familiar to the person, place, or era relevant to the investigation.

that it couldn't hurt them. Negative answers receive no response—positives activate the Mel.

"Are you a patient here?" Immediately the meter began to light up and buzz.

"Did you have an operation?" Same response.

"The doctors tried hard to figure out how to help you. Do you understand that they were trying to help and not hurt?" A long sustained response emanated from the Mel on this one.

"Are you a man?" *Yes.*

"Did you have a family?" *Yes.*

If it had been only one or two questions I could have dismissed the responses, but I know I made a connection with a spirit who lived and died at Waverly Hills, whose family watched his life slowly slip away. Who, for whatever reason, decided to remain in the place where he took his last labored breath.

The environment in the room began to change. There was a drastic drop in temperature and air pressure. The air felt heavy and stale. I noticed a change in my breathing pattern.

Our cameraman, Jimmy, became visibly shaken. Jimmy and Evan, the sound technician, were obviously being affected by what was happening.

Show producers had told them "not to interfere" with us as we investigated the sanatorium. They were to document, not direct, our actions, and, being consummate professionals, they had been largely invisible to us.

But at this point, with the Mel buzzing obediently in response to my questioning, Jimmy and Evan knew that something unusual was happening. Something *not* normal. Something *paranormal*. I stifled a giggle at the sight of them visibly shaken, but I had to keep in the moment. The spirits deserved my attention and respect. I wasn't going to stop until *they* decided the session was over.

After several more minutes of this interaction, the Mel became dormant again. The conversation was apparently over. The heavi-

Paranormal Activities

Elementals: supernatural beings that were never living people; that is, they are not the souls or spirits of once-living humans.
Although angels, fairies, and animal spirits are technically "inhuman," they are not typically associated with the negativity surrounding elementals.

ness slipped away. The room became noticeably warmer. The
spirits were gone. At least for now.

Theresa returned from her solo investigation of the fifth floor
and joined us in the surgical suite. I filled her in on what had
happened.

"Did you get it on camera?" was her immediate response.
Spoken like a true team leader.

"Of course!" I exclaimed. "And so did they!" I smiled and
pointed to our stricken two-man crew, who were now, for better
or worse, members of the paranormal club.

Personal Experience—
Theresa: Time for a Second Opinion

The surgical suite had been a hotbed of paranormal activity on
our *Paranormal Challenge* visit. Now we were back and it was
my turn. With Cathi by my side and the Mel Meter in my hand,
we tried to duplicate her earlier encounter.

The energy in the air was palpable. It was as if the room had
been filled with electricity, vibrating silently around us. A quiet-
ness came over us, making any incidental sound seem incongru-
ously loud. The only voices echoing through the dark corridors
were our own.

The warm August air was comfortable, and the muffled calls of night owls and coyotes seeped in through the glass, providing a spooky soundtrack for our activities.

An effulgent moon hung low in the night sky, illuminating details of the suite: cracks in the cement floor, exposed wires from the Eye of God light fixture dangling from the ceiling, a surprisingly large insect scurrying about.

Moonlight spilled into the hallway, and inky black shadows danced in the doorway each time a cloud crossed the moon. The temperature changed suddenly and drastically like a cold breeze blowing in, but I felt it *under* my shirt, as if it were coming from inside.

"Cathi, do you feel that chill?"

"Sure do."

Cathi set the Mel Meter in the same position as it had been on the previous, fateful session. We tried for several minutes to establish contact. If there were ghosts in our midst they weren't talking, at least not through the Mel. But there *was* action in the hallway. Tall shadows darted across the doorway. Dark, human-like forms with spidery limbs and elongated heads peeked from around the corners every so often.

We were being watched.

We decided to change tactics and, channeling our inner Thomas Edison, pulled out the spirit box radio. Maybe we'd have better luck with this device, aptly nicknamed "the telephone to the dead."

With the spirit box, answers can be more specific and detailed than with the yes/no beeps and lights of the Mel Meter, transmitting words or even complete sentences as it rapidly scans the dial.

The goal was to try to reconnect with the same entity with which Cathi had conversed on our previous visit. Cathi set the spirit box on the floor and we began our session.

"How many spirits are in this room with us?" I asked.

"*Ten . . . eight*," intoned the box.

Paranormal Activities

EVP Ranking System

Class A: an EVP that is clear, loud, and easily understood or decipherable without the aid of software manipulation.

Class B: an EVP that is audible but possibly vague or debatable. It can be heard but its meaning may be questionable to some.

Class C: an EVP that is basically an unexplainable sound or only slightly audible words. There is something on the tape but it is nearly impossible to decipher what is being said.

"Did you work here at the hospital?"

Cathi sensed that this wasn't the phantom patient from our previous visit, the one who had carried on consistently for a quarter of an hour.

"Doctor, are you in?" she asked.

"*In*," the spirit spoke over the radio.

"Doctor, where did you get your medical degree?"

Nice question, Cathi. This one needed a very specific answer.

"*Berkeley.*"

We were dumbfounded by this answer. I wasn't even sure if Berkeley had a medical school at that point. Turns out they did. A very good one at that.

I joined in on the questioning, still reeling from the previous answer.

"What happens in this room?"

"*Death . . . probably.*"

"What procedures are scheduled for today?"

"*GET OUT!*"

I guess our session with the doctor was over.

Was this the spirit of a doctor who had worked at the hospital?

I believe it was, but I can't be sure. Nevertheless, the fact remains that someone (or something) was with us in that surgery suite. Our diagnosis was confirmed by a second opinion handed down from the other side.

Take the Haunted Tour—The Fifth Floor

The fifth floor of Waverly Hills is basically an open roof with a smaller enclosed area at its center. The open side was used as an outdoor recreation area for the Waverly children; the covered area housed less desirable patients and a nurses' station.

It is from here we get reports of a ghostly game of catch. There are several videos online of a rubber or plastic ball moving on its own, sometimes stopping, changing directions, and then rolling back to its starting point. In season two of *Fact or Faked: Paranormal Files*, investigators Ben Hansen, Austin Porter, and Lanisha Cole conducted an investigation at Waverly Hills, drawn to the case by two of these very compelling videos, which they aired on the show.

One showed a ball moving under its own power in the children's area of the fifth floor. The team set up an experiment to see if they could verify or disprove this video by finding a natural explanation. They tested the movement of wind in the area and the level of the cement floor. Although it did move slightly, they could not duplicate the erratic movement of the ball as seen in the videos.

A night investigation left the team with more questions than answers. Lanisha attempted to communicate with the spirit of Timmy, the playful child ghost said to hang out in the building. She brought a large plastic ball with which he could play.

Lanisha announced to Timmy that she was leaving the ball for him as she left the area.

Moments later, Austin, who was monitoring the cameras from

Tools of the Trade

Mel Meter: a multitool device that detects electromagnetic fluctuations and alerts the user with a series of beeps and lights. It has a temperature sensor that gives a digital readout of ambient temperatures, and a feature that can sense any anomalies in the electromagnetic current. The Mel Meter was developed by Gary Galka and named for his daughter Melanie, who died tragically in an automobile accident when she was a teenager. Galka created the Mel Meter specifically to communicate with the spirit of his daughter, Mel.

a centralized area, watched the ball move out of the corner, turn toward the doorway, and roll out of the room—all under its own power!

Austin literally jumped out of his seat as he announced that something was moving the ball, rolling it across the room and out the door!

The fifth floor is also the location of Waverly's most notorious room: room 502. Cramped and graffiti laden, it has lent its name to a heavy metal band and a horror film and inspired an assortment of urban legends. A distraught nurse, unwed, pregnant, and infected with tuberculosis, hanged herself back in 1928. Her lifeless body was found swinging in front of the elevator doors, right outside room 502.

The Mattinglys confirm this tale, adding that a fetus was discovered in the hospital's well system shortly after the nurse's body was found. The prevailing theory is that this woman aborted the baby because of what she felt were overwhelmingly bleak circumstances, and then her guilt and pain drove her to take her own life.

Visitors to the sanatorium report seeing the apparition of a distraught woman dressed in an old-fashioned white nurse's uniform, her appearance accompanied by intense feelings of sadness and unease in witnesses.

There is historic documentation that two nurses died at Waverly Hills. Both were single, and both perished under mysterious or tragic circumstances. Besides the nurse who took her life outside room 502, another plunged to her death from the roof of the hospital. It is unknown if she jumped, fell, or was pushed. These tragic figures feed into the emotional whirlwind of the fifth floor.

Personal Experience—
Theresa: Swinging Times and Rooftop Rendezvous

While Cathi and Darla investigated on the fourth floor during our *Paranormal Challenge* visit, I made my way to the roof. It was pitch black and I had no flashlight with me. I tried to navigate my way in the dark to the stairwell that would take me to the top of the building.

It was so difficult keeping my bearings that I ended up in the opposite wing of the building. Finally, after getting lost and nearly falling down a flight of stairs with a camera strapped to my back, I made it to the roof. My intent was to contact the spirit of the suicidal nurse by connecting with her woman-to-woman.

On the other side of the roof, adjacent to the nurses' station, is an area where some of the most violent patients were segregated from the general population. Not just a disease of the lungs, TB affected the blood, the bones, and the brain as well. If the bacterium moved into the brain, the patients would often go mad, and there was little that could be done for them.

My first priority was to scope out the entire roof area, using the fleeting moonlight before it disappeared behind clouds.

I stood silently in the spot where the children's swings had once swung happily in the breeze. I thought of the iconic swing set photo displayed in the Waverly Hills museum. The black-and-white photo is emblematic of the dark reality and light of hope embodied in these children. I could almost hear their carefree laughter—for a moment they weren't patients, just kids playing.

I went back inside and parked myself in front of room 502. I set up my recorder and started to ask questions aloud. I divulged my own struggles with pregnancy, my wish for acceptance from family, and the eventual birth of a happy, healthy child.

My experience was the opposite of the poor nurse's. I was able to make a decent life for myself and my son. I didn't feel shame or remorse. I didn't lose hope.

Curious sounds seemed to be everywhere. I couldn't determine if they were coming from the outdoors or from the room in front of me. I didn't capture anything unusual on my digital recorder.

But the ghost nurse made her presence known to me. A surge of despair welled inside me. I was somehow connected with the nurse's spirit, feeling her extreme emotional pain.

It wasn't until I left the area that I began to feel like myself again.

CONCLUSION

It's a given that Waverly Hills Sanatorium is haunted. Anyone I know who's been to the location agrees that it is rife with paranormal activity. It has been featured on countless television programs, cable specials, radio broadcasts, and even a number of documentary films.

The Booth Brothers filmed their award-winning para-documentary *SPOOKED: The Ghosts of Waverly Hills* in 2004. This was a thorough account of the dark history and supernatural activity of the facility. It included eyewitness testimony, historical reenactments, and former patient interviews. This film's huge impact played an important part in bringing Waverly to the attention of the paranormal community.

Syfy's *Ghost Hunters* has filmed at the sanatorium three times, including a live Halloween event in 2009. The Ghost Adventures Crew had an interesting lockdown there. In 2011, *Fact or Faked: Paranormal Files* investigated some of the more famous claims of the facility with absolutely stunning results. The team's scientific approach to explaining or "debunking" the paranormal phenomena lent much credence to the haunted reputation of Waverly Hills.

And our own episode of *Paranormal Challenge* had its moments as well.

Shadow People in the corridors, phantom footsteps in the body chute, the Creeper climbing the walls and ceilings, cries of the suicide nurse, the mischievous ghost of a child named Timmy, the ill-fated homeless man and his dog. These are but a handful of the ghosts reported at Waverly Hills—it seems there's not one square inch of the building that isn't haunted!

Waverly Hills Sanatorium offers students of the paranormal a unique place to study and learn, a place to develop investigation skills and experiment with new techniques. It is also a place where we can explore the often overlooked *human* side of hauntings. The souls of the sanatorium were victims of a cruel disease that cut them down in the prime of life, or the unsung heroes who served selflessly to ease their painful plight.

Tina and Charlie Mattingly, the owners of the sanatorium, work tirelessly to preserve the dignity of these poor souls. They demand respect, forbid provocation, and seek to restore this important piece of history. It is important that we preserve our past, count our blessings, and tread lightly between the excitement of the paranormal and the fragility of life.

Waverly Hills Sanatorium is a place worthy of attention and deserving of your support. Proceeds collected from public and private ghost hunts and tours go back into preserving this important piece of our nation's history. Come to Waverly and see for yourself why we've placed this magnificent building so very high on our list of America's most haunted.

What You Need to Know Before You Go:

Waverly Hills Sanatorium
4400 Paralee Ln., Louisville, KY 40272

Contact Information:
(502) 933-2142
therealwaverlyhills.com
info@therealwaverlyhills.com

Office Hours:
Monday/Tuesday/Thursday/Friday, 9 A.M. to 5 P.M.; closed 1 P.M.
   to 2 P.M.
Wednesday, 9 A.M. to 1 P.M.

Tours and Ghost Hunts:
Daytime Historical Guided Tours: one Sunday each month from
   March through August, beginning at 2:30 P.M. Not
   recommended for children under 6.
Two-Hour Private Paranormal/Historical Guided Tours: Friday
   and Saturday nights from March through August. Minimum
   25 people.
Two-Hour Public Paranormal/Historical Guided Tours:
   Friday and Saturday nights from March through August.
   Not recommended for children under 10. No flash
   photography.

Full-Night Public Paranormal Investigations/Ghost Hunts:
Saturday nights from March through August, midnight to
8 A.M. Age 18 and over only.

Half-Night Public Paranormal Investigations/Ghost Hunts:
Friday nights from March through August, midnight to 4 A.M.
Age 18 and over only.

**Private Paranormal Investigations/Ghost Hunts and Historical
Tours:** Sundays through Thursdays from March through
August. Full Night, 8 P.M. to 4 A.M. Minimum 10 people.
Half Night, midnight to 4 A.M. Minimum 20 people.

Waverly Hills Sanatorium operates as a Halloween attraction
during the fall. Please contact Waverly Hills for exact hours of
operation and pricing info.

Lodging:
Comfort Inn Louisville, (502) 447-2096
4444 Dixie Highway, Louisville, KY 40216
comfortinn.com

America's Best Value Inn Louisville, (502) 449-7376
1735 Stewart Ave., Louisville, KY 40216
americasbestvalueinn.com

Holiday Inn Louisville Southwest, (877) 859-5095
4110 Dixie Highway, Louisville, KY 40216
holidayinn.com

Days Inn & Suites Louisville Airport, (800) 329-1949
4051 Cane Run Rd., I-264 Exit 5, Louisville, KY 40216
daysinn.com/hotels

#1

The Ohio State Reformatory

Mansfield, Ohio

INTRODUCTION

From its idealistic conception to its ignominious demise and beyond, the Ohio State Reformatory (OSR) at Mansfield has always been an iconic structure. Although it once represented a brighter path for thousands of wayward young men who passed through its corridors of stone and steel, despair and violence play an equal role in its legacy.

The cold stares of prisoners long removed from their cages seem to follow visitors as they walk the stark, desolate cell blocks. Decades after their sentences were complete, a number of inmates linger on in the form of Mansfield's many ghosts.

OSR opened for business amid much local fanfare in September 1896. On December 31, 1990, it was closed by a federal court order because of "brutalizing and inhumane conditions." Over 154,000 inmates passed through its gates over the years, but more than two hundred never checked out, victims of disease, murder, accidents, and suicide.

Built with an idealistic eye toward the rehabilitation of young, first-time offenders—the middle cog in a "graded" state penal system between the juvenile Boys Industrial School and the hard-core Ohio Penitentiary—the reformatory was intended to be much more than just a warehouse for convicts. It was a self-contained city featuring a working farm, a tailor shop, a cannery, a shoe factory, a furniture factory, and a print shop, the whole of which doubtless contributed to the improvement of its more improvable denizens over the decades.

The castlelike structure, reflecting Romanesque, Victorian Gothic, and Queen Anne influences, was designed by famed architect and Freemason Levi Scofield of nearby Cleveland with the lofty goal of leading young delinquents to a "rebirth of their spiritual lives."

Sadly, within a few decades OSR had gained a reputation as one of the country's more beleaguered prisons, plagued with overcrowding, violence, disease, and federal civil rights violations, living up to the popular inmate nickname "Dracula's Castle."

Not surprisingly, a number of murders and suicides erupted out of these conditions. Most spectacularly, a twenty-two-year-old inmate named Lockhart immolated himself in his cell in order to escape the confines of the reformatory in 1960.

The tumultuous past of the prison includes the murder of two guards and the killing of the reformatory's farm boss and family, who were kidnapped and shot to death by vengeful parolees in the middle of the notorious Mad Dog killing spree of 1948. But by far the most perplexing death at the reformatory was that of Helen Glattke, wife of longtime superintendent Arthur Glattke who died as the result of a gunshot wound in 1950. Though her death was ruled accidental, questions remain, and her spirit is thought to be one of the most active at the prison.

The visually striking, 250,000-square-foot stone structure—which boasts the world's largest freestanding steel cell block—has been the setting of numerous TV and video productions and the feature films *The Shawshank Redemption, Air Force One, Harry and Walter Go to New York, Fallen Angels, Tango and Cash,* and *The Dead Matter.*

The facility has been operated since 1995 by the nonprofit Mansfield Reformatory Preservation Society (MRPS), whose members work tirelessly to keep this piece of history alive, giving the reformatory new life as a historical landmark and world-renowned paranormal hot spot.

MRPS has worked to remove debris, replace roofing, and restore the Superintendent's Quarters and central guard room between the East and West cell blocks, funded by tour and ghost hunting fees. Paranormal investigators and thrill seekers have flocked to OSR in droves for sold-out public overnight ghost hunts since 1998.

Take the Haunted Tour—The Administration Building

Inside the central Administration Building was an infirmary, a library, a chapel, and a large open room on the top (fourth) floor with smaller adjoining rooms on one side and large windows on the other, which was used variously as a tuberculosis isolation ward, a guard's dormitory, and even a shooting range (bullet holes have been found in the walls and ceiling).

Personal Experience—
Theresa: If They Can Touch You, They Can Hurt You

In 2007 I was a member of Paranormal Researchers of Ohio (PRO), a long-standing and well-respected investigative team out of Cleveland founded by mother and daughter Pat Murray and Carrie Hebert.

On her previous visit, Carrie had been startled by the sudden appearance—"right in my face"—of a man dressed in prison blues as she investigated a "vacant" cell, causing her to "scream and run like a little girl."

I made the eighty-mile journey south to Mansfield for a public ghost hunt on a frosty night in November 2007, with PRO member Laura; Carrie, who now sought investigative redemption; and about 150 other enthusiasts, to see what we could scare up at the prison.

A thin blanket of snow covered the ground, and we were anticipating another helping of white stuff before morning. Only a small portion of the imposing stone edifice is heated, so the temperature outside is reflected within. But the cold didn't chill our enthusiasm—we sensed that this was going to be an epic evening.

The festivities began with a fascinating, detailed tour of the entire complex, with special emphasis on the historic and ghostly hotspots, led by OSR ghost-hunt coordinator Scott Sukel, who has roamed these halls since 1998 and calls Mansfield Reformatory his "own private paranormal laboratory."

We were also each given an excellent map of the complex created by Scott, so we could navigate the prison's 250,000 square feet as efficiently as possible on our own in the dark.

After Scott's time in the spotlight, another volunteer, Chris Vance, became our personal guide and regaled us with more history, detail, and stories. Chris warned us that as women we needed to be "extra careful." Female visitors, volunteers, and workers at the reformatory often report being touched, slapped, pinched, and otherwise manhandled by unseen hands.

We shrugged it off, but his warning was prophetic.

We headed to the so-called Tuberculosis Ward and spent almost an hour taking pictures and conducting EVP sessions with a digital audio recorder. The three of us spread out in an effort to cover every nook and cranny of the spacious but oddly tight-feeling room. With each step I took in the gloom the energy seemed to change, and then a palpable sadness engulfed me.

The sick and dying had long since gone, but I could feel their despair oozing from the pocked and peeling walls, thickening the air. Suddenly, I felt intense pressure upon my chest, and drawing breath became alarmingly difficult. I had to fight the compulsion to cough.

Was I empathetically experiencing the painful, labored breathing of someone stricken with tuberculosis? I had never felt anything like it before.

A few long, scary moments later, the pressure lifted and I could breathe freely, gratefully again.

When we had thoroughly explored the area, we decided to move down to the chapel on the next level. I walked out the door into a corridor and down a cramped flight of stairs leading to a narrow hallway and another flight of stairs, my still-trembling hands guiding my descent in the murk.

On one side of the corridor was a smooth stone wall and on the other a wooden handrail. I took several steps down the hallway toward the next set of stairs, and then three quick, hard yanks on my ponytail jolted me from behind, my head jerking back uncomfortably with each pull.

As startled as I was by this, my immediate reaction was annoyance. "Ha ha, very funny," I said as I turned around to confront Carrie, who I assumed was playing a joke on me.

As I finished the last word, I stopped in my tracks. Carrie was at least eight feet behind me, intently reviewing pictures on her camera.

She looked up at me, bewildered. "What did you say?"

"Did you just pull my hair?" I asked.

"What? No. I'm having problems with this stupid camera."

Laura, who was right behind Carrie, noticed my puzzled look and said, "You look like you've seen a ghost."

The blood drained from my stricken face and I began to shake. "Someone just pulled my hair. I thought you were playing a joke."

"I wasn't even near you, Theresa," Carrie replied.

"Yeah, I see that now."

The three of us examined the hallway, trying to figure out a logical explanation. There was nothing nearby for my hair to catch upon, and neither did it get tangled in my coat. I wasn't near the wall. And there was no one—visible—behind me.

Even as we shifted to investigator mode and tried to "debunk" the incident, I knew it was futile. This was not a case of misidentified sensation. I hadn't imagined it. My hair was pulled and my head yanked backward—three times. Someone or something wanted my attention, and got it.

The entire incident took only a few moments, but when I play back this memory in my mind, it unfolds in detailed slow motion. I remember the sensation, the terror welling inside me, the reaction I got from my friends, the puzzled looks on their faces, and how they changed when they realized what had occurred.

It was at this moment that my view of ghosts and the paranormal changed irrevocably. Now it was tangible, physical, objective. I realized not only that ghosts were real—definitely, very real—but that they can touch you. And if they can touch you, they can hurt you—or worse. I was only a few feet from stairs in the dark, and three yanks could have just as easily been a shove.

This wasn't just fun and games. This was something beyond our current logic and physics. A spiritual fire ignited in me, and that was the moment I decided to dedicate my life to an understanding of the paranormal.

About an hour later we ran into our personal tour guide, Chris, at another area of the prison. I was still quite shaken up but charged with a burst of energy that propelled me through the rest of the evening. Chris didn't seem surprised at all when I told him what had happened to me. For a moment I thought he didn't believe me, but then I realized this was a story he had heard before.

"I warned you that something might happen," he said with a grin. "Consider yourself lucky that only your hair got pulled!" He reminded me that other women had been pinched, prodded, and even smacked on the rear by invisible agents at the reformatory. Chris suggested I write up what had happened in OSR's visitor evidence book.

As I logged my experience in the book, I was shocked to see how many other women had experienced the same thing in the same area of the reformatory. This made me feel quite a bit better about what had happened to me: I knew I wasn't crazy.

This experience remains among the most profound of my career, and I was honored to share it on an episode of the Biography Channel's *My Ghost Story*.

Personal Experience—
Scott Sukel (OSR Ghost Hunt Coordinator): Human Punching Bag

About ten years ago I was showing the last handful of people around on a public ghost hunt at about 4:30 in the morning. The building was dead. They wanted to check out the third floor of the west administration building before heading home.

We went up there and the group scattered to different rooms trying to pick up any last bits of evidence for the evening. I was just standing there in the middle of the hall. The next thing I knew, something punched me in the left kidney so hard that it put me down on the ground and made a bruise that lasted several weeks.

I've never felt anything like it. I tried to pick myself up and brush it off, not letting the guests know exactly what had happened. My priority changed immediately to getting them out of there safely because I didn't know if this thing was going to lash out at anyone else.

I went to the doctor, and there was nothing physically wrong with me that could have caused the pain and bruising. I don't know what hit me. I don't know why it hit me. I don't know if I was at the right place at the right time, or the wrong place at the wrong time. It just depends on how you look at it.

Take the Haunted Tour—The Superintendent's Quarters

The Tragic and Mysterious Demise of Helen Glattke

Not all resident spirits of the reformatory are former inmates. One of its most famous lived the comfortable, even stylish life of a superintendent's wife. Perhaps she couldn't bear to leave, or perhaps she has a story yet to tell.

Arthur Glattke and Helen Bauer met while working on the Ohio gubernatorial campaign of Democrat Martin Davey. Davey won office in 1934 and appointed Glattke—who had been a high school coach and teacher in Toledo—superintendent, or warden, of the Ohio State Reformatory in 1935. He and Helen were married that same year.

At the reformatory, the Glattkes, who had two sons, lived in the front, castlelike portion of the facility, away from the dark realities of the cell blocks, from the time of their marriage until Helen's death in 1950.

Around 10:15 Sunday morning, November 5, 1950, Mrs. Glattke, a Catholic, was getting ready for church. The official report states that while reaching up to her closet shelf for a jewelry box, she accidentally dislodged a hidden .32-caliber semiautomatic handgun, which fired a bullet into her left lung as it hit the floor.

She died of complications from the injury at Mansfield General Hospital two days later at age forty-one.

Whispers circulated among inmates and staff that the superintendent had been involved in an extramarital relationship and that there had been a vocal argument about it just the night before. It was rumored that Helen had come home early from work, discovered the indiscretion, and wanted a divorce. Some alleged that Arthur had his wife killed to cover up this affair or to preclude a career-threatening divorce.

There is no evidence—beyond the persistent rumors—that Helen Glattke was murdered, nor that her death was anything but an accident. Oddly, no outside investigation was ever conducted, although a number of gun experts have stated it is "very unlikely" that a .32-caliber semiautomatic pistol could have discharged in the manner stated in the official account.

But of course, "very unlikely" is not the same as "impossible," and "very unlikely" things happen every day of the week—perhaps twice on Sunday.

On February 10, 1959, Arthur Glattke, a large man who had been a star football lineman at Wittenberg University in the 1920s, suffered a heart attack at his office desk and died shortly thereafter at Mansfield General Hospital.

Some believe Arthur was haunted by the spirit of Helen. A ghost thought to be Helen's has been reported around the Ohio State Reformatory since shortly after her death. Even while the prison was still in operation, employees and visitors claimed to smell her distinctive, rose-scented perfume emanating through the hallways of her former living quarters, and ghost hunters have caught glimpses of her walking through her pink bathroom as she did many times while alive.

After Arthur's death, people claimed to hear muffled conversations between a man and a woman all through the superintendent's house, perhaps echoing their reported argument from the night before her death.

However, Dr. Ted Glattke, son of Arthur and Helen, told investigator Rebecca Muller in 2005, "I find it hard to think of a spirit staying in a place, rather than staying with the people who are important to that spirit. I think that 'haunting' a house or the Ohio State Reformatory is a concept left over from a time when people didn't move very far from their birthplaces . . . What if the OSR were completely destroyed? I have little respect for the stories that I've seen because of all the inaccurate pieces, such as the places where my parents died [neither died at OSR], and the sensationalism regarding their lives."

In a recent phone conversation, Ted, a retired professor of audiology at the University of Arizona, told us that he had no memory of the fateful day when his mother was shot. He believes he must have been outside at the time.

Dr. Glattke also told us that his father was devastated by the loss of his wife, and a household once alive with visitors, parties, and live performances (tap dancers loved the tile floors!) became somber, sedate, and insular in the aftermath.

Personal Experience—
Theresa: Sorrowful Cries and Rose Perfume

In July 2010 Cathi Weber and I were making our way wearily from the central guard room to the administration wing at the tail end of an investigation, just on the verge of dawn, when we were startled out of drowsiness by the piercing, sustained cry of a woman inside the Superintendent's Quarters.

The sorrow at the heart of this cry spoke volumes to us as women: a mother's pain, a wife's anguish. She wanted us to hear and feel. We did.

Cathi and I searched in vain for a source of the audible "anomaly" but found nothing and no one. When we caught up with the other remaining investigators, who had been off in the cell blocks, we were shocked to find that they had heard the cry as well, assuming it had come from us.

We assured them it had not.

In March 2012, Cathi and I once again encountered what we believed to be the spirit of Helen Glattke. We were eager to return to the exact spot where we had heard her wail nearly two years before. A room-by-room investigation of the quarters led us to Helen's bedroom, the scene of her accident.

As I crossed the threshold of the doorway I was immediately hit with the overwhelming scent of rose perfume, so strong I could taste it. I called to Cathi to come and see if she too noticed the smell. She did.

As experienced investigators we immediately ruled each other out as the source of the floral fragrance. No serious ghost hunter should wear perfume or scented lotion on an investigation, as they make it impossible to detect phantom smells.

The rose perfume we detected had an antique quality about it, like that in the decorative bottles my grandmother left out on her dressing table, the kind Helen Glattke was known to wear. It dissipated quickly, only to manifest again in other areas of the room. I followed the meandering scent into the brown-and-beige checkered hallway, to the doorway of another room, and eventually to the threshold of the closet where Helen was fatally shot.

Sadly, there is not yet any practical way to document smells, so Cathi and I had to settle for photographs, which interestingly yielded strange rodlike anomalies in several of them.

Scott Sukel has also been touched by the rose. In 2004 he was conducting an orientation tour for fifteen ghost hunt guide volunteers. As they descended the stairs into the living area, they crossed an invisible barrier beyond which all four rooms of the quarters were awash in the powerful rose perfume scent.

Inside the barrier the scent was as strong as could be; outside it there was no smell at all. Everyone in the group experienced the same smell and division point.

If you visit the reformatory, be sure to use all your senses while investigating. This is one of the few places in United States where anomalous auditory, visual, olfactory, and tactile paranormal experiences are reported on a regular basis.

Take the Haunted Tour—The Hospital Ward

Personal Experience—
Theresa: A Cry, a Cold Spot, an Eerie Light

On a cold March night in 2012, Cathi Weber and I were exploring the old hospital ward area accompanied by Jamie Pasiak, son of "ghost cop" Stacey Jones.

Jamie grew up surrounded by the paranormal, but this was his first time investigating the reformatory. Cathi had "felt drawn" to the ward. An image was forming in her head of a dark-skinned man with an unusual name, waiting for someone to visit him in this often overlooked area of the prison.

After years of working together I've learned to trust her instincts. As usual, she was right. It wasn't long before we heard what sounded like a man's cry in one of the smaller rooms of the infirmary.

As we searched for the source of the cry, it suddenly became cold to my left. I called to my companions to see if they could feel the temperature change as well. They both felt what we determined to be about a ten-degree drop in air temperature. This cold spot then vanished only to reemerge in another area of the room.

We tried in vain to track the source of the cold air. We covered the space left to right, front to back: no source. However, Jamie noticed a strange light seeping through the bottom of a large piece of plywood covering the entrance to one of the guard turrets, which is in a fragile, dangerous state and off limits to the public.

The three of us watched as this light appeared and disappeared several times over the course of about ten minutes. There was no light source behind the plywood. It was a brick-and-iron stairwell that contained no windows, no holes.

The three of us were spooked but determined to carry on with the investigation. Recorders in hand, we asked questions of any lingering spirits.

"At dinner last week your mother broke down in tears. How do you feel about that?" asked Cathi.

All ghosts, like all people, have mothers. The iciest hearts will melt (or cringe) when you mention their mothers.

"*Our mom's not here,*" moaned a clear, male voice when Cathi played back her recorder.

Between the cries, the traveling cold spots, the strange light phenomenon, and the plaintive EVP, we all agreed that we were not alone in the infirmary.

Take the Haunted Tour—The Chapel

The reformatory had its own chapel where inmates could gather and worship. For some, these spiritual interludes were a much-needed break from the grind of prison living.

The chapel was also open to the public, who sat segregated from the prisoners in a balcony, as if looking down in judgment on the inmates below.

Personal Experience—
Scott Sukel: Imported Worshipper

Over the years people have experienced shadow figures and apparitions in the chapel. The past few years we have started to get a lady who sits in these pews. Various people have seen her—I've seen her. We've heard her laugh, cry, sob, sing, and she's always sitting in these pews. Sunday, March 25, 2012, we had a hunt, and about halfway through, a woman guest asked me who the lady was sitting in the front-right pew—she wasn't with their group. That was quite perplexing.

Take the Haunted Tour—The Toilet Room

One of the more peculiar areas of the reformatory is dubbed the Toilet Room. This room has been designated as a storage area for the many old porcelain thrones removed from cells and elsewhere throughout the prison. This plumber's nightmare is a well-known hot spot of paranormal activity.

Personal Experience—
Scott Sukel: Dr. Shadow

The Toilet Room is on what used to be the first floor of the hospital. When inmates were sick they would get a slip. Every morning guards would line up the inmates with sick slips and walk them down to what is now the Toilet Room. There was a doctor there named Dr. Salts.

According to the book *My Thirty Hard Years, 1933–1963*, by former assistant superintendent Dana W. Allen, the inmates didn't only go down there because they were actually sick. They would also go down there so they could stand in line with other inmates with whom they wouldn't normally have contact. That way they could jump them, or pass notes to them, or whatever.

According to Allen, Dr. Salts could pretty much look at you and tell if you were actually sick or if you were down there with ulterior motives. If you weren't sick, he had this concoction of Epsom salts and castor oil that you would have to drink in front of him. Salts was 6'7" and 350 pounds. That's about the size of the shadow I've seen many times in here.

Personal Experience—
Theresa: Toilet Room Terrors

On my very first visit to the reformatory in October 2006, my husband J and I watched a young man hide behind the Toilet Room door with the intent of ambushing his friend in the spirit of fearful fun. But when the time came to spring forth, the young man couldn't budge the large steel door.

Sounds of footsteps and shuffling emanated from the back of the room as shadows lurched around him in the gloom. The tables now thoroughly turned, the would-be frightener's fear rose, and he screamed to be let out.

His pal, the intended target of the joke, safely on the outside of the door, shouted to him that the door wasn't locked—in fact, it had no lock at all. The trapped man pounded ineffectually on the heavy door as several would-be rescuers tugged in vain to get it open.

"Please, God, get me out of here! There's something in here with me!" he implored.

"Push the door. Dude, it's not locked!" bellowed his friend with a hint of impatience.

"It won't move, please. Hurry!"

"Then try pulling it!"

"I did. It's stuck!"

We examined the door, but there was no lock, no latch, nothing jammed or stuck that would prevent it from opening. A crowd gathered around the recalcitrant door. The trapped man's cries became childlike whimpers.

"Step back and we'll try to pull it open from this side," we called out to him.

Then, as if it had suddenly changed its mind, the steel door slowly swung open. No one, on either side, was touching it. After a stunned moment, the Toilet Room hostage realized he was free and bounded out of the room in a blur of limbs and terror.

He was shaken and scared but physically unhurt, repeating that there had been someone or something in that room with him—something that kept the door from opening.

And then that something opened it.

Take the Haunted Tour—The Cell Blocks

The two main cell blocks spread out from the central administration building like the wings of a bird, ready to flap away to freedom. The East and West cell blocks are almost mirror images of each other with one exception: the East block stands a vertiginous six tiers high, holding the distinction of being the world's largest freestanding steel cell block. The West block is nearly as towering at five tiers.

Both cell blocks have long since been emptied, but many visitors still feel the presence of the inmates who once called them home. Each cell seems poised like a rat trap, ready to spring shut upon any visitor who strays too close. The metallic clang of cell doors slamming is commonly reported on the blocks, even though most of the rusty doors have long since lost the capacity to close.

The cell blocks have many ghostly tales to tell. As with many institutions, overcrowded conditions came to plague the reformatory. These conditions helped fuel an atmosphere of tension and violence. Fighting was commonplace among the men, and the strong preyed on the weak in a Darwinian race to the bottom.

The Mansfield Reformatory Preservation Society's museum is filled with artifacts collected from inmates over the years. The resourcefulness of some of these men is astounding. Anything from a bar of soap to a toothbrush could be turned into a deadly weapon, and was.

Most inmates learned to withstand the oppression and constant threat of violence, but for others it was simply too much. Suicide became a viable option.

Ghost Adventures—
The Burning Time

In a powerful and disconcerting episode of the Travel Channel's *Ghost Adventures* filmed at the reformatory and aired in November 2009, Zak Bagans, Nick Groff, and Aaron Goodwin interviewed former prisoner D. J. Fly, who did his time in the 1960s and early 1970s in cell 14 of the West cell block.

As Fly told the GAC on the narrow walkway outside his former cell, on January 30, 1960, his neighbor in cell 13, a man named James Lockhart, unilaterally decided his term was up and made a spectacularly dramatic exit.

Having managed to secure flammable liquid, likely turpentine or paint thinner from the prisoner furniture shop, Lockhart anointed his clothing, body, and mattress, then ignited himself into a human torch. An unwilling participant in the conflagration was neighbor Fly, trapped in his adjacent cage as noxious fumes, billowing smoke, and agonized shrieks from the living inferno choked, blinded, and horrified him.

As the flames and heat rose, Fly splashed water on himself from his sink faucet while screaming for salvation. Guards, two of whom were injured themselves in the process, rescued Fly, and eventually managed to extinguish Lockhart, but it was too late. Portions of Lockhart's skin stuck to the cell floor, and chunks sloughed off like overcooked meat as guards removed his smoldering remains.

The stench of chemical fire and charred flesh lingered for days after the body was removed and ultimately buried in the cemetery on the prison grounds.

Fly swears Lockhart never really did escape. As the GAC's cameras continued rolling, the aging former prisoner spoke to his unseen, late crony in cell 13, saying he knew he was still there in the cell, that he wasn't going anywhere, and that he still thought about him.

Then, with forceful brushing-off motions, Fly told Lockhart to get off him and strode out of the cell past Zak onto the walkway.

Addressing the cell from the outside, Fly said he had done all he could to free Lockhart, squinting in effort, pain, or memory.

Zak asked Fly softly if he thought Lockhart was still in the cell.

Fly sighed in the affirmative.

That night during the "lockdown," as the team passed the death cell, the words *drag, pass,* and *fly* appeared on Zak's video goggles device, seemingly relevant to the gruesome Lockhart tale. Upon review, the video appeared to reveal a mist figure passing behind Zak in the gloom as he spoke on camera.

If indeed Lockhart's spirit remains imprisoned in cell 13, his tale of "escape" is almost too sad and pathetic to bear.

Personal Experience—
Scott Sukel: Stalked by a Shadow Figure

I'm a photographer by trade, and if you show me a picture I can probably figure out an explanation for any anomalies. About one hundred thousand pictures have been submitted here from ghost hunts over the years, but I have found only seven I can't explain photographically.

What appears in those seven are phenomena that have been reported for decades, including a shadow guy on the fourth tier of the East cell block, and a figure going into a cell on the West cell block.

My coolest experience was seeing a shadow figure up on the fourth tier of the East cell block on the north side. One night in 2010 I was closing up—it was about 5:30 in the morning and I was the only one in the building.

I was walking down to close up the Toilet Room and I heard somebody walking, crunching on the paint chips on the fourth tier. I looked up, didn't see anything, and thought there must be a big old raccoon up there or something.

I kept walking, looked up again, and saw a shadow figure, pretty much pacing me. I stopped—it stopped. I walked—it walked. Finally, I got about halfway down, stopped, and said, "That's okay, keep on going." It sat there for a second or two, then started walking again.

I kept walking toward the Toilet Room—when you get to the end on the fourth tier, there's a catwalk over to the library. The shadow figure went to the catwalk and stood there watching me as I walked. I closed the Toilet Room up, keeping one eye on that guy, and then it occurred to me, "Oh shit, I have to go up there and close those doors too."

I announced, "I'm just going up to the second floor to close that door, and leave me alone, all right?"

As I headed up the stairs to the second floor, I heard footsteps heading off to the library. I closed the second-floor door, then ran like a schoolgirl off to the Bullpen [central meeting area]. That was the most extended paranormal experience I've had.

CELLS OF INFAMY

There are several notorious cells on the East and West cell blocks: the aforementioned cell 13—where Lockhart set himself on fire— and cell 14, where his unfortunate neighbor D. J. Fly lived; and "Cell X."

Cell X, located on the second tier of the East cell block, is where investigators Dustin Pari and Dave Tango from *Ghost Hunters* famously chased phantom footsteps and darting shadows in an episode that aired in October 2005.

In the same episode, team leaders Jason and Grant heard footsteps overhead and banging noises on the second tier of the West cell block, and Grant later heard whispers from Cell X.

If you visit the block today you can see the cell clearly marked with the X by the investigators, and maybe you'll run into a noisy shadow or two.

Take the Haunted Tour—Solitary Confinement

Solitary confinement, better known as "the Hole," is hidden away in the lower levels of the reformatory. The Hole is a series of single-man cells lined up along two back-to-back corridors. The cells are dark, dank, and cramped, little more than stone boxes enclosed by heavy iron doors. Designed for short-term disciplinary isolation of the prison's most violent inmates, the Hole was sometimes over capacity, most notably after a prisoner uprising in 1957.

It was tough enough for one man to be confined in such a small place for any length of time, but it was far worse if you were saddled with a roommate. One account tells of two inmates going into a cell, but only one coming out. One inmate had snapped and murdered the other, shoving his body under the bunk.

Personal Experience—
Theresa: Curses in the Hole

Meet Mike Evans

On the 2010 visit with Cathi Weber, our good friend and psychic Jackie Williams was on hand to share her impressions of the reformatory. Jackie wasted no time zeroing in on some of the strongest energies in the building and we followed like lemmings, descending into the bowels of OSR, Solitary.

Jackie is a strong woman, confident in her abilities and unafraid to confront the darkness. It's exceedingly more difficult when, like Cathi and me, you can't "see" what you're hunting.

"Should I bark or something when I find one?" Jackie asked sarcastically.

"Well, yeah, I guess."

"Ah-roo ah-roo ah-roo." Jackie vocalized like a bloodhound, pointing into a tiny black cell.

I began an EVP session in the cell.

Jackie stood in the narrow hallway, looking amused.

"What's so funny?"

According to Jackie, the resident spirit had answered every question I had asked, but I had heard none of it. Feeling that I was ignoring him, the spirit had become indignant and had ordered me out of his cell.

Jackie gave us a detailed description of this spirit, named Mike, who was literally screaming obscenities in my ear. He was young, early twenties, longish dirty blond hair, very thin—even emaciated—about six feet tall, and had been sent to the reformatory sometime in the 1970s for burglary, among other things.

He didn't like me one bit. I took Jackie's advice and moved on to another cell.

Mike Evans Digs Jordan Murphy

On another visit, in November 2011, I was leading a group of forty-three people who came down from Cleveland on a bus for a tour and ghost hunt. I was a teacher of occult and supernatural topics for Polaris Career Center, and a perk of the job was organizing and leading tours to some of the area's more interesting haunted locations, the most popular of which was Mansfield.

After a tour of the prison, we spread out to explore at our leisure. Joining me that evening were Cathi, Joe Cihy, Jordan Murphy, and Daniel Hooven, experienced paranormal investigators all.

We started our investigation in Solitary. Jordan and Daniel had never been to Mansfield and were anxious to begin. The five of us found just how dark and claustrophobic Solitary could be.

I was hoping to have another encounter with our indignant friend Mike, though it was going to be a lot harder without our "ghost hound" Jackie with us.

We decided to do an EVP session. On the front side of Solitary, Cathi and I entered separate cells. Cathi heard the sound of shuffling in her cell but felt drawn to other cells on the opposite wall, to which we moved our little entourage.

Jordan and Daniel took turns going solo in the cells we felt most strongly about. We were all running digital recorders and videotaping. After a few "quick-burst" EVP sessions—immediate playback and review of the recordings—it was evident that the dark cells were far from vacant.

In all my years as a paranormal investigator, I have never received the astounding volume of responses we did that night down in Solitary. Question after question, session after session, we captured numerous EVPs.

It didn't seem to matter what we asked, there was almost

always an answer. Typically, we'd be lucky to capture one or two EVPs in a night.

It may have been the presence of three women in the group, or the "Pandora's box," the nickname given to a coveted older-model digital recorder we used that night, or that the entities were familiar with Cathi and me, but whatever the case, we directly communicated with spirits.

Many of the responses were screamed and unintelligible, but some were unmistakable. "My name is Daniel, what's your name? Do you have a name or were you just a number?"

In response we heard clearly, "*Mike . . . Evans.*"

The voice told us that his prison number began with "*Seven . . . nine . . .*" He seemed to know more about us than we knew about him. Mike also seemed to enjoy having young, lovely Jordan in his cell.

The reaction was quite different whenever I asked a question or entered his space.

His answers became more and more disturbing, filled with swearing and screaming: "*Shut up, you fucking bitch,*" and other more creative obscenities.

Cathi took a gentle, maternal role, while I was more bold and assertive. I don't normally use provocation, but it seemed acceptable in this instance. We offered Mike some of the trigger objects we had brought with us, including a worn deck of cards, some highly desired cigarettes, even a pocketknife.

"What did you do to land in Solitary?" Cathi asked. "Do you miss your mom? What's your message?"

I was shocked when we played back the recording.

After the maternal reference, we picked up a heart-wrenching response.

"*Mother.*"

I was taken aback by the sadness in the voice, but my sympathy was short lived. The next message he had for us was a loud, forceful scream, bone-chilling and angry.

Cathi's questions received some clear, concise answers, while mine were met with cussing and obscenities. I believe we were communicating with the same spirit, Mike, whom I had angered a year before.

Paranormal Stars and More Mike Evans

Cathi and I again returned to OSR in March 2012. The reformatory was host to a weekend event chock-full of celebrity guests and paranormal experts hosted by Darkness Radio personality Dave Schrader.

The celebrity lineup included psychic Chris Fleming, author and *Ghost Adventures* writer Jeff Belanger, "paranormal cop" Stacey Jones, psychics Michael and Marti Parry, *Ghost Adventures* tech whiz Billy Tolley, *Ghost Adventures* co-star Aaron Goodwin, and EVP experts Mark and Debby Constantino. This well-respected husband-and-wife team have made a career out of their work in electronic voice phenomena.

The weekend included charity auctions, speeches, seminars, and demonstrations, finished off by two nights of ghost hunting with some of the best people working in the field today.

The crowd fanned out into the prison, where the experts guided and assisted with paranormal experiments and investigations. After a couple of hours exploring on our own, we decided to see what was happening with the Constantinos down in Solitary.

About a dozen investigators were crammed into the hallway leading to the upper and lower cells of the Hole. The Constantinos were using several different digital recorders for EVP sessions and invited the crowd to participate.

I immediately jumped in. "Can you ask if there is an inmate named Mike Evans or something similar, with a prison number beginning with seventy-nine?"

"No, *you're* gonna ask that!" Mark pointed to me.

He told us they had captured an EVP from a Mike in an earlier session. After quieting the group, I posed the question to any unseen spirits in Solitary.

There was a pause. Then a few more questions. Mark asked the spirit to identify himself, and then came the moment of truth.

When the recordings were played back, after my question, and again after Mark's, a voice said, "*Mike . . . Evans.*"

The questioning continued. Mark seemed to think we were upsetting the spirit. More questions, more EVPs. The Constantinos had certainly lived up to their reputations, as had my old "friend"—three visits to Solitary, three encounters with Mike Evans.

I looked to Cathi, but she was fussing behind me. Suddenly she exclaimed, "I'm getting touched back here! Someone's caressing my back."

Another woman chimed in, "I felt it too!"

All this was happening at once. The crowd was charged up, as were the spirits down in Solitary. We had objective evidence compounded by personal experience coinciding with previous experience. A dozen eyewitnesses and some of the most well-respected experts in the field working the equipment corroborated.

The Concrete Mike Evans

In May 2012, Cathi and I made another journey to the reformatory, this time with a specific goal in mind. During a recent routine walk-through of the building, OSR ghost hunt director Scott Sukel had made a startling discovery.

Rainy weather had precipitated a condensation problem in Solitary, causing paint to peel from the walls and ceilings of a number of the cells, revealing decades-old graffiti left to posterity by former occupants.

With Scott absent on this particular evening, volunteer guide

Ron Paul, following directions relayed via text message by Scott, led us to the cell in question.

The three of us scanned the wet walls meticulously with our flashlights—nothing. Water dripping slowly on us from above caused us to look up.

And there it was. Among the cryptic messages, crudely etched pictures, and a menagerie of names was the one I had hoped to find: *EVANS . . . 72–74.*

Could this be my Mike Evans? After exhaustive research and dead-end leads, we had found something *literally* concrete. The writing was on the wall—or the ceiling, to be exact.

We found two separate instances of *Evans* graffiti in the cell. Ron told us that some inmates made repeated visits to Solitary, and the reformatory itself. Year after year, prison staff painted over the walls and ceilings of the cells, preparing a fresh canvas for those sequestered in the stone-and-iron cages.

As the years wore on, the layers of paint peeled back like pages in a book, revealing clues about those who had left their marks: prison records of an unofficial but very real sort.

With most of the reformatory inmate records destroyed and lost to history, this is the closest thing to confirmation I will likely be able to find. Everything in my being tells me that this is "my" Mike Evans. He has made numerous attempts to be recognized, to be remembered, inside and outside the reformatory.

CONCLUSION

What *is* a ghost? What creates a haunting?

In the case of the Ohio State Reformatory, the paranormal activity seems to have been born out of several factors. First, a sheer volume of people went in and out of the facility. Next, the emotional and psychological residue that remains in a place with such a charged atmosphere is enormous. Like walking into a room after two people have had a heated argument, you can "feel" the tension in the air, but on a much larger scale. Fear, anger, sadness, despair, all these emotions create energy. Some of it still lingers in the air at OSR, stuck in a loop, repeating over and over again. This "residual" type of haunting is common in places like the reformatory.

Theorists believe that a human spirit can remain earthbound or "stuck" when his or her death involves extreme violence, suddenness, or anguish. A number of Mansfield inmates certainly fit that bill. For some, death was an end to torment, but for others the pain tragically continues.

It seems also that in certain cases, remaining earthbound is a choice. Sometimes the dead feel the need to communicate with the living. They need to tell their story, deliver their message, or accomplish some sort of important task before they can move on. It may take years, decades, even centuries before this type of haunting can be resolved. Helping this type of ghost to move on could be the single most important accomplishment of a paranormal researcher.

OSR also has environmental conditions that may contribute to paranormal activity, including underground springs and the granite used in the building, which can generate an electrical field via the piezoelectric effect.

Electromagnetic fields and running natural water are thought to be energy sources from which spirits can draw in order to manifest themselves, communicate with the living, and so on.

Finally, OSR would appear to be home to entities darker than ghosts, though ghosts can be plenty mean—scratching, yanking, or punching someone in the left kidney! A person cruel in life will be a ghost cruel in death.

Throughout OSR, there have been numerous reported manifestations of negative energy, which are not ghosts per se. Negative energy is just energy, possibly left over from some great tragedy or a combination of energies left by a group of very unhappy souls—like prisoners. It is not the surviving consciousness of a once-living person—you cannot interact with it the way you could a ghost or spirit. It might appear in the form of a "shadow person," but one that wasn't any one person's shadow.

This type of entity can usually be displaced by changing the negative atmosphere into a positive one, though in the case of a place like the reformatory, that might require something like a global convention of Sunday school teachers.

What You Need to Know Before You Go:

The Ohio State Reformatory
100 Reformatory Rd., Mansfield, OH 44905

Contact Information:
(419) 522-2644
info@mrps.org
mrps.org

Open daily from May 1 to September 1, 11 A.M. to 5 P.M.
Self-Guided Tours: Guests can walk the tour route at their own
   pace while exploring about 70 percent of the building (does
   not include the entire building or special areas seen on guided
   tours).
Guided Tours: An informative guided exploration of some of the
   most popular sections of the building. No tour covers the
   entire building, but each gives access to specialized areas of the
   reformatory: West Cell Block Tour, Hollywood Tour (includes
   movie sets from *The Shawshank Redemption*), East Cell Block

Tour, and Behind the Scenes Tour (includes access to historic artifacts and the touch museum). Saturday and Sunday only.

All the tour guides and staff at OSR are amazing. All have a deep love and respect for the building and should be commended for their work. Even more impressive is that they are all volunteers. Every single one.

Ghost Hunts:

Public ghost hunts: 8 P.M. to 5 A.M. Please check the calendar on the website for dates.

Private ghost hunts: Limited to 100 people.

Public ghost hunts sell out extremely quickly, as do available dates for private hunts. Please check the website for availability and schedule of events.

Besides the tours and ghost hunts, many public and private events are often scheduled at the reformatory, so please check the calendar often.

The **Haunted Prison Experience** (a separate entity from MPRS) runs from late September through Halloween. There are no reformatory events during this time.

The building contains hazards including but not limited to steep steps, uneven surfaces, and lead-based paints. It is not recommended for children under 7 or women who are pregnant.

For more information on Mansfield and nearby attractions, contact the Mansfield and Richland County Convention and Visitors Bureau at mansfieldtourism.com.

Lodging:

Best Western Richland Inn Mansfield, (419) 756-6670
180 E. Hanley Rd., Mansfield, OH 44903
bestwestern.com

La Quinta Inn & Suites, (419) 774-0005, (800) 531-5900
120 Stander Ave., Mansfield, OH 44903
lq.com

Country Inn & Suites, (419) 747-2227, (800) 456-4000
2069 Walker Lake Rd., Mansfield, OH 44906
countryinns.com/mansfieldoh

Travelodge, (419) 756-7600, (800) 578-7878
90 W. Hanley Rd., Mansfield, OH 44903
travelodge.com

The Olde Stone House Bed and Breakfast, (419) 517-0013
291 Stewart Rd. N., Mansfield, OH 44905
theoldestonehousebandb.com

Spruce Hill Inn and Cottages, (419) 756-2200
3230 Possum Run Rd., Mansfield, OH 44903
sprucehillinn.com

Theresa Argie, aka "The Haunted Housewife," is a seasoned storyteller, parahistorian, researcher, and ghost hunter who has finally found a way to make being "the weird one" work to her advantage. She has traveled all over the country in search of ghosts, seeking above all to give a voice to the dead and let their stories be told. Theresa and her Haunted Housewives partner Cathi Weber have met some of the most amazing and influential people in the paranormal community along with a wonderful menagerie of everyday folk who've had an unforgettable encounter with the extraordinary. Theresa firmly believes that if we don't embrace our past, we have no future. The dead speak. It is in our best interest to listen.

Eric Olsen is a popular and influential journalist, pundit, author, and media personality covering the width and breadth of contemporary culture with wit and insight for over three decades. Also a seminal Internet entrepreneur, Olsen founded and guided Blogcritics.org, TheMortonReport.com, and Americas-Most-Haunted.com and was publisher of Technorati.com. In recent years, Olsen has become a leading chronicler of the paranormal world, acting upon a fascination with the strange and spooky that dates back to childhood. Olsen is married to legendary blogger Dawn Olsen, and has four wondrous children: Kristen, Christopher, Lily, and Alex.